the SEWING BOOK

the SEWING BOOK

ALISON SMITH **MBE**

CONTENTS

346

354

104

INTRODUCTION

The Sewing Book provides a comprehensive guide to all sewing techniques, whether it be for dressmaking, tailoring, crafts, or soft furnishings. If you are new to sewing, you'll find many tips to help and guide you; if you have been sewing for many years, there will be lots of new ideas to try. I also hope the book will be a valuable reference for all students studying textiles and fashion.

Having sewn since my teenage years and taught dressmaking and fashion for all my adult life, I am truly passionate about sewing. It can be so therapeutic – relaxing and satisfying. The ability to produce a unique item of clothing or something for your home is truly rewarding.

The book is divided into three sections. The first, Tools, covers all the equipment required to sew, including sewing machines; gives an up-to-date guide to fabrics – their properties, care, and how to sew them; and explains how to alter patterns to make clothes that fit you perfectly.

The next section is Techniques, with over 300 different sewing techniques to try, all in a step-by-step photographic format, covering everything from basic stitches and seams to professional tailoring techniques. Each chapter begins with a visual directory of what the techniques are used for, be it types of pleats or pockets, necklines or sleeves, or buttonhole shapes.

Dotted throughout the Techniques section are 10 gorgeous projects that range from quick and easy cushions through to a shift dress and a Roman blind. Whatever your level of experience, there will be something to suit you. All the projects use techniques that appear in the second section of the book and will help you practise your sewing skills and develop new ones. The final section contains patterns for the projects, as well as a useful glossary of sewing terms.

Enjoy and happy sewing.

ABOUT **THIS BOOK**

For the photographs, we have used sewing threads of a contrast colour to the fabric in order for the stitching to be visible. I recommend that you use a thread that matches your fabric as closely as possible.

All techniques and projects are graded by difficulty level, from * for the simple and straightforward to ***** for the more complex and challenging ones.

The visual directories at the start of each chapter show what the techniques within may be used for. They also show you the construction of the technique, with red dashed lines to indicate top-stitching and grey dotted lines to help you understand the structure beneath the fabric.

The fabric quantity given for each project is the minimum needed. If using fabric with a large-scale or directional pattern, you may need to buy extra to make sure the pattern works well on the finished item.

Always cut fabric on the straight grain unless instructed otherwise. The cutting layouts show fabric folded selvedge to selvedge for most projects, but this is not necessary for plain fabrics. Seam allowances are 1.5cm (⅝in) unless otherwise indicated.

Neatening of seams is not always shown in the photographs because this can distract from the technique (seam neatening is only shown when it forms part of the technique). I recommend that you neaten your seams using your preferred technique.

Many of the techniques shown may vary from those given on your pattern, but you might like to try an alternative technique. They are many to choose from.

TOOLS

SEWING EQUIPMENT

As well as a basic kit – tape measure, scissors, pins, needles, threads, and seam ripper – you will need an iron for pressing. For keen sewers, a sewing machine, and possibly an overlocker, are essential, and there are also other handy gadgets available.

BASIC **SEWING KIT**

A well-equipped sewing kit will include all of the items shown below and many more, depending on the type of sewing that you do regularly. It is important that a suitable container is used to keep your tools together, so that they will be readily to hand, and to keep them tidy.

◀ **Seam ripper**
Also called a stitch ripper, to remove any stitches that have been sewn in the wrong place. Various sizes of seam rippers are available. Keep the cover on when not in use to protect the sharp point.
See p.16

Pins ▼
Needed by every sewer to hold the fabric together prior to sewing it permanently. There are different types of pins for different types of work.
See p.23

▲ **Tape measure**
Essential, not only to take body measurements, but also to help measure fabric, seams, etc. Choose one that gives both metric and imperial. A tape made of plastic is best as it will not stretch.
See p.18

Cutting shears ▶
Required for cutting fabric. When buying, select a pair that feels comfortable in your hand and that is not too heavy.
See p.17

▼ **Zip**
It is always a good idea to keep a couple of zips in your sewing kit. Black, cream, and navy are the most useful colours.
See pp.284–293

▲ **Safety pins**
Keep a variety of sizes. They are useful for emergency repairs as well as threading elastics.
See p.23

Thimble ▲
This is useful to protect the end of your finger when hand sewing. Thimbles are available in various shapes and sizes.
See p.21

Sewing gauge ▲
A handy gadget for small measurements. The slide can be set to measure hem depths, buttonhole diameters, and much more.
See p.18

Threads ▲

A selection of threads for hand sewing and machine/overlocker sewing in a variety of colours. Some threads are made of polyester, while others are cotton or rayon.
See pp.24–25

Embroidery scissors ▼

Small pair of scissors with very sharp points, to clip threads close to the fabric.
See p.17

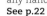

◀ Needles

A good selection of different types of needles for sewing by hand. This will enable you to tackle any hand-sewing project.
See p.22

Pin cushion ▶

To keep your needles and pins safe and clean. Choose one that has a fabric cover and is firm. Keep magnetic ones away from computerized machines.
See p.23

Haberdashery ▼

All the odds and ends a sewer needs, including everything from buttons and snaps to trimmings and elastic. A selection of buttons and snaps in your basic kit is useful for a quick repair.
See pp.26–27

Buttonhole chisel ▲

An exceedingly sharp mini-chisel that gives a clean cut through machine buttonholes. Place a cutting mat underneath when using this tool, or you might damage the blade.
See p.16

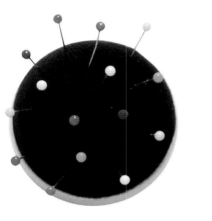

BUILD UP FROM YOUR BASIC SEWING KIT

▶ **CUTTING TOOLS pp.16–17**
Appliqué scissors
Bent-handled shears
Cutting mat
Paper scissors
Pinking shears
Rotary cutter
Snips
Trimming scissors

▶ **MEASURING TOOLS p.18**
Flexible ruler
Gridded ruler
Other tape measures

▶ **MARKING AIDS p.19**
Chalk pencil
Chalk propelling pencil
Drafting ruler
Heat-sensitive ink pen
Tailor's chalk
Tracing wheel and carbon paper
Water/air-soluble pen

▶ **USEFUL EXTRAS pp.20–21**
14-in-1 measure
Awl
Beeswax
Collar point turner
Dressmaker's dummy
Emergency sewing kit
Glue pen
Liquid sealant
Loop turner
Pattern paper
Pliers
Tape maker
Tweezers

▶ **NEEDLES AND THREADERS p.22**

▶ **PRESSING AIDS pp.28–29**
Clapper
Iron
Ironing board
Mini iron
Pressing cloth
Pressing mat
Pressing mitten
Seam roll
Tailor's ham
Velvet mat

CUTTING **TOOLS**

There are many types of cutting tools, but one rule applies to all: buy good-quality products that can be re-sharpened. Cutting shears should fit the span of your hand so that you can comfortably open the whole of the blade with one action, which is very important for clean and accurate cutting lines. A seam ripper is essential for removing misplaced stitches or for unpicking seams for mending. Rotary cutters, used in conjunction with a special cutting mat and ruler, are invaluable for cutting multiple straight edges.

▽ Snips
A very useful, small, spring-loaded tool that easily cuts the ends of thread. Not suitable for fabrics.

Applique scissors ▲
Use these scissors to trim upper fabric layers. The duck bill prevents snipping into the under layer.

▽ Rotary cutter
Available with different sizes of retractable blades. It must be used in conjunction with a special cutting mat to protect the blade and cutting surface.

▽ Buttonhole chisel
A smaller version of a carpenter's chisel, to cut cleanly and accurately through buttonholes. As this is so sharp it must be used with a self-healing cutting mat.

◀ Seam ripper
A sharp, pointed hook to slide under a stitch, with a small cutting blade at the base to cut the thread. Various sizes of seam ripper are available, to cut through light to heavyweight fabric seams.

▽ Cutting mat
A self-healing mat to use with the rotary cutter. This mat can also be used under the buttonhole chisel.

◀ **Bent-handled shears**
This type of shear has a blade that can sit flat against the table when cutting out, due to the angle between the blade and handle. Popular for cutting long, straight edges.

Pinking shears ▶
Similar in size to cutting shears but with a blade that cuts with a zigzag pattern. Used for neatening seams and decorative edges.

▼ **Cutting shears**
The most popular type of shear, used for cutting large pieces of fabric. The length of the blade can vary from 20–30cm (8–12in).

▲ **Trimming Scissors**
These scissors have a 10cm (4in) blade and are used to trim away surplus fabric and neaten ends of machining.

▼ **Embroidery scissors**
Small and very sharp scissors used to get into corners and clip threads close to the fabric.

◀ **Paper scissors**
Use these to cut around pattern pieces – cutting paper will dull blades of fabric scissors and shears.

MEASURING **TOOLS** AND **MARKING AIDS**

A huge range of tools enables a sewer to measure accurately. Choosing the correct tool for the task in hand is important, so that your measurements are precise. The next step is to mark your work using the appropriate marking technique or tool. Some tools are very specific to one job while others are specific to types of sewing.

MEASURING TOOLS

There are many tools available to help you measure everything from the width of a seam or hem, to body dimensions, to the area of a window. One of the most basic yet invaluable measuring tools is the tape measure. Be sure to keep yours in good condition – once it stretches or gets snipped on the edges, it will no longer be accurate and should be replaced.

▼ Extra-long tape
This is usually twice the length of a normal tape measure, at 300cm (10ft) long. Use it when making soft furnishings. It's also useful to help measure the length of bridal trains.

▲ Metal tape for windows
A metal tape that can be secured when extended is used to measure windows and soft furnishings.

Sewing gauge ▲
A handy small tool about 15cm (6in) long, marked in centimetres and inches, with a sliding tab. Use as an accurate measure for small measurements such as hems.

Retractable tape ▷
Very useful to have in your handbag when shopping as you never know when you may need to measure something!

Tape measure ▲
Available in various colours and widths. Try to choose one that is the same width as standard seam allowance (1.5cm/⅝in), because it will prove exceedingly useful.

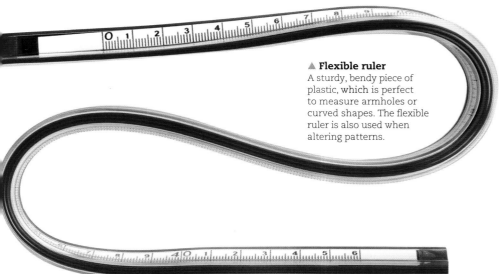

▲ Flexible ruler
A sturdy, bendy piece of plastic, which is perfect to measure armholes or curved shapes. The flexible ruler is also used when altering patterns.

Gridded ruler ▼
This type of ruler is larger than a normal ruler and is marked with a centimetre or inch grid. Used in conjunction with the rotary cutter and mat, and also for marking bias strips.

MARKING AIDS

Marking certain parts of your work is essential, to make sure that things like pockets and darts are placed correctly and seamlines are straight as drawn on the pattern. With some marking tools, such as pens and a tracing wheel and carbon paper, it is always a good idea to test on a scrap of fabric first to make sure that the mark made will not be permanent.

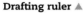

▼ Chalk propelling pencil
Chalk leads of different colours can be inserted into this propelling pencil, making it a very versatile marking tool. The leads can be sharpened.

Drafting ruler ▲
A plastic curved tool, also called a pattern marking ruler, used primarily when drafting or altering patterns.

◀ Tailor's chalk
Also known as French chalk, this solid piece of chalk in either a square or triangular shape is available in a large variety of colours. The chalk easily brushes off fabric.

◀ Water/air-soluble pen
This resembles a felt marker pen. Marks made can be removed from the fabric with either a spray of water or by leaving to air-dry. Be careful – if you press over the marks, they may become permanent.

◀ Chalk pencil
Available in blue, pink, and white. As it can be sharpened like a normal pencil, it will draw accurate lines on fabric.

Heat-sensitive ink pen ▶
This pen draws clear fine lines on fabric and will vanish once ironed. However, test it first as the ink can reappear in cold conditions.

Tracing wheel and carbon paper ▼
These two items are used together to transfer markings from a paper pattern or a design on to fabric. Not suitable for all types of fabric though, as marks may not be able to be removed easily.

USEFUL **EXTRAS**

There are many more accessories that can be purchased to help with your sewing, and knowing which products to choose and for which job can be daunting. The tools shown here can be useful aids, although it depends on the type of sewing that you do – dressmaking, craft work, making soft furnishings, or running repairs – as to whether you would need all of them in your sewing kit.

Beeswax
When hand sewing, this will prevent the thread from tangling, and will strengthen it. First draw the thread through the wax, then press the wax into the thread by running your fingers along it.

Awl
This sharp tool is used to make holes in fabric for eyelet insertion or for the rounded end of a keyhole buttonhole.

Tape maker
Available in 12, 18, and 25mm (½, ¾, and 1in) widths, this tool evenly folds the edges of a fabric strip, which can then be pressed to make binding.

Tweezers
These can be used for removing stubborn tacking stitches that have become caught in the machine stitching. An essential aid to threading the overlocker.

Loop turner
A thin metal rod with a latch at the end. Use to turn narrow fabric tubes or to thread ribbons through a slotted lace.

Emergency sewing kit
All the absolute essentials to fix loose buttons or dropped hems while away from your sewing machine. Take it with you when travelling.

Liquid sealant
Used to seal the cut edge of ribbons and trims to prevent fraying. Also useful to seal the ends of overlock stitching.

Glue pen
Similar to a glue pen for paper, this will hold fabric or trims temporarily in place until they can be secured with stitches. It will not damage the fabric or make the sewing needle sticky.

Collar point turner ▷
This is excellent for pushing out those hard-to-reach corners in collars and cuffs.

Thimble ▲
An essential item for many sewers, to protect the middle finger from the end of the needle. Choose a thimble that fits your finger comfortably as there are many varieties to choose from.

▲ **Pliers**
Specially designed pliers with various heads are used to attach eyelets, metal snaps, and rivets.

▲ **14-in-1 measure**
A strange-looking tool that has 14 different measurements on it. Use to turn hems or edges accurately. Available in both metric and imperial.

▲ **Dressmaker's dummy**
An adjustable form that is useful when fitting garments as it can be adjusted to personal body measurements. Excellent to help in the turning up of hemlines. Available in female, male, and children's shapes and sizes.

Pattern paper ▷
This can be plain or printed with dots and crosses at regular intervals. The paper can be used for drafting patterns, or for altering or tracing patterns.

TOOLS

NEEDLES AND PINS

Using the correct pin or needle for your work is so important, as the wrong choice can damage fabric or leave small holes. Needles are made from steel and pins from steel or occasionally brass. Look after them by keeping pins in a pin cushion and needles in a needle case – if kept together in a small container they could become scratched and blunt.

NEEDLES AND THREADERS

Needles are available for all types of fabrics and projects. A good selection of needles should be to hand at all times, whether it be for emergency mending of tears, or sewing on buttons, or adding trimmings to special-occasion wear. With a special needle threader, inserting the thread through the eye of the needle is simplicity itself.

Sharps
A general-purpose hand-sewing needle, with a small, round eye. Available in sizes 1 to 12. For most hand sewing use a size 6 to 9.

Crewel
Also known as an embroidery needle, a long needle with a long, oval eye that is designed to take multiple strands of embroidery thread.

Milliner's or straw
A very long, thin needle with a small, round eye. Good for hand sewing and tacking as it doesn't damage fabric. A size 8 or 9 is most popular.

Betweens or quilting
Similar to a milliner's needle but very short, with a small, round eye. Perfect for fine hand stitches and favoured by quilters.

Beading
Long and exceedingly fine, to sew beads and sequins to fabric. As it is prone to bending, keep it wrapped in tissue when not in use.

Darner's
A long, thick needle that is designed to be used with wool or thick yarns and to sew through multiple layers.

Tapestry
A medium-length, thick needle with a blunt end and a long eye. For use with wool yarn in tapestry. Also for darning in overlock threads.

Chenille
This looks like a tapestry needle but it has a sharp point. Use with thick or wool yarns for darning or heavy embroidery.

Bodkin
A strange-looking needle with a blunt end and a large, fat eye. Use to thread elastic or cord. There are larger eyes for thicker yarns.

Self-threading needle
A needle that has a double eye. The thread is placed in the upper eye through the gap, then pulled into the eye below for sewing.

Wire needle threader
A handy gadget, especially useful for needles with small eyes. Also helpful in threading sewing-machine needles.

Automatic needle threader
This threader is operated with a small lever. The needle, eye down, is inserted and the thread is wrapped around.

PINS

There is a wide variety of pins available, in differing lengths and thicknesses, and ranging from plain household pins to those with coloured balls or flower shapes on their ends.

Household
General-purpose pins of a medium length and thickness. Can be used for all types of sewing.

Quilting
A long pin of medium thickness, designed to hold multiple layers of fabric together.

Pearl-headed
Longer than household pins, with a coloured pearl head. They are easy to pick up and use.

Lace or bridal
A fine, short pin designed to be used with fine fabrics, such as those for bridal gowns, because the pin will not damage the fabric.

Flowerhead
A long pin of medium thickness with a flat, flower-shaped head. It is designed to be pressed over, as the head lays flat on the fabric.

Extra fine
Extra long and extra fine, this pin is favoured by many professional dressmakers, because it is easy to use and doesn't damage finer fabrics.

Glass-headed
Similar to pearl-headed pins but shorter. They have the advantage that they can be pressed over without melting.

Dressmaker's
Similar to a household pin in shape and thickness, but slightly longer. These are the pins for beginners to choose.

Safety pins
Available in a huge variety of sizes and made either of brass or stainless steel. Used for holding two or more layers together.

Staple
A strong pin that looks like a very large staple, used for pinning loose covers to furniture. Take care as staple pins are very sharp.

Spiral
Shaped like a spiral with a very sharp point at one end to enable it to be twisted in and out easily. Used to secure loose covers to furniture.

Pin cushion
Choose a fabric cover: a foam cushion may blunt pins. Magnetic ones should not be put on a computerized sewing machine.

TOOLS

THREADS

There are so many threads available and knowing which ones to choose can be confusing. There are specialist threads designed for special tasks, such as machine embroidery or quilting. Threads also vary in fibre content, from pure cotton to rayon to polyester. Some threads are very fine while others are thick and coarse. Failure to choose the correct thread can spoil your project and lead to problems with the stitch quality of the sewing machine or overlocker.

Cotton thread
A 100% cotton thread. Smooth and firm, this is designed to be used with cotton fabrics and is much favoured by quilters.

Polyester all-purpose thread
A good-quality polyester thread that has a very slight "give", making it suitable to sew all types of fabrics and garments, as well as soft furnishings. The most popular type of thread.

Silk thread
A sewing thread made from 100% silk. Used for machining delicate silk garments. It is also used for tacking or temporary stitching in areas that are to be pressed, such as jacket collars, because it can be removed without leaving an imprint.

Elastic thread
A thin, round elastic thread normally used on the bobbin of the sewing machine for stretch effects such as shirring.

Embroidery thread
Often made from a rayon yarn for shine. This is a finer thread designed for machine embroidery. Available on much larger reels for economy.

Overlocker thread
A dull yarn on a larger reel designed to be used on the overlocker. This type of yarn is normally not strong enough to use on the sewing machine.

Top-stitching thread
A thicker polyester thread used for decorative top-stitching and buttonholes. Also for hand sewing buttons on thicker fabrics and some soft furnishings.

Metallic thread
A rayon and metal thread for decorative machining and machine embroidery. This thread usually requires a specialist sewing-machine needle.

HABERDASHERY ITEMS

The term haberdashery covers all of the bits and pieces that a sewer tends to need, for example fasteners such as buttons, snaps, hooks and eyes, and Velcro™. But haberdashery also includes elastics, ribbons, trimmings of all types, and boning.

BUTTONS

Buttons can be made from almost anything – shell, bone, coconut, nylon, plastic, brass, silver. They can be any shape, from geometric to abstract to animal shapes. A button may have a shank or have holes on the surface to enable it to be attached to fabric.

OTHER FASTENERS

Hooks and eyes (below left), snaps (below centre), and Velcro™ (below right) all come in a wide variety of forms, differing in size, shape, and colour. Some hooks and eyes are designed to be seen, while snaps and Velcro™ are intended to be hidden fasteners.

TRIMMINGS, DECORATIONS, FRINGES, AND BRAIDS

Decorative finishing touches – fringes, strips of sequins, ric-rac braids, feathers, pearls, bows, flowers, and beads – can dress up a garment, embellish a bag, or personalize soft furnishings. Some are designed to be inserted into seams while others are surface-mounted.

RIBBONS

From the narrowest strips to wide swathes, ribbons are made from a variety of yarns, such as nylon, polyester, and cotton. They can be printed or plain and may feature metallic threads or wired edges.

ELASTIC

Elastic is available in many forms, from very narrow, round cord to wide strips (below left). It may have buttonhole slots in it (below right) or even have a decorative edge.

BONING

You can buy various types of boning in varying widths. Polyester boning (bottom left), used in boned bodices, can be sewn through, while nylon boning (bottom right), also used on boned bodices, has to be inserted into a casing. Specialist metal boning (below left and right), which may be either straight or spiral, is for corsets and bridal wear.

PRESSING **AIDS**

Successful sewing relies on successful pressing. Without the correct pressing equipment, sewing can look too "home-made", whereas if correctly pressed any sewn item will have a neat, professional finish.

▲ Mini iron
Useful to get into small corners and gathers. Use in conjunction with the pressing mat.

◀ Iron
A good-quality steam iron is a wonderful asset. Choose a reasonably heavy iron that has steam and a shot of steam facility.

▲ Ironing board
Essential to iron on. Make sure the board is height-adjustable.

◀ Pressing mat
A heat-resistant mat for pressing small items.

◀ Tailor's ham
A ham-shaped pressing cushion that is used to press darts and the curved shape of collars and shoulders, and in making tailored garments.

▲ Seam roll
This tubular pressing aid is used to press seams open on fabrics that mark, as the iron only touches the seam on top of the roll. Also used for sleeve and trouser seams.

▲ Clapper
A wooden aid that pounds creases into a heavy fabric after steaming. The top section is used to help press collar seams and points.

Pressing cloth ▶
Choose a cloth made from silk organza or muslin as you can see through it. The cloth will stop the iron marking fabric and prevent burning delicate fabrics.

▼ Velvet mat
A pressing mat with a tufted side to aid the pressing of pile fabrics, such as velvet.

Pressing mitten ▶
Slips on to your hand to enable more control over where you are pressing.

TOOLS

SEWING **MACHINE**

A sewing machine will quickly speed up any job, whether it be a quick repair or a huge home-sewing project. Most sewing machines today are aided by computer technology, which enhances stitch quality and ease of use. Always spend time trying out a sewing machine before you buy, to really get a feel for it.

Threading guides
Markings to help guide you in threading the machine.

Tension dial
To control the stitch tension on the upper thread, i.e. how fast the thread feeds through the sewing machine.

Automatic needle threader
A pull-down gadget to aid threading the machine needle.

Buttonhole sensor
A pull-down sensor that automatically judges the size of the buttonhole required to fit the button chosen.

Needle
The machine needle. Replace it regularly to ensure good stitch quality. **See p.32**

Presser foot
To hold the fabric in place while stitching. Various feet can be used here to aid different sewing processes. **See pp.32–33**

Dog feeds
These metal teeth grip the fabric and feed it through the machine.

Removable free arm
This section of the machine will pull away to give a narrow work bed that can be used when inserting sleeves. It also contains a useful storage section.

Shank
To hold the various feet in place.

Needle plate
A transparent removable cover reveals the bobbin. This plate is gridded to help stitch seams of various widths.

JANOME

Spool holder
To hold your sewing
thread in place.

Bobbin winder
Winds the thread from
the spool on to the bobbin,
keeping it under tension.
See p.32

LCD screen
An illuminated screen
that indicates which
stitch you are using.

Balance wheel
This can be turned towards
you to move the needle up
or down manually.

Buttons
To provide
various
functions, such
as reverse,
locking stitch,
needle-in, and
automatic
thread cutting.

Touch buttons
Use these to change the type
of stitch you are using and to
increase and decrease size
and width of stitch.

Speed control
A slide, to control the
speed of your machine.

Stitch library
All the different stitches this
machine can stitch. You just
have to key in the number.

SEWING-MACHINE ACCESSORIES

Many accessories can be purchased for your sewing machine to make certain sewing processes so much easier. There are different machine needles not only for different fabrics but also for different types of threads. There is also a huge number of sewing-machine feet, and new feet are constantly coming on to the market. Those shown here are some of the most popular.

Plastic bobbin
The bobbin is for the lower thread. Some machines take plastic bobbins, others metal. Always check which sort of bobbin your machine uses as the incorrect choice can cause stitch problems.

Metal bobbin
Also known as a universal bobbin, this is used on many types of sewing machine. Be sure to check that your machine needs a metal bobbin before you buy.

Machine needles
There are different types of sewing machine needle to cope with different fabrics. Machine needles are sized from 60 to 100, a 60 being a very fine needle. There are special needles for machine embroidery and also for metallic threads.

Overedge foot
A foot that runs along the raw edge of the fabric and holds it stable while an overedge stitch is worked.

Embroidery foot
A clear plastic foot with a groove underneath that allows linear machine embroidery stitches to pass under.

Free embroidery or darning foot
A foot designed to be used when the dog feeds on the machine are lowered. This enables a free motion stitch to be worked.

Buttonhole foot
This extends and the button is placed in the back of the foot. The machine will stitch a buttonhole to fit due to the buttonhole sensor.

Blind hem foot
Use this foot in conjunction with the blind hem stitch to create a neat hemming stitch.

Rolled hem foot
This foot rolls the fabric while stitching with a straight stitch or a zigzag stitch.

Walking foot
This strange-looking foot "walks" across the fabric, so that the upper layer of fabric does not push forward. Great for matching checks and stripes and also for difficult fabrics.

Zip foot
This foot fits to either the right or left-hand side of the needle to enable you to stitch close to a zip.

Concealed zip foot
A foot that is used to insert a concealed zip – the foot holds open the coils of the zip, enabling you to stitch behind them.

Pin tuck foot
A foot with grooves underneath to allow multiple pin tucks to be sewn.

Piping foot
A deep groove in this foot allows a piping cord to fit underneath, enabling close stitching to the cord.

Ribbon foot
A foot that will feed either one or two ribbons evenly under the machine needle to ensure accurate stitching.

Beading foot, narrow
This foot has a narrow groove and is used to attach small beads or decorative cords.

Beading foot, wide
Beads on a string will fit under the foot, which has a wide groove, and they can then be zigzag stitched over.

Ultra-glide foot
A foot made from Teflon™ that glides over the fabric. Useful for synthetic leathers.

OVERLOCKER

This machine is often used in conjunction with the sewing machine as it gives a very professional finish to your work. The overlocker has two upper threads and two lower threads (the loopers), with a knife that removes the edge of the fabric. Used extensively for neatening the edges of fabric, it can also be used for construction of stretch knits.

OVERLOCKER STITCHES

As the overlocker works, the threads wrap around the edge to give a professional finish. The 3-thread stitch is used primarily for neatening. A 4-thread stitch can also be used for neatening, as well as for construction due to its having the extra thread.

▶ **3-THREAD OVERLOCK STITCH**

▶ **4-THREAD OVERLOCK STITCH**

OVERLOCKER ACCESSORIES

You can purchase additional feet for the overlocker, such as a cording foot to aid decorative techniques.

Overlocker needles
The overlocker uses a ballpoint needle, which creates a large loop in the thread for the loopers to catch and produce a stitch. If a normal sewing machine needle is used it could damage the overlocker.

Overlocker foot
The standard foot used for most processes.

Cording foot
A foot with a coil on one side through which a thin cord or fishing line is fed. Use in conjunction with a rolled hem setting for decorative effects.

Thread guides
To guide the thread from the reels.

Tension dials
There are four tension dials, one for each thread.

Thread guides
To guide the thread through the machine.

Stitch length
To set the size of the machine stitch.

Differential feed
This dial controls the ratio between the two layers of fabric feeding under the foot.

Knives
The two knives that cut away the fabric edge.

Balance wheel
This can be turned manually backwards to disengage a stitch.

Waste catcher
A removable tray that collects the edge of the fabric as it is trimmed off.

EMBROIDERY **MACHINE**

A machine that does not sew but embroiders, this enables you to produce embellished clothing or homewares. Computer-controlled, the machine has plenty of built-in embroidery designs and there are many more designs that can be purchased to use with it. The machine works best with special embroidery threads and bobbin threads.

EMBROIDERY DESIGNS

Here are some examples of the many types of design that can be stitched out, to personalize and embellish clothing and accessories as well as placemats, tablecloths, serviettes, baby blankets, pillows, and many other items.

EMBROIDERY MACHINE ACCESSORIES

Hoops of varying shapes and sizes fit on to the machine carriage to enable the embroidery to be stitched.

A gridded template on the bottom of the embroidery hoop aids placement of the design.

Once the fabric is stretched in the hoop, the ring is pressed down and secured. The fabric must be held taut.

Spool holder
To hold the machine embroidery thread.

Bobbin winder
To wind the bobbins. An embroidery machine requires bobbin thread, which is a slightly finer thread.

LCD screen
A touch screen from which you choose your design and programme the machine. The screen allows you to build up your own design by combining different components.

Scissor cutter
This button cuts the embroidery threads when you need to change colours or have completed your design.

Tension dial
To control the tension in the upper thread.

JANOME

Start/stop button
This machine has no foot control as it will sew on its own! Use this button to start and stop it.

Automatic needle threader
To aid threading the machine needle.

Needle and foot
The machine needle and embroidery foot.

Hoop
The embroidery hoop in position.

FABRICS

Whether making clothes, soft furnishings, or crafts, it's important to choose the right fabric for your project. You need to consider weight and drape of the fabric, the width, the cost, and the care – some have to be dry-cleaned.

TOOLS

WOOL FABRICS

A natural fibre, wool comes primarily from sheep – Australian merino sheep's wool is considered to be the best. However, we also get wool fibres from goats (mohair and cashmere), rabbits (angora), camels (camel hair), and alpaca. A wool fibre is either short and fluffy, when it is known as a woollen yarn, or it is long, strong, and smooth, when it is called worsted. The term virgin (or new) wool denotes wool fibres that are being used for the first time. Wool may be reprocessed or reused and is then often mixed with other fibres.

PROPERTIES OF WOOL

- **Comfortable to wear** in all climates as it is available in many weights and weaves
- **Warm in the winter** and cool in the summer, because it will breathe with your body
- **Absorbs moisture** better than other natural fibres – will absorb up to 30 per cent of its weight before it feels wet
- **Flame-resistant**

- **Relatively** crease-resistant
- **Ideal to tailor** as it can be easily shaped with steam
- **Often blended** with other fibres to reduce the cost of fabric
- **Felts if exposed** to excessive heat, moisture, and pressure
- **Will be bleached** by sunlight with prolonged exposure
- **Can be damaged** by moths

CASHMERE

Wool from the Kashmir goat, and the most luxurious of all the wools. A soft yet hard-wearing fabric available in different weights.

Cutting out: as cashmere often has a slight pile, use a nap layout

Seams: plain, neatened with overlocker stitch or pinking shears (a zigzag stitch would curl the edge of the seam)

Thread: a silk thread is ideal, or a polyester all-purpose thread

Needle: machine size 12/14, depending on the thickness of the fabric; sharps for hand sewing

Pressing: steam iron on a steam setting, with a pressing cloth and seam roll

Use for: jackets, coats, men's wear; knitted cashmere yarn for sweaters, cardigans, underwear

CHALLIS

A fine wool fabric, made from a worsted yarn that has an uneven surface texture. Challis is often printed as well as plain.

Cutting out: a nap layout is not required unless the fabric is printed

Seams: plain, neatened with overlocker or zigzag stitch; a run and fell seam can also be used

Thread: polyester all-purpose thread

Needle: machine size 11/12; sharps for hand sewing

Pressing: steam iron on a steam setting, with a pressing cloth; fabric will stretch while warm so handle with care

Use for: dresses, jackets, garments with pleating or draping detail

CREPE

A soft fabric made from a twisted yarn, which is what produces the uneven surface. It is important to preshrink this fabric prior to use by giving it a good steaming, because it will have stretched on the bolt and it is prone to shrinkage.

Cutting out: a nap layout is not required

Seams: plain, neatened with overlocker (a zigzag stitch may curl the edge of the seam)

Thread: polyester all-purpose thread

Needle: machine size 12; sharps or milliner's for hand sewing

Pressing: steam iron on a wool setting; a pressing cloth is not always required

Use for: all types of clothing

NEEDLES AND PINS pp.22–23 • **THREADS pp.24–25** • **PRESSING AIDS pp.28–29**

FLANNEL

A wool with a lightly brushed surface, featuring either a plain or twill weave.

Cutting out: use a nap layout

Seams: plain, neatened with overlocker or zigzag stitch or Hong Kong finish

Thread: polyester all-purpose thread

Needle: machine size 14; sharps for hand sewing

Pressing: steam iron on a wool setting with a pressing cloth; use a seam roll as the fabric is prone to marking

Use for: coats, jackets, skirts, men's wear

GABARDINE

A hard-wearing suiting fabric with a distinctive weave. Gabardine often has a sheen and is prone to shine. It can be difficult to handle as it is springy and frays badly.

Cutting out: a nap layout is advisable as the fabric has a sheen

Seams: plain, neatened with overlocker or zigzag stitch

Thread: polyester all-purpose thread or 100 per cent cotton thread

Needle: machine size 14; sharps for hand sewing

Pressing: steam iron on a wool setting; use just the toe of the iron and a silk organza pressing cloth as the fabric will mark and may shine

Use for: men's wear, jackets, trousers

MOHAIR

From the wool of the Angora goat. A long, straight, and very strong fibre that produces a hairy cloth or yarn for knitting.

Cutting out: use a nap layout, with the fibres brushing down the pattern pieces in the same direction, from neck to hem

Seams: plain, neatened with overlocker or pinking shears

Thread: polyester all-purpose thread

Needle: machine size 14; sharps for hand sewing

Pressing: steam iron on a wool setting; "stroke" the iron over the wool, moving in the direction of the nap

Use for: jackets, coats, men's wear, soft furnishings; knitted mohair yarns for sweaters

TARTAN

An authentic tartan belongs to a Scottish clan, and each has its own unique design that can only be used by that clan. The fabric is made using a twill weave from worsted yarns.

Cutting out: check the design for even/uneven check as it may need a nap layout or even a single layer layout

Seams: plain, matching the pattern and neatened with overlocker or zigzag stitch

Thread: polyester all-purpose thread

Needle: machine size 14; sharps for hand sewing

Pressing: steam iron on a wool setting; may require a pressing cloth, so test first

Use for: traditionally kilts, but these days also skirts, trousers, jackets, soft furnishings

CUTTING OUT pp.76–83 ● **MACHINE STITCHES AND SEAMS pp.92–109**

TWEED, MODERN

A mix of chunky and nobbly wool yarns. Modern tweed is often found in contemporary colour palettes as well as plain, and with interesting fibres in the weft such as metallics and paper. It is much favoured by fashion designers.

Cutting out: use a nap layout

Seams: plain, neatened with overlocker or zigzag stitch; the fabric is prone to fraying

Thread: polyester all-purpose thread

Needle: machine size 14; sharps for hand sewing

Pressing: steam iron on a wool setting; a pressing cloth may not be required

Use for: jackets, coats; also skirts, dresses, soft furnishings

TWEED, TRADITIONAL

A rough fabric with a distinctive warp and weft, usually in different colours, and often forming a small check pattern. Traditional tweed is associated with the English countryside.

Cutting out: a nap layout is not required unless the fabric features a check

Seams: plain, neatened with overlocker or zigzag stitch; can also be neatened with pinking shears

Thread: polyester all-purpose thread or 100 per cent cotton thread

Needle: machine size 14; sharps for hand sewing

Pressing: steam iron on a steam setting; a pressing cloth may not be required

Use for: jackets, coats, skirts, men's wear, soft furnishings

VENETIAN

A wool with a satin weave, making a luxurious, expensive fabric.

Cutting out: use a nap layout

Seams: plain, neatened with overlocker or zigzag stitch

Thread: polyester all-purpose thread or 100 per cent cotton thread

Needle: machine size 14; sharps for hand sewing

Pressing: steam iron on a steam setting with a silk organza cloth to avoid shine; use a seam roll under the seams to prevent them from showing through

Use for: jackets, coats, men's wear

WOOL WORSTED

A light and strong cloth, made from good-quality thin, firm filament fibres. Always steam prior to cutting out as the fabric may shrink slightly after having been stretched around a bolt.

Cutting out: use a nap layout

Seams: plain, neatened with overlocker or zigzag stitch or Hong Kong finish

Thread: polyester all-purpose thread

Needle: machine size 12/14, depending on fabric; milliner's or sharps for hand sewing

Pressing: steam iron on a wool setting, with a pressing cloth; use a seam roll to prevent the seam from showing through

Use for: skirts, jackets, coats, trousers

NEEDLES AND PINS **pp.22–23** • THREADS **pp.24–25** • PRESSING AIDS **pp.28–29**

COTTON FABRICS

One of the most versatile and popular of all fabrics, cotton is a natural fibre that comes from the seed pods, or bolls, of the cotton plant. It is thought that cotton fibres have been in use since ancient times. Today, the world's biggest producers of cotton include the United States, India, and countries in the Middle East. Cotton fibres can be filament or staple, with the longest and finest used for top-quality bed linen. Cotton clothing is widely worn in warmer climates as the fabric will keep you cool.

PROPERTIES OF COTTON

▸ **Absorbs moisture** well and carries heat away from the body

▸ **Stronger wet than dry**

▸ **Does not build up** static electricity

▸ **Dyes well**

▸ **Prone to shrinkage** unless it has been treated

▸ **Will deteriorate** from mildew and prolonged exposure to sunlight

▸ **Creases easily**

▸ **Soils easily,** but launders well

BRODERIE ANGLAISE

A fine, plain-weave cotton that has been embroidered in such a way as to make small holes. Usually white or a pastel colour.

Cutting out: may need a nap layout to place embroidery at hem edge

Seams: plain, neatened with overlocker or zigzag stitch; a French seam can also be used

Thread: polyester all–purpose thread

Needle: machine size 12/14; sharps for hand sewing

Pressing: steam iron on a cotton setting; a pressing cloth is not required

Use for: baby clothes, summer skirts, blouses

CALICO

A plain weave fabric that is usually unbleached and quite stiff. Available in many different weights, from very fine to extremely heavy.

Cutting out: a nap layout is not required

Seams: plain, neatened with overlocker or zigzag stitch

Thread: polyester all–purpose thread

Needle: machine size 11/14, depending on thickness of thread; sharps for hand sewing

Pressing: steam iron on a steam setting; a pressing cloth is not required

Use for: toiles (test garments), soft furnishings

CHAMBRAY

A light cotton that has a coloured warp thread and white weft thread. Chambray can also be found as a check or a striped fabric.

Cutting out: a nap layout should not be required

Seams: plain, neatened with overlocker or zigzag stitch

Thread: polyester all-purpose thread

Needle: machine size 11; sharps for hand sewing

Pressing: steam iron on a cotton setting; a pressing cloth is not required

Use for: blouses, men's shirts, children's wear

CHINTZ

A floral print or plain cotton fabric with a glazed finish that gives it a sheen. It has a close weave and is often treated to resist dirt.

Cutting out: use a nap layout

Seams: plain, neatened with overlocker or zigzag stitch; a run and fell seam can also be used

Thread: polyester all-purpose thread or 100 per cent cotton thread

Needle: machine size 14; milliner's for hand sewing

Pressing: steam iron on a cotton setting; a pressing cloth may be required due to sheen on fabric

Use for: soft furnishings

CUTTING OUT pp.76–83 ● **MACHINE STITCHES AND SEAMS pp.92–109**

TOOLS

CORDUROY

A soft pile fabric with distinctive stripes (known as wales or ribs) woven into it. The name depends on the size of the ribs: baby or pin cord has extremely fine ribs; needle cord has slightly thicker ribs; corduroy has 10–12 ribs per 2.5cm (1in); and elephant or jumbo cord has thick, heavy ribs.

Cutting out: use a nap layout with the pile on the corduroy brushing up the pattern pieces from hem to neck, to give depth of colour

Seams: plain, stitched using a walking foot and neatened with overlocker or zigzag stitch

Thread: polyester all-purpose thread

Needle: machine size 12/16; sharps or milliner's for hand sewing

Pressing: steam iron on a cotton setting; use a seam roll under the seams with a pressing cloth

Use for: trousers, skirts, men's wear

CRINKLE COTTON

Looks like an exaggerated version of seersucker (see p.46), with creases added by a heat process. Crinkle cotton may require careful laundering as it often has to be twisted into shape when wet to put the creases back in.

Cutting out: a nap layout is not required unless the fabric is printed

Seams: plain, neatened with overlocker or zigzag stitch

Thread: polyester all-purpose thread

Needle: machine size 12; milliner's for hand sewing

Pressing: steam iron on a cotton setting; take care not to press out the crinkles

Use for: blouses, dresses, children's wear

DAMASK

A cotton that has been woven on a jacquard loom to produce a fabric usually with a floral pattern in a self colour. May have a sheen to the surface.

Cutting out: use a nap layout

Seams: plain, neatened with overlocker or zigzag stitch

Thread: polyester all-purpose thread or 100 per cent cotton thread

Needle: machine size 14; sharps for hand sewing

Pressing: steam iron on a cotton setting; a pressing cloth may be required if the fabric has a sheen

Use for: home furnishings; coloured jacquards for jackets, skirts

DENIM

Named after Nîmes in France. A hard-wearing twill-weave fabric with a coloured warp and white weft, usually made into jeans. Available in various weights and often mixed with an elastic thread for stretch. Denim is usually blue, but is also available in a variety of other colours.

Cutting out: a nap layout is not required

Seams: run and fell or top-stitched plain

Thread: polyester all-purpose thread with top-stitching thread for detail top-stitching

Needle: machine size 14/16; sharps for hand sewing

Pressing: steam iron on a cotton setting; a pressing cloth should not be required

Use for: jeans, jackets, children's wear

DRILL

A hard-wearing twill or plain-weave fabric with the same colour warp and weft. Drill frays badly on the cut edges.

Cutting out: a nap layout is not required

Seams: run and fell; or plain, neatened with overlocker or zigzag stitch

Thread: polyester all-purpose thread with top-stitching thread for detail top-stitching

Needle: machine size 14; sharps for hand sewing

Pressing: steam iron on a cotton setting; a pressing cloth is not required

Use for: men's wear, casual jackets, trousers

GINGHAM

A fresh, two-colour cotton fabric that features a check of various sizes. A plain weave made by having groups of white and coloured warp and weft threads.

Cutting out: usually an even check, so nap layout is not required but recommended; pattern will need matching

Seams: plain, neatened with overlocker or zigzag stitch

Thread: polyester all-purpose thread

Needle: machine size 11/12; sharps for hand sewing

Pressing: steam iron on a cotton setting; a pressing cloth should not be required

Use for: children's wear, dresses, shirts, home furnishings

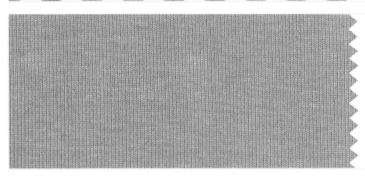

JERSEY

A fine cotton yarn that has been knitted to give stretch, making the fabric very comfortable to wear. Jersey will also drape well.

Cutting out: a nap layout is recommended

Seams: 4-thread overlock stitch; or plain seam stitched with a small zigzag stitch and then seam

allowances stitched with a zigzag

Thread: polyester all-purpose thread

Needle: machine size 12/14; a ballpoint needle may be required for overlocker and milliner's for hand sewing

Pressing: steam iron on a wool setting; it may shrink on cotton setting

Use for: underwear, drapey dresses, leisurewear, bedding

COTTON LAWN

A plain-weave fabric woven from fine, high-density yarns, which results in a silky, smooth feel.

Cutting out: a nap layout is not required unless the fabric has a one-way print

Seams: plain, neatened with overlocker or zigzag stitch; French

Thread: pure cotton thread; or a polyester all-purpose thread

Needle: machine size 11; or a milliner's size 9 for hand sewing

Pressing: steam iron on a cotton setting; a pressing cloth should not be required

Use for: blouses, shirts, dresses, children's wear, interlining

MADRAS

A check fabric made from a fine cotton yarn, usually from India. Often found in bright colours featuring an uneven check. An inexpensive cotton fabric.

Cutting out: use a nap layout and match the checks

Seams: plain, neatened with overlocker or zigzag stitch

Thread: polyester all-purpose thread

Needle: machine size 12/14; sharps for hand sewing

Pressing: steam iron on a cotton setting; a pressing cloth is not required

Use for: shirts, skirts, home furnishings

CUTTING OUT pp.76–83 • **MACHINE STITCHES AND SEAMS pp.92–109**

MUSLIN

A fine, plain, open-weave cotton. Can be found in colours but usually sold a natural/unbleached or white. Makes great pressing cloths and interlinings. It is a good idea to wash prior to use.

Cutting out: a nap layout is not required

Seams: 4-thread overlock stitch; or plain seam, neatened with overlocker or zigzag stitch; a French seam could also be used

Thread: polyester all-purpose thread

Needle: machine size 11; milliner's for hand sewing

Pressing: steam iron on a cotton setting; a cloth is not required

Use for: curtaining and other household uses

SEERSUCKER

A woven cotton that has a bubbly appearance woven into it, due to stripes of puckers. Do not over-press, or the surface effect will be damaged.

Cutting out: use a nap layout, due to puckered surface effect

Seams: plain, neatened with overlocker or zigzag stitch

Thread: polyester all-purpose thread

Needle: machine size 11/12; milliner's for hand sewing

Pressing: steam iron on a cotton setting (be careful not to press out the wrinkles)

Use for: summer clothing, skirts, shirts, children's wear

SHIRTING

A closely woven, fine cotton, with coloured warp and weft yarns making stripes or checks.

Cutting out: use a nap layout if fabric has uneven stripes

Seams: plain, neatened with overlocker or zigzag stitch; a run and fell seam can also be used

Thread: polyester all-purpose thread

Needle: machine size 12; milliner's for hand sewing

Pressing: steam iron on a cotton setting; a pressing cloth is not required

Use for: ladies' and men's shirts

TOWELLING

A cotton fabric with loops on the surface; top-quality towelling has loops on both sides. It is highly absorbent. Wash before use to preshrink and make it fluffy.

Cutting out: use a nap layout

Seams: 4-thread overlock stitch; or plain seam, neatened with overlocker or zigzag stitch

Thread: polyester all-purpose thread

Needle: machine size 14; sharps for hand sewing

Pressing: steam iron on a cotton setting; a pressing cloth is not required

Use for: bathrobes, beachwear

VELVET

A pile-weave fabric, made by using an additional yarn that is then cut to produce the pile. Difficult to handle and can be easily damaged if seams have to be unpicked.

Cutting out: use a nap layout with the pile brushing up from hem to neck, to give depth of colour

Seams: plain, stitched using a walking foot (stitch all seams from hem to neck) and neatened with overlocker or zigzag stitch

Thread: polyester all-purpose thread

Needle: machine size 14; milliner's for hand sewing

Pressing: only if you have to; use a velvet board, a bit of steam, toe of iron, and silk organza cloth

Use for: jackets, coats

NEEDLES AND PINS **pp.22—23** ● THREADS **pp.24—25** ● PRESSING AIDS **pp.28—29**

LINEN FABRICS

Linen is a natural fibre that is derived from the stem of the flax plant. It is available in a variety of qualities and weights, from very fine linen to heavy suiting weights. Coarser than cotton, it is sometimes woven with cotton as well as being mixed with silk.

PROPERTIES OF LINEN

▶ **Cool and comfortable** to wear
▶ **Absorbs moisture well**
▶ **Shrinks when washed**
▶ **Does not ease well**

▶ **Has a tendency** to crease
▶ **Prone to fraying**
▶ **Resists moths** but is damaged by mildew

COTTON AND LINEN MIX

Two fibres may have been mixed together in the yarn or may have mixed warp and weft yarns. It has lots of texture in the weave. Silk and linen mix is treated in the same way.

Cutting out: a nap layout should not be required

Seams: plain, neatened with overlocker or zigzag stitch

Thread: polyester all-purpose thread

Needle: machine size 14; sharps for hand sewing

Pressing: a steam iron on a steam setting, with a silk organza pressing cloth

Use for: summer-weight jackets, tailored dresses

DRESS-WEIGHT LINEN

A medium-weight linen with a plain weave. The yarn is often uneven, which causes slubs in the weave.

Cutting out: a nap layout is not required

Seams: plain, neatened with overlocker or zigzag stitch or a Hong Kong finish

Thread: polyester all-purpose thread with a top-stitching thread for top-stitching

Needle: machine size 14; sharps for hand sewing

Pressing: steam iron on a cotton setting (steam is required to remove creases)

Use for: dresses, trousers, skirts

PRINTED LINENS

Many linens today feature prints or even embroidery. The fabric may be light- to medium weight, with a smooth yarn that has few slubs.

Cutting out: use a nap layout

Seams: plain, neatened with overlocker or zigzag stitch

Thread: polyester all-purpose thread

Needle: machine size 14; sharps for hand sewing

Pressing: steam iron on a cotton setting (steam is required to remove creases)

Use for: dresses, skirts

SUITING LINEN

A heavier yarn is used to produce a linen suitable for suits for men and women. Can be a firm, tight weave or a looser weave.

Cutting out: a nap layout is not required

Seams: plain, neatened with overlocker or a zigzag stitch and sharps hand-sewing needle

Thread: polyester all-purpose thread with a top-stitch thread for top-stitching

Needle: machine size 14; sharps for hand sewing

Pressing: steam iron on a cotton setting (steam is required to remove creases)

Use for: men's and women's suits, trousers, coats

CUTTING OUT **pp.76—83** • MACHINE STITCHES AND SEAMS **pp.92—109**

SILK FABRICS

Often referred to as the queen of all fabrics, silk is made from the fibres of the silkworm's cocoon. This strong and luxurious fabric dates back thousands of years to its first development in China, and the secret of silk production was well protected by the Chinese until 300 CE. Silk fabrics can be very fine or thick and chunky. They need careful handling as some silk fabrics can be easily damaged.

PROPERTIES OF SILK

▶ **Keeps you warm** in winter and cool in summer
▶ **Absorbs moisture** and dries quickly
▶ **Dyes well,** producing deep, rich colours
▶ **Static electricity** can build up and fabric may cling
▶ **Will fade in prolonged** strong sunlight

▶ **Prone to shrinkage**
▶ **Best dry-cleaned**
▶ **Weaker when** wet than dry
▶ **May water-mark**

CHIFFON

A very strong and very fine, transparent silk with a plain weave. Will gather and ruffle well. Difficult to handle.

Cutting out: place tissue paper under the fabric and pin the fabric to the tissue, cutting through all layers if necessary; use extra-fine pins

Seams: French

Thread: polyester all-purpose thread

Needle: machine size 9/11; fine milliner's for hand sewing

Pressing: dry iron on a wool setting

Use for: special-occasion wear, over-blouses

CREPE DE CHINE

Medium weight, with an uneven surface due to the twisted silk yarn used. Drapes well and often used on bias-cut garments.

Cutting out: if to be bias-cut, use a single layer layout; otherwise use a nap layout

Seams: a seam for a difficult fabric or French

Thread: polyester all-purpose thread

Needle: machine size 11; milliner's or betweens for hand sewing

Pressing: dry iron on a wool setting

Use for: blouses, dresses, special-occasion wear

DUCHESSE SATIN

A heavy, expensive satin fabric used almost exclusively for special-occasion wear.

Cutting out: use a nap layout

Seams: plain, with pinked edges

Thread: polyester all-purpose thread

Needle: machine size 12/14; milliner's for hand sewing

Pressing: steam iron on a wool setting with a pressing cloth; use a seam roll under the seams to prevent shadowing

Use for: special-occasion wear

DUPION

Similar to hand-woven dupion (see p.49) but woven using a much smoother yarn to reduce the amount of nubbly bits in the weft.

Cutting out: use a nap layout to prevent shadowing

Seams: plain, neatened with overlocker or zigzag stitch

Thread: polyester all-purpose thread

Needle: machine size 12; milliner's for hand sewing

Pressing: steam iron on a wool setting, with a pressing cloth as fabric may water-mark

Use for: dresses, skirts, jackets, special-occasion wear, soft furnishings

◀ NEEDLES AND PINS **pp.22–23** • THREADS **pp.24–25** • PRESSING AIDS **pp.28–29**

DUPION, HAND-WOVEN

The most popular of all the silks. A distinctive weft yarn with many nubbly bits. Available in hundreds of colours. Easy to handle, but it does fray badly.

Cutting out: use a nap layout as the fabric shadows

Seams: plain, neatened with overlocker or zigzag stitch

Thread: polyester all-purpose thread

Needle: machine size 12; milliner's for hand sewing

Pressing: steam iron on a wool setting, with a pressing cloth to avoid water-marking

Use for: dresses, special-occasion wear, jackets, soft furnishings

GEORGETTE

A soft, filmy silk fabric that has a slight transparency. Does not crease easily.

Cutting out: place tissue paper under the fabric and pin fabric to tissue, cutting through all layers if necessary; use extra-fine pins

Seams: French

Thread: polyester all-purpose thread

Needle: machine size 11; milliner's for hand sewing

Pressing: dry iron on a wool setting (fabric can be damaged by steam)

Use for: special-occasion wear, loose-fitting overshirts

HABUTAI

Originally from Japan, a smooth, fine silk that can have a plain or a twill weave. Fabric is often used for silk painting.

Cutting out: a nap layout is not required

Seams: French

Thread: polyester all-purpose thread

Needle: machine size 9/11; very fine milliner's or betweens for hand sewing

Pressing: steam iron on a wool setting

Use for: lining, shirts, blouses

MATKA

A silk suiting fabric with an uneven-looking yarn. Matka can be mistaken for linen.

Cutting out: use a nap layout as silk may shadow

Seams: plain, neatened with overlocker or zigzag stitch or Hong Kong finish

Thread: polyester all-purpose thread

Needle: machine size 12/14; milliner's for hand sewing

Pressing: steam iron on a wool setting with a pressing cloth; a seam roll is recommended to prevent the seams from showing through

Use for: dresses, jackets, trousers

ORGANZA

A sheer fabric with a crisp appearance that will crease easily.

Cutting out: a nap layout is not required

Seams: French or a seam for a difficult fabric

Thread: polyester all-purpose thread

Needle: machine size 11; milliner's or betweens for hand sewing

Pressing: steam iron on a wool setting; a pressing cloth should not be required

Use for: sheer blouses, shrugs, interlining, interfacing

CUTTING OUT pp.76–83 • **MACHINE STITCHES AND SEAMS pp.92–109**

SATIN

A silk with a satin weave that can be very light to quite heavy in weight.

Cutting out: use a nap layout in a single layer as fabric is slippy

Seams: French; on thicker satins, a seam for a difficult fabric

Thread: polyester all-purpose thread (not silk thread as it becomes weak with wear)

Needle: machine size 11/12; milliner's or betweens for hand sewing

Pressing: steam iron on a wool setting, with a pressing cloth as fabric may water-mark

Use for: blouses, dresses, special-occasion wear

SILK AND WOOL MIX

A fabric made by mixing wool and silk fibres or wool and silk yarns. The fabric made may be fine in quality or thick, like a coating.

Cutting out: use a nap layout

Seams: plain, neatened with overlocker or zigzag stitch

Thread: polyester all-purpose thread

Needle: machine size 11/14, depending on fabric; sharps for hand sewing

Pressing: steam iron on a wool setting; seams will require some steam to make them lie flat

Use for: suits, skirts, trousers, coats

TAFFETA

A smooth, plain-weave fabric with a crisp appearance. It makes a rustling sound when worn. Can require special handling and does not wear well.

Cutting out: use a nap layout, with extra-fine pins in seams as they will mark the fabric

Seams: plain; fabric may pucker, so sew from the hem upwards, keeping the fabric taut under the machine; neaten with overlocker or pinking shears

Thread: polyester all-purpose thread

Needle: machine size 11; milliner's or betweens for hand sewing

Pressing: cool iron, with a seam roll under the seams

Use for: special-occasion wear

LEATHER AND SUEDE

Leather and suede are natural fabrics derived from either a pig or a cow and are sold as skins. Depending on the curing process that has been used, the skin will be either a suede or a leather. The fabrics require special handling.

Leather

Suede

LEATHER AND SUEDE

As the pattern pieces cannot be pinned on to leather and suede, you will need to draw around them using tailor's chalk. After cutting out, the chalk will rub off and will not damage the skin.

Cutting out: a complete pattern is required, left- and right-hand halves; use a nap layout for suede, as it will brush one way

Seams: lapped or plain, using a walking foot or an ultra-glide foot; neatening is not required

Thread: polyester all-purpose thread

Needle: machine size 14 (a special leather needle may actually damage the skin); hand sewing is not recommended

Pressing: steam iron, with a silk organza pressing cloth

Use for: skirts, trousers, jackets, soft furnishings

MAN-MADE FABRICS

The term "man-made" applies to any fabric that is not 100 per cent natural. Many of these fabrics have been developed over the last hundred years, which means they are new compared to natural fibres. Some man-made fabrics are made from natural elements mixed with chemicals while others are made entirely from non-natural substances. The properties of man-made fabrics vary from fabric to fabric.

ACETATE

Introduced in 1924, acetate is made from cellulose and chemicals. The fabric has a slight shine and is widely used for linings. Acetate can also be woven into fabrics such as acetate taffeta, acetate satin, and acetate jersey.

Properties of acetate:
• dyes well
• can be heat-set into pleats
• washes well

Cutting out: use a nap layout due to sheen on fabric

Seams: plain, neatened with overlocker or zigzag stitch, or 4-thread overlock stitch

Thread: polyester all-purpose thread

Needle: machine size 11; sharps for hand sewing

Pressing: steam iron on a cool setting (fabric can melt)

Use for: special-occasion wear, linings

ACRYLIC

Introduced in 1950, acrylic fibres are made from ethylene and acrylonitrile. The fabric resembles wool and makes a good substitute for machine-washable wool. Often seen as a knitted fabric, the fibres can be mixed with wool.

Properties of acrylic:
• little absorbency
• tends to retain odours
• not very strong

Cutting out: a nap layout may be required

Seams: 4-thread overlock stitch on knitted fabrics; plain seam on woven fabrics

Thread: polyester all-purpose thread

Needle: machine size 12/14, but a ballpoint needle may be required on knitted fabrics; sharps for hand sewing

Pressing: steam iron on a wool setting (fabric can be damaged by heat)

Use for: knitted yarns for sweaters; wovens for skirts, blouses

NYLON

Developed by DuPont in 1938, the fabric takes its name from a collaboration between New York and London. Nylon is made from polymer chips that are melted and extruded into fibres. The fabric can be knitted or woven.

Properties of nylon:
• very hard-wearing
• does not absorb moisture

• washes easily, although white nylon can discolour easily
• very strong

Cutting out: a nap layout is not required unless the fabric is printed

Seams: plain, neatened with overlocker or zigzag stitch

Thread: polyester all-purpose thread

Needle: machine size 14, but a ballpoint needle may be required for knitted nylons; sharps for hand sewing

Pressing: steam iron on a silk setting (fabric can melt)

Use for: sportswear, underwear

SCUBA

A relatively new fabric, scuba is a lofty double-knit fabric of finely spun polyester fibres that create a super smooth handle, low sheen, and a full-bodied drape. It is often digitally printed to great effect.

Properties of scuba:
• takes dye well, especially digital prints

• holds its shape after construction
• does not absorb moisture well

Cutting out: a nap layout is not required unless the fabric is printed

Seams: plain seam; no need to neaten but you can pink the edge or overlock

Thread: polyester all-purpose thread

Needle: machine size 14; some scubas may require a ballpoint needle

Pressing: steam iron, with a pressing cloth (fabric can melt)

Use for: skirts and dresses

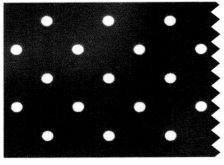

POLYESTER

One of the most popular of the man-made fibres, polyester was introduced in 1951 as a washable man's suit! Polyester fibres are made from petroleum by-products and can take on any form, from a very fine sheer fabric to a thick, heavy suiting.

Properties of polyester:
- non-absorbent
- does not crease
- can build up static
- may "pill"

Cutting out: a nap layout is only required if the fabric is printed

Seams: French, plain, or 4-thread overlock, depending on the weight of the fabric

Thread: polyester all-purpose thread

Needle: machine size 11/14; sharps for hand sewing

Pressing: steam iron on a wool setting

Use for: workwear, school uniforms

RAYON

Also known as viscose and often referred to as artificial silk, this fibre was developed in 1889. It is made from wood pulp or cotton linters mixed with chemicals. Rayon can be knitted or woven and made into a wide range of fabrics. It is often blended with other fibres.

Properties of rayon:
- is absorbent
- is not static
- dyes well
- frays badly

Cutting out: a nap layout is only required if the fabric is printed

Seams: plain, neatened with overlocker or zigzag stitch

Thread: polyester all-purpose thread

Needle: machine size 12/14; sharps for hand sewing

Pressing: steam iron on a silk setting

Use for: dresses, blouses, jackets

SPANDEX

Introduced in 1958, this is a lightweight, soft fibre than can be stretched 500 per cent without breaking. A small amount of spandex is often mixed with other fibres to produce wovens with a slight stretch.

Properties of spandex:
- resistant to body oils, detergents, sun, sea, and sand
- can be difficult to sew
- can be damaged by heat
- not suitable for hand sewing

Cutting out: use a nap layout

Seams: 4-thread overlock stitch or a seam stitched with a small zigzag

Thread: polyester all-purpose thread

Needle: machine ballpoint size 14 or a machine stretch needle

Pressing: steam iron on a wool setting (spandex can be damaged by a hot iron)

Use for: swimwear, foundation wear, sportswear

SYNTHETIC FURS

Created using a looped yarn that is then cut on a knitted or a woven base, synthetic fur can be made from nylon or acrylic fibres. The furs vary tremendously in quality and some are very difficult to tell from the real thing.

Properties of synthetic furs:
- easy to sew
- require careful sewing

- can be heat-damaged by pressing
- not as warm as real fur

Cutting out: use a nap layout, with the fur pile brushed from the neck to the hem; cut just the backing carefully and not through the fur pile

Seams: plain, with a longer stitch and a walking foot; no neatening is required

Thread: polyester all-purpose thread

Needle: machine size 14; sharps for hand sewing

Pressing: if required, use a cool iron (synthetic fur can melt under a hot iron)

Use for: outerwear

SYNTHETIC LEATHER AND SUEDE

Made from polymers, these are non-woven fabrics. Some synthetic leathers and suedes can closely resemble the real thing.

Properties of synthetic leather and suede:
- do not fray
- do not ease well

- can be difficult to sew by hand, so this is not recommended

Cutting out: use a nap layout

Seams: plain, stitched using a walking foot and neatened with pinking shears; can also use top-stitched seams and lapped seams

Thread: polyester all-purpose thread

Needle: machine size 11/14

Pressing: steam iron on a wool setting, with a pressing cloth

Use for: jackets, skirts, trousers, soft furnishings

FABRIC CONSTRUCTION

Most fabric is made by either knitting or weaving. A knitted fabric is constructed by interlocking looped yarns. For a woven fabric, horizontal and vertical yarns go under and over each other. The warp yarn, which is the strongest, runs vertically and the weft crosses it at right angles. There are also non-woven fabrics created by a felting process where tiny fibres are mixed and squeezed together, then rolled out.

PLAIN WEAVE

As the name suggests, this is the simplest of all the weaves. The weft yarn passes under one warp yarn, then over another one.

SATIN WEAVE

This has a long strand known as a float on the warp yarn. The weft goes under four warp yarns, then over one. This weave gives a sheen on the fabric.

HERRINGBONE WEAVE

The distinctive herringbone zigzag weave is made by the weft yarn going under and over warp yarns in a staggered pattern.

TWILL WEAVE

The diagonal twill weave is made by the weft yarn going under two warp yarns, then over another two, with the pattern moved one yarn across each time.

WARP KNIT

This is made on a knitting machine, where one yarn is set to each needle (latch). The knit is formed in a vertical and diagonal direction.

WEFT KNIT

Made in the same way as knitting by hand on needles, this uses one yarn that runs horizontally.

CUTTING OUT **pp.76–83** ● MACHINE STITCHES AND SEAMS **pp.92–109**

INTERFACINGS

An interfacing is a piece of fabric that is attached to the main fabric to give it support or structure. An interfacing fabric may be woven, knitted, or non-woven. It may also be fusible or non-fusible. A fusible interfacing (also called iron-on) can be bonded to the fabric by applying heat, whereas a non-fusible interfacing needs to be sewn to the fabric with a tacking stitch. Always cut interfacings on the same grain as the fabric, regardless of its construction.

FUSIBLE INTERFACINGS

Be sure to buy fusibles designed for the home sewer, because the adhesive on the back of fusible interfacings for commercial use cannot be released with a normal steam iron. Do all pattern marking after the interfacing has been applied to the fabric.

WOVEN

A woven fusible is always a good choice for a woven fabric as the two weaves will work together. Always cut on the same grain as the fabric. This type of interfacing is suitable for crafts and for more structured garments.

LIGHTWEIGHT WOVEN

A very light, woven fusible that is almost sheer, this can be difficult to cut out as it tends to stick to the scissors. It is suitable for all light-to medium-weight fabrics.

KNITTED

A knitted fusible is ideally suited to a knit fabric as the two will be able to stretch together. Some knitted fusibles only stretch one way, while others will stretch in all directions. A knitted fusible is also a good choice on fabrics that have a percentage of stretch.

NON-WOVEN

Non-woven fusibles are available in a wide variety of weights – choose one that feels lighter than your fabric. You can always add a second layer if one interfacing proves to be too light. This interfacing is suitable for supporting collars and cuffs, and facings on garments.

▶ HOW TO APPLY A FUSIBLE INTERFACING

1 Place fabric on pressing surface, wrong side up, making sure it is straight and not wrinkled.

2 Place the chosen interfacing sticky side down on the fabric (the sticky side feels gritty).

3 Cover with a dry pressing cloth and spray the cloth with a fine mist of water.

4 Place a steam iron, on a steam setting, on top of the pressing cloth.

5 Leave the iron in place for at least 10 seconds before moving it to the next area of fabric.

6 Check to see if the interfacing is fused to the fabric by rolling the fabric – if the interfacing is still loose in places, repeat the pressing process.

7 When the fabric has cooled down, the fusing process will be complete. Then pin the pattern back on to the fabric and transfer the pattern markings as required.

NON-FUSIBLE INTERFACINGS

These sew-in interfacings require tacking to the wrong side of facings or the main garment fabric around the seam allowances. They are useful for sheer or fine fabrics where the adhesive from a fusible interfacing might show through.

ALPACA

A tailoring canvas made from wool and alpaca, this interfacing is excellent to use in difficult fabrics such as velvet, because the alpaca can be steamed into shape.

VOILE AND BATISTE

Voile (shown) is a lightweight, semi-sheer, 100 per cent cotton fabric. It is perfect as an underlining or for interfacing silks and cotton lawns. It can also be used in heirloom sewing and smocking. Batiste is very similar but slightly firmer, and can be used in the same ways.

MUSLIN

A cotton muslin interfacing is a good choice on summer dresses as well as for special-occasion wear. Muslin can also be used to line fine cotton dresses.

ORGANZA

A pure silk organza makes an excellent interfacing for sheer fabric to give support and structure. It can also be used for structure in much larger areas such as bridal skirts.

NON-WOVEN SEW-IN INTERFACING

A non-woven material is ideal for crafts and small areas of garments, such as cuffs and collars. Use it in garments when a woven or fusible alternative is not available.

 HOW TO APPLY A NON-FUSIBLE INTERFACING

1 Place the interfacing on to the wrong side of the fabric, aligning the cut edges.

2 Pin in place.

3 Using a basic tacking stitch, tack the interfacing to the fabric or facing at 1cm (⅜in) within the seam allowance.

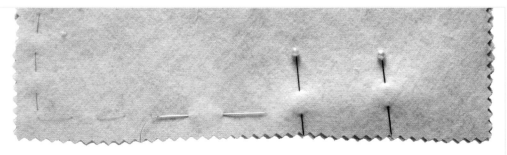

STITCHES FOR HAND SEWING **pp.88–91** ● APPLYING INTERFACING TO A FACING **p.153** ● LININGS AND INTERFACINGS **pp.322–333**

PATTERNS

Patterns are available not only for clothes but for a whole range of crafts and soft furnishing projects. It is always a good idea to test out a pattern in calico before using the real fabric – this is known as making a toile.

READING **PATTERNS**

Paper patterns are available for clothing, crafts, and home furnishings. A pattern has three main components: the envelope, the pattern, and the instructions. The envelope gives an illustration of the finished item, together with fabric suggestions and requirements. The pattern sheets inside the envelope contain a wealth of information, while the instructions tell you how to construct the item.

READING A PATTERN ENVELOPE

The envelope front illustrates the finished item that can be made from its contents. This may be a line drawing or a photograph. Different versions will be labelled as views. The reverse of the envelope usually depicts an illustration of the back view and the body measurement chart used for that pattern. There is also a chart to help you purchase the correct amount of fabric. Suitable fabrics are also listed alongside "notions", or haberdashery. Smaller independent pattern companies may list this information differently.

Number of pattern pieces

Code number for ordering

Description of garment or item, giving details of style and different views included in pattern

List of pattern sizes in metric and imperial measurements for bust, waist, and hips in each size

Suggested fabrics suitable for garment or item as well as unsuitable fabrics

Notions required for each view

5678
15 PIECES

MISSES' UNLINED JACKET, SKIRT, SHORTS, AND PANTS. Unlined, semi-fitted, V-neck jacket has short sleeves, front buttons, optional waistline darts, and optional breast pocket. Straight skirt, above mid-knee, and trousers or shorts with straight legs, have waistband, front pleats, side seam pockets, and back zip.

FABRICS: Jacket, skirt, shorts, and trousers: wool crepe, soft cottons, sheeting, linen, silk, silk types, and lightweight woollens. Skirt, shorts, and trousers also challis, jacquards, and crepe. Unsuitable for fabrics printed with obvious diagonals. Allow extra fabric in order to match plaids, stripes, or one-way design fabrics.

Use nap yardages/layouts for shaded, pile, or one-way design fabrics. *with nap. ** without nap
NOTIONS: Thread. Jacket: three 1.2 cm (⅜ in) buttons; 6mm (¼in) shoulder pads. Skirt, trousers: pkg of 3.2 cm (1¼ in) waistband interfacing; 18 cm (7 in) zip; and one hook and eye closure.

METRIC

Body measurements	(6	8	10)	(12	14	16)	(18	20	22)	
Bust	78	80	83	87	92	97	102	107	112	cm
Waist	58	61	63.5	66	71	76	81	86	94	cm
Hip	81	84	86	91	96.5	102	107	112	117	cm

Fabric needed		(6	8	10)	(12	14	16)	(18	20	22)	
Jacket	115 cm*/**	1.70	1.70	1.70	1.80	1.80	2.10	2.20	2.20	2.20	m
	150 cm*/**	1.30	1.30	1.30	1.40	1.70	1.70	1.70	1.80	1.80	m
Interfacing		1 m of 55–90 cm lightweight fusible or non-fusible									
Skirt A	115 cm*/**	1.6	1.6	1.6	1.6	1.9	1.9	1.9	1.9	2	m
	150 cm*/**	1.2	1.2	1.3	1.3	1.3	1.3	1.4	1.4	1.5	m
Shorts B	115 cm*/**	1.6	1.6	1.6	1.6	1.9	1.9	1.9	1.9	2	m
	150 cm*/**	1.2	1.2	1.3	1.3	1.3	1.3	1.4	1.4	1.5	m
Pants B	115 cm*/**	2.4	2.4	2.4	2.4	2.4	2.4	2.4	2.7	2.7	m
	150 cm*	2	2	2	2	2.1	2.1	2.2	2.3	2.3	m
	150 cm**	1.6	1.6	1.8	2	2	2.1	2.2	2.3	2.3	m

Garment measurements	(6	8	10)	(12	14	16)	(18	20	22)	
Jacket bust	92	94.5	97	101	106	111	116	121	126	cm
Jacket waist	81	83	86	89.5	94.5	100	105	110	116	cm
Jacket back length	73	73.5	74	75	75.5	76	77	77.5	78	cm
Skirt A lower edge	99	101	104	106	112	117	122	127	132	cm
Skirt A length	61	61	61	63	63	63	65	65	65	cm
Shorts B leg width	71	73.5	76	81	86.5	94	99	104	109	cm
Shorts B side length	49.5	50	51	51.5	52	52.5	53.5	54	54.5	cm
Pants B leg width	53.5	53.5	56	56	58.5	58.5	61	61	63.5	cm
Pants B side length	103	103	103	103	103	103	103	103	103	cm

IMPERIAL

Body measurements	(6	8	10)	(12	14	16)	(18	20	22)	
Bust	30½	31½	32½	34	36	38	40	42	44	in
Waist	23	24	25	26½	28	30	32	34	37	in
Hip	32½	33½	34½	36	38	40	42	44	46	in

Fabric needed		(6	8	10)	(12	14	16)	(18	20	22)	
Jacket	45 in*/**	1⅞	1⅞	1⅞	1⅞	1⅞	2⅜	2⅜	2⅜	2⅜	yd
	60 in*/**	1½	1½	1½	1⅝	1⅞	1⅞	1⅞	2	2	yd
Interfacing		1⅛ yd of 22–36 in lightweight fusible or non-fusible									
Skirt A	45 in*/**	1¾	1⅞	1⅞	1⅞	2	2	2	2	2⅜	yd
	60 in*/**	1¼	1¼	1⅜	1⅜	1⅜	1⅜	1½	1½	1⅝	yd
Shorts B	45 in*/**	1¾	1¾	1¾	1⅞	2	2	2	2	2⅜	yd
	60 in*/**	1¼	1¼	1⅜	1⅜	1⅜	1⅜	1½	1½	1⅝	yd
Pants B	45 in*/**	2⅝	2⅝	2⅝	2⅝	2⅝	2⅝	2⅝	2⅞	2⅞	yd
	60 in*	2¼	2¼	2¼	2¼	2¼	2¼	2⅜	2½	2½	yd
	60 in**	1¾	1¾	1⅞	2⅛	2⅛	2¼	2⅜	2½	2½	yd

Garment measurements	(6	8	10)	(12	14	16)	(18	20	22)	
Jacket bust	36¼	37¼	38¼	39¾	41¾	43¾	45¼	47¾	49¾	in
Jacket waist	31¾	32¾	33¾	35¼	37¼	39¼	41¼	43¼	45¼	in
Jacket back length	28¾	29	29¼	29½	29¾	30	30¼	30½	30¾	in
Skirt A lower edge	39	40	41	42	44	46	48	50	52	in
Skirt A length	24	24	24	24¾	24¾	24¾	25½	25½	25½	in
Shorts B leg width	28	29	30	32	34	37	39	41	43	in
Shorts B side length	19½	19¾	20	20¼	20½	20¾	21	21¼	21½	in
Pants B leg width	21	21	22	22	23	23	24	24	25	in
Pants B side length	40½	40½	40½	40½	40½	40½	40½	40½	40½	in

Outline drawing of garment or item, including back views, showing darts and zip positions

Garment measurements box gives actual size of finished garment

Chart to follow for required fabric quantity, indicating size across top, and chosen view and correct width down the side

FIGURE SHAPES

Most people fall into one of these four basic figure shapes. Pattern books and envelopes may feature these symbols and they can be used to help you choose suitable patterns for your figure.

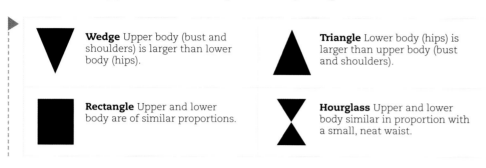

Wedge Upper body (bust and shoulders) is larger than lower body (hips).

Triangle Lower body (hips) is larger than upper body (bust and shoulders).

Rectangle Upper and lower body are of similar proportions.

Hourglass Upper and lower body similar in proportion with a small, neat waist.

SINGLE-SIZE PATTERNS

Some patterns contain a garment or craft project of one size only. If you are using a single-size pattern, cut around the tissue on the thick black cutting line before making any alterations.

Zip markings indicate length of seam opening for zip

Darts are marked with lines, and sometimes with dots or circles that match when darts are folded

Alteration lines indicate best place to lengthen or shorten pattern pieces

Pattern pieces without grainline have place-to-fold line to be positioned directly on fold of fabric, parallel to selvedges

Notches are usually single on front armhole and double on back armhole

Straight arrow must be placed on straight grain

Positions and number of notches on both sides should match to ensure correct edges are joined together

Dart cutting line

Open dart is very wide, and fabric is cut away with pattern following cutting line

MULTI-SIZE PATTERNS

Many patterns today have more than one size printed on the tissue. Each size is clearly labelled and the cutting lines are marked with a different type of line for each size.

Where there is one line only, it applies to all sizes

Straight arrow to be placed along straight grain of fabric, parallel to selvedges

Where there is a choice of size lines, desired size line should be selected and followed

Alteration lines

PATTERN MARKINGS

Each pattern piece will have a series of lines, dots, and other symbols printed on it. These symbols are to help you alter the pattern and join the pattern pieces together. The symbols are universal across all major paper patterns.

Cutting line

Multi-size cutting lines

Grainlines

Place-to-fold line

Alteration lines

Seamline or stitching line

Seam allowance

Buttonhole

Combined button and buttonhole

Button position

Dart

Pleat

Tuck

Bust point or hipline

Waist or hipline

Markings to be transferred from pattern pieces to the fabric for matching or to indicate detail

Single notches

Double notches

Triple notches

Alternative notch marking

Zip placement

BODY **MEASURING**

Accurate body measurements are needed to determine the correct pattern size to use and if any alterations are required. Pattern sizes are usually chosen by the hip or bust measurement; for tops follow the bust measurement, but for skirts or trousers use the hip measurement. If you are choosing a dress pattern, go by whichever measurement is the largest.

TAKING BODY MEASUREMENTS

1 You'll need a tape measure and ruler as well as a helper for some of the measuring, and a hard chair or stool.

2 Wear underwear that fits you well, especially a good-fitting bra.

3 Tie a piece of elastic or ribbon snugly around your waist prior to taking any measurements. The elastic will find your natural waist, which may not be where you think it is.

4 Do not wear any shoes.

HOW TO MEASURE YOUR HEIGHT

Most paper patterns are designed for a woman 165 to 168cm (5ft 5in to 5ft 6in). If you are shorter or taller than this you may need to adjust the pattern prior to cutting out your fabric.

1 Remove your shoes.

2 Stand straight, with your back against the wall.

3 Place a ruler flat on your head, touching the wall, and mark the wall at this point.

4 Step away and measure the distance from the floor to the marked point.

▶ CHEST

Measure above the bust, high under the arms, keeping the tape measure flat and straight across the back.

▶ FULL BUST

Make sure you are wearing a well-fitting bra and measure over the fullest part of the bust. If your cup size is in excess of a B, you will probably need to do a bust alteration, although some patterns are now cut to accommodate larger cup sizes.

▶ WAIST

This is the measurement around the smallest part of your waist. Wrap a piece of elastic or ribbon around first to find your natural waist, then measure.

HIPS

This measurement must be taken around the fullest part of the hips, between the waist and legs.

HIGH HIP

Take this just below the waist and just above the hip bones to give a measurement across the tummy.

SHOULDER

Hold the end of the tape measure at the base of your neck (where a necklace would lie) and measure to the dent at the end of your shoulder. To find this dent raise your arm slightly.

NECK

Measure around the neck – snugly but not too tight – to determine collar size.

BACK WAIST

Take this measurement down the centre of the back, from the lumpy bit at the top of the spine, in line with the shoulders, to the waist.

OUTSIDE LEG

Measure the side of the leg from the waist, over the hip, and straight down the leg to the ankle bone.

INSIDE LEG

Stand with your legs apart and measure the inside of one leg from the crotch to the ankle bone.

ARM

Bend your elbow and place your hand on your hip, then measure from the end of the shoulder over the elbow to the wrist bone.

CROTCH DEPTH

Sit upright on a hard chair or stool and measure from the waist vertically down to the chair.

CROTCH LENGTH

Stand with your legs slightly apart. Measure from your centre front waist, between your legs, to the centre back waist.

ALTERING PATTERNS **pp.62–73** • MAKING A TOILE **pp.74–75** • MARKING A HEMLINE **p.263**

TOOLS

ALTERING **PATTERNS**

It is unlikely that your body measurements will be exactly the same as those of your chosen pattern, so you will need to alter the pattern to accommodate your figure. Here is how to lengthen and shorten pattern pieces, and how to make specific alterations at the bust, waist and hips, shoulders and back, and to sleeves and trousers.

EQUIPMENT

▸ **In addition to scissors and pins or tape**, you will need a pencil, an eraser, a ruler that is clearly marked, and possibly a set square. For many alterations you will also need pattern paper.

▸ **After pinning or taping the piece of pattern tissue to the paper**, you can redraw the pattern lines. Trim away the excess tissue or paper before pinning the pattern pieces to the fabric for cutting out.

EASY MULTI-SIZE PATTERN ALTERATIONS

Using a multi-size pattern has many advantages because you can cut on different size lines for different parts of your body. For example, you can combine sizes to accommodate a larger hip or a thinner waist.

▸ **INDIVIDUAL PATTERN ADJUSTMENT**

To adjust for a wider hip measurement, when cutting from one size to another, make the lines a gentle curve to follow the contours of the body.

▸ **BETWEEN SIZES**

If your body measurements fall between two pattern sizes, cut carefully between the two cutting lines for the different sizes.

LENGTHENING AND SHORTENING PATTERNS

If you are shorter or taller, or your arms or legs are shorter or longer, than the pattern pieces, you will need to adjust the paper pattern prior to cutting out. There are lines printed on the pattern pieces that will guide you as to the best places to adjust. However, you will need to compare your body shape against the pattern. Alter the front and back by the same amount at the same points, and always check finished lengths.

▸ **FOR A FITTED SLEEVE**

On a sleeve with elbow shaping, alter by half required amount halfway between elbow and underarm.

Elbow shaping

Alter by other half of required amount halfway between elbow and wrist.

▸ **FOR A STRAIGHT SLEEVE**

To keep wrist area intact, alter partway down sleeve, or at hem.

▸ **FOR A BODICE**

Alter back neck to waist length below bust dart but above waist (through waist dart if there is one).

Bust dart

Waist

Waist dart

Underarm

Wrist

Hem

▶ FOR A FITTED DRESS

Mark between bust and waist to alter back neck to waist length.

Bust dart

Waist

Hipline

Alter below hipline if not altering at hem.

Alter below hem if not altering at hipline.

▶ FOR A PRINCESS DRESS

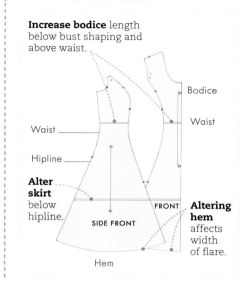

Increase bodice length below bust shaping and above waist.

Bodice

Waist

Hipline

Waist

Alter skirt below hipline.

Altering hem affects width of flare.

FRONT

SIDE FRONT

Hem

▶ FOR SHORTS

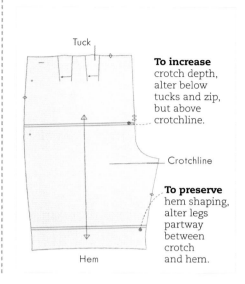

Tuck

To increase crotch depth, alter below tucks and zip, but above crotchline.

Crotchline

To preserve hem shaping, alter legs partway between crotch and hem.

Hem

▶ FOR A SKIRT

Hipline

Alter below hipline or at hem.

Hem

▶ FOR SHAPED-LEG TROUSERS

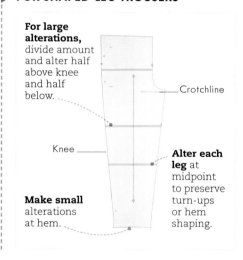

For large alterations, divide amount and alter half above knee and half below.

Crotchline

Knee

Alter each leg at midpoint to preserve turn-ups or hem shaping.

Make small alterations at hem.

▶ FOR STRAIGHT TROUSERS

Increase crotch below tucks, but above crotchline.

Tucks

Make large alterations midway down leg to retain leg width.

Crotchline

Hem

▶ HOW TO LENGTHEN A PATTERN PIECE

1 First work out the amount you want to add by comparing your measurements to those of the pattern.

2 Cut through the lengthening and shortening lines on the tissue paper, following the lines carefully.

3 Place some pattern paper behind the tissue and spread the pattern pieces apart to leave a gap of the required amount. Make sure the gap is level along the cut lines.

4 Pin or tape the pattern pieces to the paper.

MAKING A TOILE pp.74–75 ● **MARKING A HEMLINE p.263**

▶ HOW TO SHORTEN A PATTERN PIECE

1 Work out the amount you want to lose. Mark this amount above the lengthening and shortening lines, then draw a line through the marks using the ruler as a guide.

2 Fold the lengthening and shortening line on to the drawn line so the two lines meet neatly.

3 Press with your fingers to crease the fold sharply, then secure the fold in the pattern piece with tape.

▶ HOW TO LENGTHEN ACROSS DARTS

1 If an adjustment is required across a dart, cut and lengthen the pattern piece.

2 Place pattern paper behind the tissue, making sure that the lines of the dart are smoothly connected.

3 Tape or pin in place.

▶ HOW TO SHORTEN ACROSS DARTS

1 Fold to shorten the pattern piece.

2 After shortening across a dart, the lines of the dart may not remain in line. If this is the case, re-draw the dart from dot to dot, using a ruler to ensure the lines are straight.

▶ HOW TO LENGTHEN A HEM EDGE

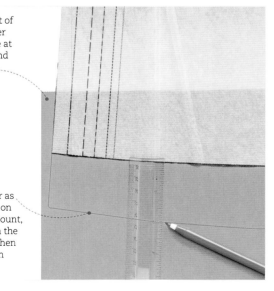

1 Place a sheet of pattern paper under the tissue at the hem edge and tape down.

2 Using a ruler as a guide, add on the required amount, marking dots on the paper first and then connecting them with a line.

▶ HOW TO SHORTEN A HEM EDGE

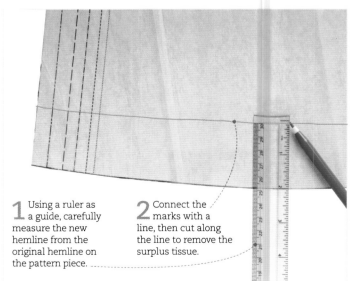

1 Using a ruler as a guide, carefully measure the new hemline from the original hemline on the pattern piece.

2 Connect the marks with a line, then cut along the line to remove the surplus tissue.

MEASURING TOOLS AND MARKING AIDS pp.18—19 ● BODY MEASURING pp.60—61

BUST

Some paper patterns today feature various cup sizes, but the majority of patterns are cut to accommodate a B cup. If you are larger than this, you will probably need to adjust your pattern before cutting out. As a general rule, when spreading the pattern pieces apart, try adjusting by 6mm (¼in) per cup size over a B cup. Other pattern alterations can be made for bust position, raising it higher or lowering it. If the bust dart is altered, the waist dart may also need to be adjusted.

▶ RAISING A BUST DART

1 If you have a high bust you may need to raise the point of the darts. The bust point is nearly always marked on the pattern pieces. Mark the new bust point on the tissue.

2 Redraw the lines of the dart to this point.

3 Lengthen waist dart by same amount as bust dart is raised.

▶ RAISING A BUST DART SUBSTANTIALLY

1 If the dart has to be raised quite a lot, it is easier to cut a rectangle out of the part of the pattern that contains the dart and then move it higher.

2 Mark the new bust point on the tissue first.

3 Use a sheet of pattern paper to fill in the gap and tape in place.

4 Raise waist dart by same amount as bust dart is raised.

▶ INCREASING A BUST DART

1 Cut the pattern as indicated, straight through the bust point.

2 Place the tissue pieces on pattern paper, then spread them apart by about 6mm (¼in) per cup size over a B cup.

3 Tape securely in place.

4 Redraw the dart to original length.

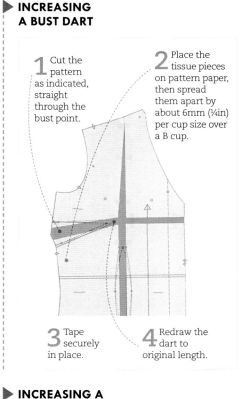

▶ LOWERING A BUST DART

1 Mark the new lower bust point on your pattern piece.

2 Redraw the dart stitching lines to this new lower point.

3 Shorten waist dart by same amount as bust dart is lowered.

▶ LOWERING A BUST DART SUBSTANTIALLY

1 First mark the new bust point on the tissue.

2 Cut out a rectangle from the pattern piece that contains the dart and move it to the lower position.

3 Fill in the gap with a sheet of pattern paper and tape in place.

4 Lower waist dart by same amount as bust dart is lowered.

▶ INCREASING A FRENCH DART

1 Cut the pattern piece along the dart line from the side seam, straight through the bust point to the centre front line.

2 Spread the tissue apart and tape to pattern paper.

3 Keep centre front straight.

4 Mark a new dart point in the centre of where the dart has been spread.

5 Redraw the dart from the original seam points.

MAKING A TOILE pp.74–75 ● **SHAPING DARTS TO FIT p.114** ● **MARKING A HEMLINE p.263**

▶ RAISING A CURVED BUST SEAM

1 Fold a pleat in the shoulder pattern to bring the bust point up by the required amount.

2 Cut the pattern on the lengthening and shortening lines and spread apart by the same amount (if this is not done the waist will be raised as well).

3 Tape the pieces to pattern paper, then redraw the armhole lower by the same measurement.

▶ LOWERING A CURVED BUST SEAM

1 Cut the shoulder pattern piece and spread apart by the required amount, then tape to a sheet of pattern paper.

2 Make a fold on the lengthening and shortening lines by the same amount.

3 Redraw the armhole higher by the same amount.

▶ ADJUSTING A CURVED SEAM

1 For a larger bust, place a sheet of pattern paper under the bust curve on the side front piece.

2 Add onto this curve 6mm (¼in) per cup size over a B cup, for example 12mm (½in) for a D cup. Redraw the curve.

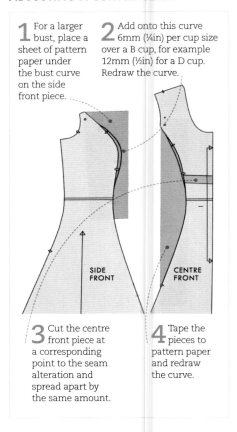

3 Cut the centre front piece at a corresponding point to the seam alteration and spread apart by the same amount.

4 Tape the pieces to pattern paper and redraw the curve.

WAIST AND HIPS

Most people's waists and hips are out of proportion when compared to the measurements of a paper pattern. To alter the pattern to suit your body shape, adjust the pieces for the waist first and then do the hip pieces.

▶ INCREASING THE WAIST AT A SEAM

1 On a fitted skirt, increase the waist at the side seams. Divide the amount to be increased by four as there are four seamlines.

2 Tape pattern paper behind the tissue pieces and add the increase on at the waist edge.

3 Draw a new seamline from this point, tapering it back into the skirt side seam.

▶ INCREASING THE WAIST ON A GORED SKIRT

1 As there are many seams on a gored skirt, divide the increase amount by the number of seamlines.

2 Tape the tissue pieces on to pattern paper and add one of these small amounts to each seamline at the waist.

▶ INCREASING THE WAIST ON A FULL-CIRCLE SKIRT

1 First carefully check the waist circumference on the pattern against your body measurements.

2 Make the waist larger by drawing a new, lower waist stitching line on the pattern pieces.

3 Be sure to adjust the finished length of the skirt, if necessary.

▶ INCREASING THE WAIST ON A FITTED DRESS

1 Place a sheet of pattern paper under the side seam section of each of the pattern pieces.

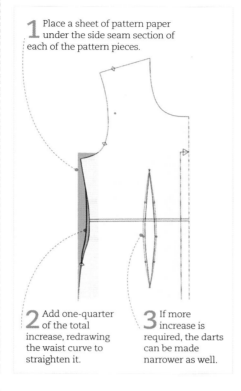

2 Add one-quarter of the total increase, redrawing the waist curve to straighten it.

3 If more increase is required, the darts can be made narrower as well.

▶ INCREASING THE WAIST ON A PRINCESS-LINE DRESS

1 Place a sheet of pattern paper under the waist section of each of the pattern pieces.

SIDE FRONT

CENTRE FRONT

2 Divide the amount to be increased by the number of seamlines.

3 Add one of these small amounts on to each seamline.

▶ DECREASING THE WAIST AT A SEAM

1 On a straight skirt, divide the amount to be decreased by four as there are four seamlines.

2 Mark the amount of decrease at the waist edge on the pattern pieces.

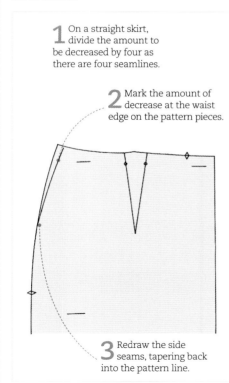

3 Redraw the side seams, tapering back into the pattern line.

▶ DECREASING THE WAIST ON A GORED SKIRT

1 Divide the amount to be decreased by the number of seamlines.

SIDE FRONT

FRONT

2 Take one of these small amounts off each seamline at the waist.

▶ DECREASING THE WAIST ON A FULL-CIRCLE SKIRT

1 Tape the pattern tissue to a sheet of pattern paper.

2 Draw the stitching line at the waist higher, which will make the waist smaller.

MAKING A TOILE pp.74–75 ● **SHAPING DARTS TO FIT p.114** ● **WAISTLINES pp.184–193**

▶ DECREASING THE WAIST ON A FITTED DRESS

1 To reduce the waist seam, you need to redraw the side seamline on each pattern piece. Divide the total decrease by four.

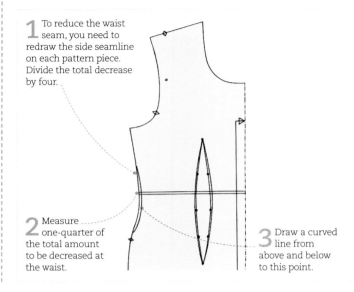

2 Measure one-quarter of the total amount to be decreased at the waist.

3 Draw a curved line from above and below to this point.

▶ DECREASING THE WAIST ON A PRINCESS-LINE DRESS

1 Divide the total amount of reduction by the number of seamlines, then mark the required amount of decrease at the waist on each pattern piece.

2 Redraw the seams, curving each one in to the marked point.

FRONT   SIDE FRONT

▶ WIDENING A FITTED SKIRT AT THE HIPLINE

1 To increase the hip dimension on a fitted skirt, divide the amount of the increase by four. Place the tissue pieces on pattern paper and increase each side seam at the hip point by the required amount.

2 Redraw the seamline from the hip increase, gradually tapering into the waistline.

3 It is more flattering to take the adjustment all the way down the skirt, so redraw the seamline straight down from the hip to the hem.

▶ ADJUSTING A FITTED SKIRT FOR EXTRA-LARGE HIPS

1 For an increase over 5cm (2in), cut each pattern piece vertically between the dart and the side seam.

2 Place on pattern paper and spread apart by one-quarter of the total amount of increase.

3 If the waist is to remain the same, draw in a second dart to remove the increase at the waist.

▶ ADJUSTING A FITTED SKIRT FOR PROMINENT HIPS

1 Place the tissue on pattern paper and add the required amount from the waist to the hip point as for a fitted skirt (see left), tapering the line back into the seam.

2 Increase the width of the dart by the same amount, redrawing the dart lines to the new centre point.

▶ ADJUSTING A FITTED SKIRT FOR A LARGE BOTTOM

1 Cut through the skirt back pattern piece, vertically through the dart to the hem.

2 Cut across the hipline, but not through the side seam.

3 Spread apart the tissue on pattern paper as much as needed and tape in place.

4 Redraw the dart.

▶ DECREASING THE HIPLINE ON A FITTED SKIRT

1 Divide the amount to be reduced by four and mark the reduction amount on each pattern piece at the hipline.

2 Redraw the side seam, tapering the line into the waist and from the hipline, drawing straight down to the hem.

▶ ADJUSTING THE HIPLINE ON A GORED SKIRT OR PRINCESS DRESS

1 Divide the amount to be reduced or added by the number of seamlines.

2 If widening, tape the pieces of tissue to pattern paper.

SIDE FRONT   CENTRE

3 Mark the reduction or addition at the hipline on each piece.

4 Redraw the seamlines, tapering them into the waist and drawing straight down to the hem.

▶ MAKING A LARGE INCREASE AT THE HIPLINE ON A FITTED DRESS

1 Make a cut into each pattern piece horizontally just below the waist by one-quarter of the total amount to be increased.

2 Cut vertically to the hem.

3 Spread the tissue apart and tape to a sheet of pattern paper.

4 Redraw the side seam.

▶ ADJUSTING AT THE HIPLINE TO ALLOW FOR A HOLLOW BACK

1 A hollow back requires a shorter centre back seam. Draw a line on the pattern piece across the hipline, from the centre back.

2 Fold along the line to make a pleat of the required reduction, tapering it to nothing at the side seam. Tape in place.

Centre back seam

Fold line

SHOULDERS, BACK, AND SLEEVES

Alterations can be made to accommodate sloping shoulders, square shoulders, rounded shoulders, and backs that may be wider or narrower than the pattern allowances. It's important to ensure that these alterations have a minimum effect on the armhole. Sleeves need to allow for movement, so should not be too tight, and pattern pieces can be enlarged as necessary. Alterations can also be made for thin arms.

▶ ADJUSTING TO FIT SQUARE SHOULDERS

1 Starting at the armhole, slash the pattern piece about 3cm (1¼in) below and parallel with the shoulder line, not cutting through the neck seamline.

2 Spread the tissue apart to make the shoulder line straighter. Tape to pattern paper.

3 Redraw the line across the gap created.

4 Raise the armhole by the amount added at the shoulder. Adjust the front shoulder pattern pieces by the same amount as the back.

▶ ADJUSTING TO FIT SLOPING SHOULDERS

1 Slash from the armhole across the pattern piece 3cm (1¼in) below the shoulder line and parallel with it.

2 Overlap the tissue by the required amount and tape in place.

3 Lower the armhole by the same amount, drawing a new seamline on the tissue. Adjust the front shoulder pattern pieces by the same amount as the back.

▶ PREPARING THE PATTERN FOR SHOULDER WIDTH ALTERATIONS

1 Draw a vertical line 20cm (8in) long from the middle of the shoulder line.

2 Next, draw a second line horizontally from the end of this line to the armhole.

▶ ADJUSTING TO FIT BROAD SHOULDERS

1 Cut along the lines that have been drawn and spread the pieces of tissue apart on pattern paper, to accommodate the increase in shoulder length.

2 Tape in place and redraw the shoulder line. Adjust the front shoulder pattern pieces by the same amount as the back.

▶ ADJUSTING TO FIT NARROW SHOULDERS

1 Cut along the drawn lines.

2 Slide the cut-out piece of tissue in to overlap the cut edges and reduce the shoulder length.

3 Tape on to pattern paper and redraw the shoulder line. Adjust the front shoulder pattern pieces by the same amount as the back.

▶ ENLARGING A FITTED SLEEVE

1 Cut the sleeve pattern piece vertically down the centre.

2 Spread apart as much as required to make the sleeve wider. Tape to pattern paper.

3 You may need to make the armhole slightly larger, by adding half this amount to each bodice side seam.

▶ ENLARGING THE HEAD ON A FITTED SLEEVE

1 Cut the pattern piece vertically down the centre, not cutting through the wrist seamline.

2 Spread the tissue apart at the top by the required amount and taper to nothing at the wrist.

3 You may need to make the armhole slightly larger, by adding half this amount to each bodice side seam.

▶ ENLARGING A FITTED SLEEVE AT THE ELBOW

1 Cut horizontally at an angle from just above the elbow dart to the centre, then cut vertically almost to the top.

2 Spread the tissue on pattern paper, leaving the sleeve head intact, and tape to the paper.

3 Redraw the underarm seam over the gap created.

▶ INCREASING AT THE UNDERARM ON A FITTED SLEEVE

1 If the underarm is tight across the bicep, cut the pattern horizontally from armhole to armhole, then cut the top piece of tissue vertically almost to the sleeve head.

2 Pull the outside points up to make a gap in the centre of the required amount, and tape to pattern paper.

3 Redraw the sleeve side seams.

4 You may need to make the armhole slightly larger, by adding half this amount to each bodice side seam.

▶ DECREASING A FITTED SLEEVE FOR THIN ARMS

1 To decrease the width of a sleeve, make a vertical pleat in the centre of the sleeve pattern piece, from wrist to sleeve head.

2 Taper the pleat to nothing at the sleeve head. Tape in place.

3 Reduce the side seams on the armhole by half this amount.

TROUSERS

Trouser alterations, to accommodate a large stomach, wide hips, a prominent or flat bottom, can be more complicated than those on other pattern pieces, and need to be done in the correct order. Crotch depth alterations are done first, followed by width alterations, then crotch length alterations, and finally trouser leg length. The crotch depth line is only marked on the back pattern pieces.

▶ INCREASING DEPTH AT CROTCH SEAM

1 Adjust both back and front pattern pieces by the same amount. Cut along the upper lengthening and shortening lines.

2 Spread the pattern tissue apart by the required amount at the centre back and centre front seams, tapering to nothing at the side seam. Tape the tissue to pattern paper.

3 Redraw the crotch edge.

▶ DECREASING DEPTH AT CROTCH SEAM

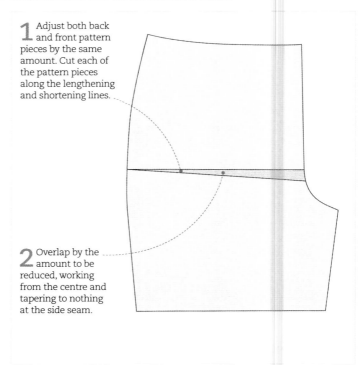

1 Adjust both back and front pattern pieces by the same amount. Cut each of the pattern pieces along the lengthening and shortening lines.

2 Overlap by the amount to be reduced, working from the centre and tapering to nothing at the side seam.

▶ INCREASING THE WAISTLINE

1 Divide the amount to be increased by eight (there are eight seamlines that you can add on to). Tape the tissue to pattern paper.

2 Add an equal amount to each seamline at the waist, tapering the new drawn line back into the seam.

▶ DECREASING THE WAISTLINE

1 Take the amount to be decreased and divide it by eight.

2 Reduce each of the waist seamlines by this amount.

3 Draw a new line from the decrease point back into the seamline on the pattern.

▶ INCREASING AT THE HIPLINE

1 Take the amount to be increased and divide it by four.

2 Place a sheet of pattern paper under the hip area on the side seam of each pattern piece.

3 Add the required amount to each of the seamlines at the hip, tapering the new seamline into the waist and thigh.

4 For straight trousers, draw the new seamline straight down from the hip to the hem.

▶ INCREASING THE BOTTOM OR TUMMY AREA

1 Adjust the back pattern pieces for a large bottom or the front pattern pieces for a full tummy. Cut through the pieces at the hipline.

2 Place the tissue on pattern paper and spread apart by the required amount, then tape the tissue to the paper.

3 Redraw the crotch edge. This adjustment may be in addition to a crotch depth adjustment.

▶ DECREASING AT THE HIPLINE

1 For fitted trousers, divide the amount to be decreased by four.

2 Reduce the side seam at the hipline on each pattern piece by one-quarter of the total reduction.

3 Taper the new drawn seamline to waist and thigh.

▶ INCREASING LENGTH AT CROTCH POINT

1 The crotch length may need to be increased by a different amount on the front and back. Tape a sheet of pattern paper under the crotch seam.

2 Add on the amount required and redraw the inside leg seam from this new crotch point, tapering into the original seamline.

▶ DECREASING LENGTH AT CROTCH POINT

1 To reduce the length of the crotch seam, make a mark on the pattern piece where the new crotch point should be.

2 Redraw the inside leg seam from this point to taper into the original seamline.

MAKING A TOILE pp.74—75 ● **WAISTLINES pp.184—193**

MAKING A TOILE

When using a new pattern for the first time, or if you have made pattern alterations, it is always a good idea to try out the pattern in calico, to make a test garment called a toile. This will tell you if the garment is going to fit you, or whether more alterations are required. It is also a good opportunity to confirm that the style suits your figure type. You will need a helper, or failing that a dressmaker's dummy.

TOILE TOO BIG

When you try the toile on, if it is too big there will be surplus fabric. Pleat and pin out the surplus fabric, making the pleating equal on both the left- and right-hand sides of the garment. Take off the toile and measure the surplus amount. Alter the pattern pieces to match, by pinning out the surplus tissue.

Back adjustment
If the back is too big, pleat and pin out the surplus fabric parallel to the centre back seam, doing this equally on both sides. The alteration can then be made down the centre back seam on the appropriate pattern pieces.

Shoulder adjustment
If the shoulder is too wide it will need a narrow shoulder adjustment (see p.70).

The waist on the bodice and skirt
If the waist is too big, this can easily be adjusted by taking more fabric into the bust dart, thus making the waist smaller. If you adjust the bust dart on the bodice, you will need to alter the skirt dart too, so they join up.

The hip on the skirt
If the hip is too loose, pleat and pin out the surplus fabric, doing this equally on both side seams. Measure the surplus amount and take in the hipline on the pattern pieces accordingly (see Decreasing the hipline on a fitted skirt, p.69).

TOILE TOO SMALL

If the toile is too small, the fabric will "pull" where it is too tight. The garment shown below is too tight over the bust and also over the high hip area. The pattern will need adjusting to allow more fabric in these areas. It is also snug at the top of the sleeve, which will need adjusting.

The bust on the bodice
If a small increase is required in the bust, unpick the side seams and measure the increase required. Then make the required alteration to the pattern pieces. If a larger increase is required the whole pattern piece will need to be altered and a new front cut out (see Increasing a bust dart, p.65). To be sure the alteration is successful, make up a new toile bodice to try.

Shoulder adjustment
If the sleeve is tight at the top, or at the underarm, it is best to alter the pattern pieces (see p.70) and then to make up a new sleeve for the toile.

The hip on the skirt
Unpick the side seams and measure the increase required. When you have adjusted the toile with extra calico to be sure the fit is right, you can alter the pattern pieces accordingly (see p.68).

HOW TO ADJUST A TOILE THAT IS TOO SMALL

If the toile is too tight, it will require more fabric to cover the contours of the body and you will need to make further alterations to the pattern pieces. For small increases (up to 4cm/1½in), you can adjust the toile as described below and then alter the pattern pieces accordingly, redrawing the seamlines. For more substantial increases, after altering the pattern pieces you will need to make up a new toile to try on.

1 Where the toile is too tight, unpick the side seam on either side, until the garment will hang without pulling.

2 Measure the gap between the stitching lines where the seam has been opened at the fullest point. It should be the same on both sides of the body.

3 Divide this measurement by four (4 seams) – for example, if the gap is 4cm (1½in) at the fullest point, then 1cm (⅜in) needs to be added to each seamline.

4 Using a marker pen, mark directly on the toile the top and bottom of the alteration. Also mark the fullest point of the alteration.

5 When the toile has been removed, add calico to the seam in the given area at the fullest point, tapering back to the original seam at either end.

6 Try the toile on again to be sure your alterations have made it fit you properly, then measure them and make adjustments to the relevant pattern pieces.

CUTTING OUT

Cutting out correctly can make or break your project. But first you need to examine the fabric in the shop, looking for any flaws, such as a crooked pattern, and checking to see if the fabric has been cut properly from the roll – that is at a right angle to the selvedge. If not, you will need to straighten the edge. If the fabric is creased, press it; if washable, wash it to avoid shrinkage later. After this preparation, you will be ready to lay the pattern pieces on the fabric, pin in place, and cut out.

FABRIC GRAIN AND NAP

It is important that the pattern pieces are cut on the correct grain, as this will make the fabric hang correctly and produce a longer-lasting item. The grain of the fabric is the direction in which the yarns or threads that make up the fabric lie. The majority of pattern pieces need to be placed with the straight of grain symbol running parallel to the warp yarn. Some fabrics have a nap due to the pile, which means the fabric shadows when it is smoothed in one direction. A fabric with a one-way design or uneven stripes is also described as being with nap. Fabrics with nap are generally cut out with the nap running down, whereas those without nap can be cut out either way.

▶ GRAIN ON WOVEN FABRICS

The selvedge is the woven, non-frayable edge that runs parallel to the warp grain.

Yarns that run the length of the fabric are called warp yarns. They are stronger than weft yarns and less likely to stretch.

Weft

Selvedge

Selvedge

Weft yarns run crossways, over and under the warp yarns.

Bias

Warp

The bias grain is diagonal – running at 45 degrees to the warp and weft. A garment cut on the bias will follow the contours of the body.

▶ GRAIN ON KNITTED FABRICS

Warp

Weft

A knitted fabric also has a grain. Some knit fabrics stretch only one way while others stretch in both directions. Patterns for knit fabrics often need to be cut following the direction of the greatest stretch.

▶ NAP DUE TO PILE

Fabrics such as velvet (shown here), corduroy, and velour will show a difference in colour, depending on whether the nap is running up or down.

▶ NAP IF ONE-WAY DESIGN

A one-way pattern that runs lengthways in the fabric will be upside-down on one side if pieces are cut when the fabric is folded across the warp grainline.

▶ NAP IF STRIPES ARE IRREGULAR

If the stripes do not match on both sides when the fabric is folded across the warp grainline, they are uneven and the fabric will need a nap layout.

CUTTING TOOLS **pp.16–17** • MARKING AIDS **p.19** • FABRICS **pp.40–52**

FABRIC PREPARATION

To check if the fabric has been cut properly from the roll, smooth it out flat, with the selvedges lying together. If the cut ends are uneven and do not match, use one of the following methods to make the edge straight. Then press the fabric.

▶ PULLING A THREAD TO OBTAIN A STRAIGHT EDGE

1 On a loose-woven fabric you can pull a weft thread to get a straight edge. First snip the selvedge, then find a single thread and tug it gently to pull it out.

2 The fabric will gather along the single weft thread until the thread can be removed completely.

3 Carefully cut along the space left by the pulled-out weft thread.

▶ CUTTING ON A STRIPE LINE

On checks and stripes, cut along the edge of one of the boldest stripes to achieve a straight edge.

▶ CUTTING ON A STITCH LINE ON KNIT FABRICS

On jersey and other knit fabrics, if you look carefully you can cut along a row of stitches.

PATTERN PREPARATION

Before cutting out, sort out all the pattern pieces that are required for the item you are making. Check them to see if any have special cutting instructions. Make pattern alterations, if necessary. If there are no alterations, just trim patterns to your size.

1 Using the pattern instruction sheet, which has drawings of the pattern pieces, select the pieces you require.

2 The instruction sheet also shows a suggested cutting-out layout for the item you are making, on different widths of fabric, with or without nap.

3 Trim multi-size pattern pieces according to the chosen size.

PATTERN LAYOUT **pp.78–79** ● STRIPES AND CHECKS **pp.80–81** ● CUTTING OUT ACCURATELY **p.82**

PATTERN LAYOUT

Fabric is usually folded selvedge to selvedge. With the fabric folded, the pattern is pinned on top, and both the right- and left-side pieces are cut out at the same time. If pattern pieces have to be cut from single layer fabric, remember to cut matching pairs. For a fabric with a design it is a good idea to have the right side of the fabric on the outside so that you can arrange the pattern pieces to show off the design. If you have left- and right-side pattern pieces, they are cut on single fabric with the fabric right side up and the pattern right side up.

▶ **PINNING THE PATTERN TO THE FABRIC**

1 The "to fold" symbol indicates the pattern piece is to be pinned carefully to the folded edge of the fabric.

2 To check the straight of grain on the other pattern pieces, place the grain arrow so that it looks parallel to the selvedge, then pin to secure at one end of the arrow.

3 Measure from the pinned end to the selvedge.

4 Measure from the other end of the arrow to the selvedge.

Fold

To fold symbol

Straight of grain arrow

Selvedges

5 Move the pattern piece slightly until this measurement is the same as the pinned end, then pin in place.

6 Once it is straight, pin around the rest of the pattern piece, placing pins in the seam allowances.

▶ **GENERAL GUIDE TO LAYOUT**

On single layer fabrics ▼

If using a single layer of fabric the pieces will need to be cut twice, reversing for the second piece.

Place the pattern pieces on the fabric with the printed side uppermost.

Selvedges

On folded fabrics ▼

Fold

☐ RIGHT SIDE OF PATTERN PIECE
☐ WRONG SIDE OF PATTERN PIECE

Cutting on folded fabric gives two pieces per pattern, or four if you cut it twice. Some pieces need to be placed on a fold, which creates double-width pieces.

▶ LAYOUT FOR FABRICS WITH A NAP OR A ONE-WAY DESIGN

Selvedges

Fold

"Top" of fabric, from which direction the nap runs

If your fabric needs to be cut out with a nap, all the pattern pieces need to be placed so the nap will run in the same direction in the made-up garment.

▶ LAYOUT ON A CROSSWAYS FOLD

Selvedge

Occasionally a fabric is folded across the grain. This is usually done to accommodate very large pattern pieces.

Fold

Selvedge

▶ LAYOUT ON A CROSSWAYS FOLD WITH A NAP

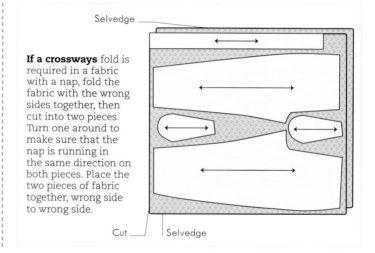

Selvedge

If a crossways fold is required in a fabric with a nap, fold the fabric with the wrong sides together, then cut into two pieces. Turn one around to make sure that the nap is running in the same direction on both pieces. Place the two pieces of fabric together, wrong side to wrong side.

Cut

Selvedge

▶ LAYOUT ON A PARTIAL FOLD

Selvedge

Selvedge

The fabric is folded part way to enable you to cut some pattern pieces on a fold and the remainder from single fabric.

Fold

STRIPES AND CHECKS

For fabrics with a stripe or check pattern, a little more care is needed when laying out the pattern pieces. If the checks and stripes are running across or down the length of the fabric when cutting out, they will run the same direction in the finished garment. So it is important to place the pattern pieces to ensure that the checks and stripes match and that they run together at the seams. If possible, try to place the pattern pieces so each has a stripe down the centre. With a check, be aware of the hemline placement on the pattern.

▶ EVEN STRIPES

When a corner of the fabric is folded back diagonally, the stripes will meet up at the fold.

▶ UNEVEN STRIPES

When a corner of the fabric is folded back diagonally, the stripes will not match at the fold.

▶ EVEN CHECKS

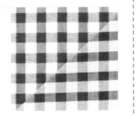

When a corner is folded back diagonally, the checks will be symmetrical on both of the fabric areas.

▶ UNEVEN CHECKS

When a corner of the fabric is folded back diagonally, the checks will be uneven lengthways, widthways, or both.

▶ MATCHING STRIPES OR CHECKS ON A SKIRT

1 Place one of the skirt pattern pieces on the fabric and pin in place.

2 Mark on the tissue the position of the boldest lines of the checks or stripes.

3 Place the adjoining skirt pattern piece alongside, with notches matching and side seams even. Transfer the marks across.

4 Move the second pattern piece away, matching up the bold lines, and pin it in place.

▶ MATCHING STRIPES OR CHECKS AT THE SHOULDER

1 Mark the boldest lines of the stripes or checks around the armhole on the front bodice pattern.

2 Place the sleeve pattern on to the armhole, matching the notches, and copy the marks on to the sleeve pattern.

3 Place the sleeve pattern on to the fabric, matching the marks to the corresponding bold lines, and pin in place.

▶ LAYOUT FOR EVEN CHECKS ON FOLDED FABRIC

Centre of sleeve is aligned with prominent colour bar

Selvedge

Centre front is aligned with prominent colour bar

Checks are matched at seams

Fabric is folded to form double layer with checks matching on both layers

Centre back is aligned with prominent colour bar

Hem foldline is aligned with prominent crossways bar

Collar and cuff can be cut on a lengthways grain

Fold

Pocket and yoke can be cut on bias grain for special effects

Fabric is folded along prominent colour bar at centre of repeat

▶ LAYOUT FOR EVEN STRIPES ON FOLDED FABRIC

Selvedge

If fabric has prominent stripe, align stripe along straight seam

Collar is cut lengthways along stripe

Yoke is cut lengthways, with seamline aligned with prominent stripe across back edge

If fabric has prominent stripe, centre of sleeve should be aligned

Cuff is cut lengthways along stripe

Fabric is folded into double layer with stripes matching on both layers

▶ LAYOUT FOR UNEVEN CHECKS OR STRIPES ON UNFOLDED FABRIC

Hem foldline is arranged level with base of prominent bar

Right side of pattern piece

Wrong side of pattern piece

Centre back is aligned with prominent lengthways bar

Pattern piece is cut out twice from single layer of fabric

Right side of pattern piece

Bars align on both collar pieces

Wrong side of pattern piece

Selvedge

PATTERN LAYOUT **pp.78—79**

CUTTING OUT ACCURATELY

Careful, smooth cutting around the pattern pieces will ensure that they join together accurately. Always cut out on a smooth, flat surface such as a table – the floor is not ideal – and be sure your scissors are sharp. Use the full blade of the scissors on long, straight edges, sliding the blades along the fabric; use smaller cuts around curves. Do not nibble or snip at the fabric.

▶ HOW TO CUT

If you are right-handed, place your left hand on the pattern and fabric to hold them in place, and cut cleanly with the scissor blades at a right angle to the fabric.

▶ MARKING NOTCHES

These symbols need to be marked on to the fabric as they are matching points. One of the easiest ways to do this is to cut the mirror image of the notches out into the fabric. Rather than cutting out each notch separately, cut straight across from point to point.

▶ MARKING DOTS

You can cut a small clip into the fabric to mark the dots that indicate the top of the shoulder on a sleeve. Alternatively, these can be marked with tailor's tacks (see opposite page).

▶ CLIPPING LINES

A small clip or snip into the fabric is a useful way to mark some of the lines that appear on a pattern, such as the centre front line and foldlines.

PATTERN MARKING

Once the pattern pieces have been cut out, you will need to mark the symbols shown on the tissue through to the fabric. There are various methods to do this. Tailor's tacks are good for circles and dots, or mark these with a water- or air-soluble pen (when using a pen, it's a good idea to test it on a piece of scrap fabric first). For lines, you can use trace tacking or a tracing wheel with dressmaker's carbon paper.

▶ TRACE TACKING

1 This is a really useful technique to mark centre front lines, foldlines, and placement lines. With double thread in your needle, stitch a row of loopy stitches, sewing along the line marked on the pattern.

2 Carefully pull away the tissue. Cut through the loops, then gently separate the layers of fabric to show the threads. Snip apart to leave thread tails in both of the fabric layers.

▶ TAILOR'S TACKS

1 As there are often dots of different sizes, it is a good idea to choose a different colour thread for each dot size. It is then easy to match the colours as well as the dots. Have double thread in your needle, unknotted. Insert the needle through the dot from right to left, leaving a tail of thread. Be sure to go through the tissue and both layers of fabric.

2 Now stitch through the dot again, this time from top to bottom to make a loop. Cut through the loop, then snip off excess thread to leave a tail.

3 Carefully pull the pattern tissue away. On the top side you will have four threads marking each dot. When you turn the fabric over, the dot positions will be marked with an X.

4 Gently turn back the two layers of fabric to separate them, then cut through the threads so that thread tails are left in both pieces of fabric.

▶ TRACING PAPER AND WHEEL

1 This method is not suitable for all fabrics as the marks may not be able to be removed easily. Slide dressmaker's carbon paper against the wrong side of the fabric.

2 Run a tracing wheel along the pattern lines (a ruler will help you make straight lines).

3 Remove the carbon paper and carefully pull off the pattern tissue. You will have dotted lines marked on your fabric.

▶ MARKER PENS

1 This method can only be used with a single layer of fabric. Press the point of the pen into the centre of the dot marked on the pattern piece.

2 Carefully remove the pattern. The pen marks will have gone through the tissue on to the fabric. Be sure not to press the fabric before the pen marks are removed or they may become permanent.

FABRICS pp.40—52 ● PATTERN LAYOUT pp.78—79

TECHNIQUES

STITCH ESSENTIALS

Seams and stitches are the essential construction elements of your work. Some stitches are created by hand, while others are made on the sewing machine or overlocker.

STITCHES FOR HAND SEWING

Although modern sewing machines have eliminated the need for a lot of hand sewing, it is still necessary to use hand stitching to prepare the fabric prior to permanent stitching – these temporary pattern marking and tacking stitches will eventually be removed. Permanent hand stitching is used to finish a garment and to attach fasteners, as well as to help out with a quick repair.

THREADING THE NEEDLE

When sewing by hand, cut your piece of thread to be no longer than the distance from your fingertips to your elbow. If the thread is much longer than this, it will knot as you sew.

1 Hold your needle in your right hand and the end of the thread in your left. Keeping the thread still, place the eye of the needle over the thread.

2 If the needle will not slip over the thread, dampen your fingers and run the moisture across the eye of the needle. Pull the thread through.

3 At the other end of the thread, tie a knot as shown (left) or secure the thread (shown right).

4 You are now ready to start sewing.

SECURING THE THREAD

The ends of the thread must be secured firmly, especially if the hand stitching is to be permanent. A knot (see left) is frequently used and is the preferred choice for temporary stitches. For permanent stitching a double stitch is a better option.

▶ **DOUBLE STITCH**

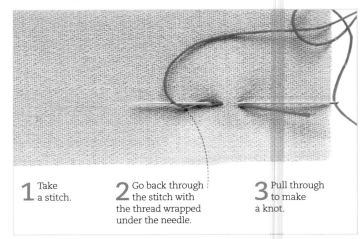

1 Take a stitch.

2 Go back through the stitch with the thread wrapped under the needle.

3 Pull through to make a knot.

▶ **BACKSTITCH**

Make two small stitches in the same place.

TACKING STITCHES

Each of the many types of tacking stitches has its own individual use. Trace tacks are used to transfer pattern markings to fabric. Basic tacks and bar tacks hold two or more pieces of fabric together. Long and short tacks are an alternative version of the basic tacking stitch, often used when the tacking will stay in the work for some time. Thread chain tacks work in a similar way to bar tacks but are much finer as they are made by looping a single thread through itself. Diagonal tacks hold folds or overlaid fabrics together, while slip tacks are used to hold a fold in fabric to another piece of fabric.

▶ BASIC TACKS

Starting with a knot, using single thread, make straight, evenly spaced stitches.

▶ DIAGONAL TACKS

Work vertically, taking horizontal stitches.

▶ SLIP TACKS

Take a stitch into the fold and then a stitch into the base fabric.

▶ LONG-AND-SHORT TACKS

Make long stitches with a short space between each one.

▶ BAR TACKS

1 Using double thread, make two or three loops between the two layers of fabric.

2 Work a buttonhole stitch (see p.91) across the loops.

▶ THREAD CHAIN TACKS

1 Start with a stitch in the fabric and make a loop.

2 Make another loop from the thread and push through the first loop, then pull to tighten the first loop.

3 Repeat the process. Eventually you will have made a thread chain.

4 To finish, take a single thread through the last loop and pull to tighten. Use the thread end to stitch the loop as required.

PATTERN MARKING pp.82—83

TECHNIQUES

HAND STITCHES

There are a number of hand stitches that can be used during construction of a garment or other item. Some are for decorative purposes while others are more functional.

▶ BACKSTITCH

A strong stitch that could be used to construct a piece of work. Work from right to left. Bring the needle up, leaving a space, and then take the thread back to the end of the last stitch. Repeat.

▶ RUNNING STITCH

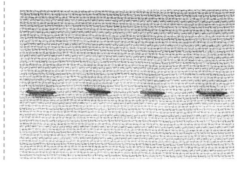

Very similar to tacking (see p.89), but used more for decorative purposes. Work from right to left. Run the needle in and out of the fabric to create even stitches and spaces.

▶ PRICK STITCH

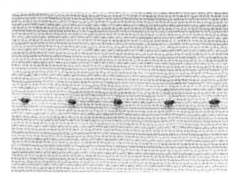

Often used to highlight the edge of a completed garment, such as a collar. Work from right to left. Make small stitches about 2mm (¹⁄₁₆in) long, with spaces between of at least three times that length.

▶ WHIP STITCH

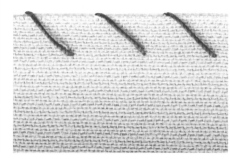

A diagonal stitch sewn with a single thread along a raw edge to prevent fraying. Work from right to left. Take a stitch through the edge of the fabric. The depth of the stitch depends on the thickness of the fabric – for a thin fabric take a shallow stitch.

▶ HERRINGBONE STITCH

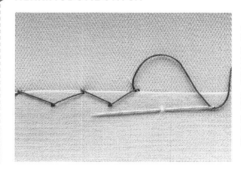

A very useful stitch as it is secure yet has some movement in it. It is used to secure hems and interlinings. Work from left to right. Take a small horizontal stitch into one layer and then the other, so the thread crosses itself.

▶ FLAT FELL STITCH

A strong, secure stitch to hold two layers permanently together. This stitch is often used to secure bias bindings and linings. Work from right to left. Make a short, straight stitch at the edge of the fabric.

▶ SLIP HEM STITCH

Also called a catch stitch, this is used primarily for securing hems. It looks similar to herringbone (above). Work from right to left. Take a short horizontal stitch into one layer and then the other.

▶ BLIND HEM STITCH

As the name suggests this is for hemming a garment. As the stitch is under the edge of the fabric it should be discreet. Work from right to left and use a slip hem stitch (left).

▶ BUTTONHOLE STITCH

1 Used to make hand-worked buttonholes and also to secure fastenings. It is always stitched on an edge with no spaces between the stitches. Work from left to right. Push the needle from the top edge into the fabric.

2 Wrap the thread behind the needle as the needle goes in and again as the needle leaves the fabric. Pull through and a knot will appear at the edge. This is an essential stitch for all sewers and is not difficult to master.

▶ BLANKET STITCH

Similar to buttonhole stitch (above) but without the knot. Blanket stitch is useful to neaten edges and for decorative purposes. Always leave a space between the stitches. Push the needle into the fabric and, as it appears at the edge, wrap the thread under the needle.

▶ CROSS STITCH

A temporary securing stitch used to hold pleats in place after construction. It can also be used to secure linings. Work a row of even diagonal stitches in one direction and then a row back over them to make crosses.

▶ SLIP STITCH/LADDER STITCH

A stitch worked in double thread from right to left to secure a gap in a seam. Take a small horizontal stitch on one side and then a small horizontal stitch on the opposite side. When tightened, the gap is seamlessly closed.

HAND-STITCHED ARROWHEADS

Difficulty level ✱✱✱✱✱

An arrowhead is a triangular shape made by working straight stitches in a set order. This is a permanent stitch placed at an area of strain or stress, such as the top of a split.

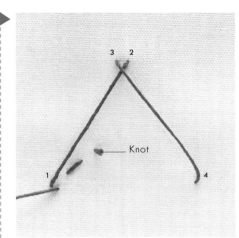

Knot

1 Mark a triangle with sides about 8mm (5⁄16in) long on the fabric. Start with a knot. Bring the needle up through **1** and down through **2**.

2 Then bring the needle up through **3** and down through **4**. Repeat the stitch.

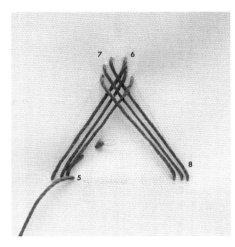

3 Continue the stitches, up through **5** and down through **6**, up through **7** and down through **8**.

4 Make about 10 alternating stitches to complete the arrowhead.

MACHINE ARROWHEADS p.93 ⬩ **MACHINE-MADE BUTTONHOLES p.306**

MACHINE STITCHES AND SEAMS

Fabric is joined together using seams, whether it be for an item of clothing, craft work, or soft furnishings. The most common seam is a plain seam, which is suitable for a wide variety of fabrics and items. However, there are many other seams to be used as appropriate, depending on the fabric and item being constructed. Some seams are decorative and can add detail to structured garments.

SECURING THE THREAD

Machine stitches need to be secured at the end of a seam to prevent them from coming undone. This can be done by hand, tying the ends of the thread, or using the machine with a reverse stitch or a locking stitch, which stitches three or four stitches in the same place.

▶ **TIE THE ENDS**

1 Pull on the top thread and it will pull up a loop – this is the bobbin thread.

2 Pull the loop through to the top.

3 Tie the two threads together.

▶ **REVERSE STITCH**

1 When starting, stitch a couple of stitches forward, then hold in the reverse button and reverse over them. Continue forward again.

2 At the end of the seam, reverse again to secure the stitches.

▶ **LOCKING STITCH**

1 When starting, press the locking stitch and stitch, then continue forward.

2 At the end of the seam, press the locking stitch again.

STITCHES MADE WITH A MACHINE

The sewing machine will stitch plain seams and decorative seams as well as buttonholes of various styles. The length and width of all buttonholes can be altered to suit the garment or craft item. Stitch length and width can also be adjusted. On most machines, the number settings equate to millimetres (used in this book), but some brands use stitches per inch.

▶ **STRAIGHT STITCH**

Used for most applications. The length of the stitch can be altered from 0.5 to 5.0 on most sewing machines.

▶ **ZIGZAG STITCH**

To neaten seam edges and for securing and decorative purposes. Both the width and the length of this stitch can be altered.

▶ **3-STEP ZIGZAG STITCH**

Made up of small, straight stitches. This stitch is decorative as well as functional, and is often found in lingerie. The stitch length and width can be altered.

▶ BLIND HEM STITCH

Made in conjunction with the blind hem foot. A combination of straight stitches and a zigzag stitch (see opposite page). Used to secure hems.

▶ OVEREDGE STITCH

Made in conjunction with the overedge foot. The stitch is used for neatening the edge of fabric. The width and length of the stitch can be altered.

▶ STRETCH STITCH

Also known as a lightening stitch. This stitch is recommended for stretch knits, but is better used to help control difficult fabrics.

▶ BASIC BUTTONHOLE STITCH

Square on both ends. Used on all styles of garment.

▶ ROUND-END BUTTONHOLE STITCH

One square end and one round end. Used on jackets.

▶ KEYHOLE BUTTONHOLE STITCH

One square end and one end shaped like a loop. Used on jackets.

▶ DECORATIVE STITCHES

CORN STITCH

FLOWER STITCH

Sewing machines are capable of producing decorative linear stitches. These can be used to enhance the surface of work or a seam as they add interest to edges. Or, when worked as many rows together, they can be used to create a piece of embroidered fabric.

STAR STITCH

▶ 3-THREAD OVERLOCK STITCH

Stitched using three threads on the overlocker. Used to neaten the edge of fabric to prevent fraying.

▶ 4-THREAD OVERLOCK STITCH

Made using four threads on the overlocker. Used to neaten edges and to construct stretch knits.

▶ MACHINE ARROWHEADS

This is a built-in stitch on many sewing machines. Used to secure weak points.

SEAM NEATENING **p.95** ● MACHINED HEMS **p.266** ● BUTTONHOLES **pp.304–311**

TECHNIQUES

HOW TO MAKE A PLAIN SEAM

Difficulty level ✳✳✳✳✳

A plain seam is usually 1.5cm (⅝in) wide, but it can be 1cm (⅜in) or even 6mm (¼in). It is important that the seam is stitched at the width indicated on the pattern, to ensure the item comes out true to size. There are guides on the plate of the sewing machine to help align the fabric.

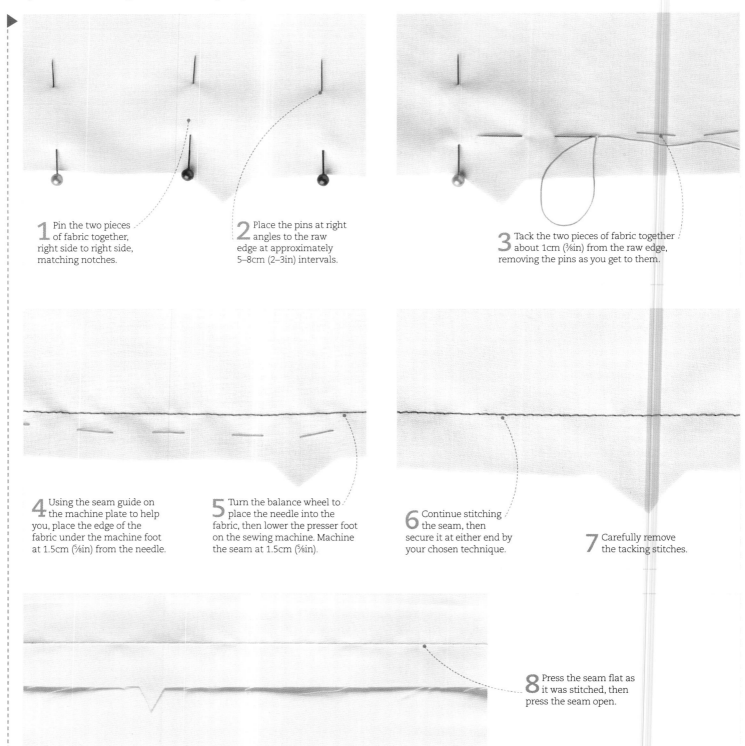

1 Pin the two pieces of fabric together, right side to right side, matching notches.

2 Place the pins at right angles to the raw edge at approximately 5–8cm (2–3in) intervals.

3 Tack the two pieces of fabric together about 1cm (⅜in) from the raw edge, removing the pins as you get to them.

4 Using the seam guide on the machine plate to help you, place the edge of the fabric under the machine foot at 1.5cm (⅝in) from the needle.

5 Turn the balance wheel to place the needle into the fabric, then lower the presser foot on the sewing machine. Machine the seam at 1.5cm (⅝in).

6 Continue stitching the seam, then secure it at either end by your chosen technique.

7 Carefully remove the tacking stitches.

8 Press the seam flat as it was stitched, then press the seam open.

SEAM NEATENING

It is important that the raw edges of the seam are neatened or finished – this will make the seam hard-wearing and prevent fraying. The method of neatening will depend on the style of item that is being made and the fabric you are using.

▶ PINKED

This method of neatening is ideal to use on fabrics that do not fray badly. Stitch 5mm (³⁄₁₆in) away from the raw edge, then use pinking shears to trim as little as possible off the edge.

▶ ZIGZAGGED

All sewing machines will make a zigzag stitch. It is an ideal stitch to use to stop the edges fraying and is suitable for all types of fabric. Stitch in from the raw edge, then trim back to the zigzag stitch. On most fabrics, use a stitch width of 2.0 and a stitch length of 1.5.

▶ OVEREDGE STITCHED

This is found on most sewing machines. Select the overedge stitch on your machine. Using the overedge machine foot and the pre-set stitch length and width, machine along the raw edge of the seam.

▶ CLEAN FINISH

This is a very hard-wearing finish and is ideal for cottons and fine fabrics. Using a straight stitch, turn under the raw edge of the seam allowance by 3mm (⅛in) and straight stitch along the fold.

▶ 3-THREAD OVERLOCKED

If you have an overlocker, you can neaten seams with a 3-thread overlock stitch. It is one of the most professional ways to finish seams and is suitable for all types of fabrics and items.

TECHNIQUES

HONG KONG FINISH

This is a great finish to use on wools and linens, to neaten the seams on unlined jackets. It is made by wrapping the raw edge with bias-cut strips.

Difficulty level ✸✸✳✳✳

1 Cut bias strips of silk organza 2cm (¾in) wide. Good-quality lining fabric can also be used.

2 Stitch the raw edge of the bias strip to the raw edge of the seam allowance using a 5mm (³⁄₁₆in) seam allowance.

3 Press over the raw edge.

4 Wrap to the wrong side of the raw edge, with the raw edge of the bias strip against the stitching of the seam.

Right side of seam allowance

Bias strip

Raw edge of seam allowance

Wrong side of seam allowance

Wrapped bias strip

5 Pin the wrapped bias strip to the fabric, then press the folded edge.

Stitching on right side of seam allowance

6 Machine the wrapped bias strip to the seam, from the upper side of the seam, stitching alongside the edge of the bias.

FRENCH SEAM

Difficulty level ✱✱✱✱✱

A French seam is a seam that is stitched twice, first on the right side of the work and then on the wrong side, enclosing the first seam. The French seam has traditionally been used on delicate garments, such as lingerie, and on sheer and silk fabrics.

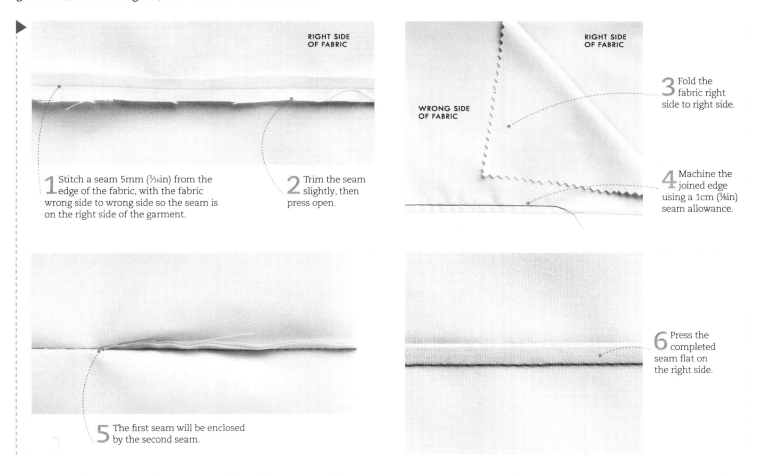

RIGHT SIDE OF FABRIC

1 Stitch a seam 5mm (³⁄₁₆in) from the edge of the fabric, with the fabric wrong side to wrong side so the seam is on the right side of the garment.

2 Trim the seam slightly, then press open.

WRONG SIDE OF FABRIC

RIGHT SIDE OF FABRIC

3 Fold the fabric right side to right side.

4 Machine the joined edge using a 1cm (³⁄₈in) seam allowance.

5 The first seam will be enclosed by the second seam.

6 Press the completed seam flat on the right side.

MOCK FRENCH SEAM

Difficulty level ✱✱✱✱✱

When this seam is completed, it looks very similar to the French seam. A mock French seam is best used on cotton or firmer fine fabrics. It is constructed on the wrong side of the work.

WRONG SIDE OF FABRIC

1 Make a 1.5cm (⁵⁄₈in) seam on the wrong side of the fabric.

2 Fold in the raw edges of both the seam allowances towards the stitching line.

3 Pin the folded edges together.

4 Machine the folded edges of the seam allowances together, without stitching through to the right side. Press.

HOW TO CUT BIAS STRIPS **p.154**

RUN AND FELL SEAM

Difficulty level ✱✱✱✱✱

Some garments require a strong seam that will withstand frequent washing and wear and tear. A run and fell seam, also known as a flat fell seam, is very strong. It is made on the right side of a garment and is used on the inside leg seam of jeans, and on men's tailored shirts.

WRONG SIDE OF FABRIC

RIGHT SIDE OF FABRIC

1 Stitch a 1.5cm (⅝in) seam on the right side of the fabric. Press open.

2 Trim the side of the seam allowance that is towards the back of the garment down to one-third of its width.

Folded edge   Trimmed edge

3 Wrap the other side of the seam allowance around the trimmed side and pin in position.

4 Machine along the folded pinned edge through all layers. Press.

5 On the right side, there will be two rows of parallel stitching.

SELF-BOUND SEAM

Difficulty level ✱✱✱✱✱

Another strong seam, this is constructed in a similar way to the run and fell seam (see above), but on the wrong side of the work. It is often used in children's wear.

1 Make a 1.5cm (⅝in) seam on the wrong side of the fabric.

2 Trim one side of the seam allowance to one-third of its width.

WRONG SIDE OF FABRIC

Trimmed seam

3 Fold under the edge on the other side of the seam.

Folded edge

4 Bring the fold on to the original seam stitching line.

5 Machine in position, stitching just to the seam allowance but not through to the right side of the work.

6 The finished seam can only be seen on the wrong side. On the right side there is just a seamline.

TOP-STITCHED SEAM

Difficulty level ✱✱✱✱✱

A top-stitched seam is very useful as it is both decorative and practical. This seam is often used on crafts and soft furnishings as well as garments.

RIGHT SIDE OF FABRIC

1 Make a 1.5cm (⅝in) seam on the wrong side of the fabric. Press the seam open.

2 Working from the right side of the work, stitch down either side of the seam. Press.

CUTTING TOOLS **p.16** ● HOW TO MAKE A PLAIN SEAM **p.94**

LAPPED SEAM

Also called an overlaid seam, a lapped seam is constructed on the right side of the garment. It is a very flat seam when it is finished.

1 Press under 1.5cm (⅝in) on one side of the seamline to the wrong side.

2 Place the folded edge of the fabric to the other half of the seamline on the right side. Pin in place.

WRONG SIDE OF FABRIC

RIGHT SIDE OF FABRIC

3 Machine close to the fold.

4 Machine again 1cm (⅜in) from the fold. Press.

SLOTTED SEAM

A slotted seam is a decorative seam, shown on the right side. The edges of the seam open to reveal an underlayer, which could be a contrasting fabric.

RIGHT SIDE OF FABRIC

WRONG SIDE OF FABRIC

1 On the wrong side of the work, make a plain seam 1.5cm (⅝in) wide using a long stitch. Press open.

WRONG SIDE OF FABRIC

2 Turn the seam back to the wrong side and cut through every fifth stitch using a seam ripper. Press the seam open again.

RIGHT SIDE OF FABRIC

3 Cut a straight grain strip of fabric 3cm (1¼in) wide (use the same fabric or a contrasting fabric). Pin it to the wrong side, behind the seam allowance.

4 Machine the strip to the seam allowance, stitching along either side of the seamline at an equal distance from it. Machine from the right side of the work.

RIGHT SIDE OF FABRIC

5 Remove the long stitches that made the original seam, to produce an open seam with parallel lines of stitching on either side.

Stitching lines

STITCHES MADE WITH A MACHINE pp.92–93

CORDED SEAM

A seam with piping in it can add interest to an otherwise plain garment. This is also a useful technique if you are joining two fabrics that are different. The piping is made first, prior to its being inserted in the seam.

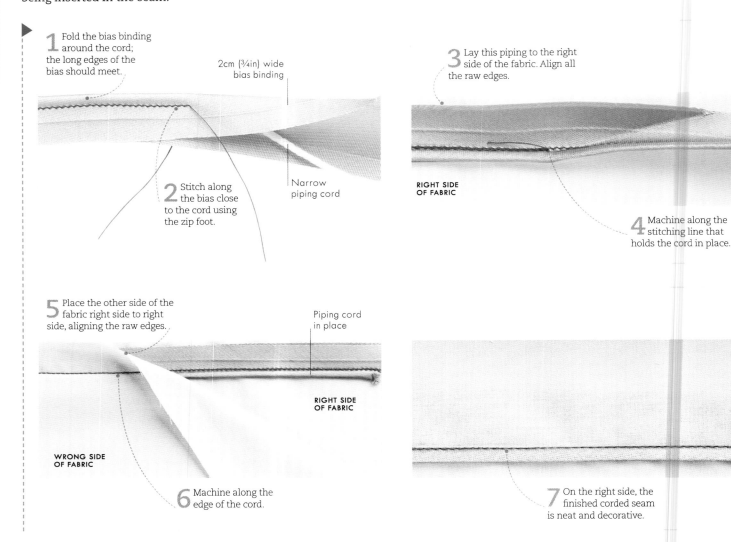

1 Fold the bias binding around the cord; the long edges of the bias should meet.

2cm (¾in) wide bias binding

Narrow piping cord

2 Stitch along the bias close to the cord using the zip foot.

3 Lay this piping to the right side of the fabric. Align all the raw edges.

RIGHT SIDE OF FABRIC

4 Machine along the stitching line that holds the cord in place.

5 Place the other side of the fabric right side to right side, aligning the raw edges.

Piping cord in place

RIGHT SIDE OF FABRIC

WRONG SIDE OF FABRIC

6 Machine along the edge of the cord.

7 On the right side, the finished corded seam is neat and decorative.

MAKING A SEAM WITH THE OVERLOCKER

Use this when constructing stretch knits.

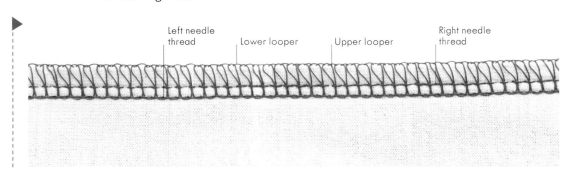

Left needle thread · Lower looper · Upper looper · Right needle thread

1 Put the fabric together, right side to right side, pin, and tack.

2 Remove all the pins as they could damage the overlocker.

3 Stitch the seam with a 4-thread overlock stitch.

SEAMS ON DIFFICULT FABRICS

Difficulty level ✷✷✷✷✷

Some fabrics require specialist care for seam construction because they are very bulky, as with a fur fabric, or so soft and delicate that they appear too soft to sew. On a sheer fabric, the seam used is an alternative to a French seam; it is very narrow when finished and presses very flat. Making a seam on suede is done by means of a lapped seam. As some suede-effect fabric has a fake fur on the other side, the seam is reversible.

▶ A SEAM ON SHEER FABRIC

1 On the wrong side of the work, make a 1.5cm (⅝in) seam.

2 Machine again 5mm (³⁄₁₆in) from the first stitching, using either a very narrow zigzag stitch or a stretch stitch. Press.

3 Trim the raw edge of the fabric close to the second row of stitching.

▶ A SEAM ON SUEDE OR SUEDE-EFFECT FABRIC

1 On all seams, trace tack the stitching line 1.5cm (⅝in) from the edge.

2 Trace tack again 1.5cm (⅝in) away from the first row of stitching.

3 Overlap one side of the seam over the other, matching the 1.5cm (⅝in) tack lines. The raw edge should touch the second row of tacks.

4 Using a walking foot and a longer-than-normal stitch length of 3.5, machine the two layers together along the tacks marking the 1.5cm (⅝in) seam allowance.

5 Stitch again 1cm (⅜in) from the first stitching line.

6 Trim the raw edge by about 3mm (⅛in).

▶ A SEAM ON FUR FABRIC

1 Pin the fabric together right side to right side, placing the pins in alternate directions to stop the fur moving.

2 Using a walking foot and a longer-than-normal stitch length, machine the seam.

3 Finger press the seam open.

4 Trim the surplus fur fabric off the seam allowances.

STITCHES MADE WITH A MACHINE pp.92—93

STITCHING CORNERS AND CURVES

Difficulty level ✱✱✱✱✱

Not all sewing is straight lines. Most items will have curves and corners that require negotiation to produce sharp, clean angles and curves on the right side. The technique for stitching a corner shown below applies to corners of all angles. On a thick fabric, the technique is slightly different, with a stitch taken across the corner, and on a fabric that frays badly the corner is reinforced with a second row of stitches.

▶ **STITCHING A CORNER**

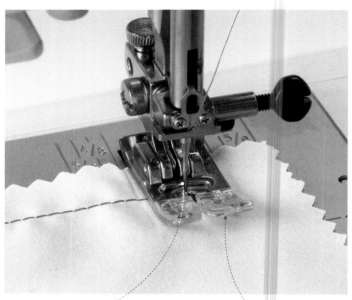

1 Pin the fabric together, right side to right side.

2 Stitch a seam at 1.5cm (⅝in).

3 On reaching the corner, insert the machine needle into the fabric.

4 Raise the presser foot and turn the fabric through 90 degrees (this is pivoting at the corner).

5 Lower the presser foot and continue stitching in the other direction.

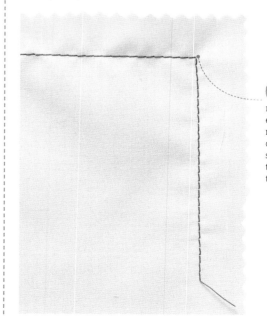

6 The stitching lines are at right angles to each other, which means the finished corner will have a sharp point when turned through to the right side.

▶ **STITCHING A CORNER ON HEAVY FABRIC**

1 On a thick fabric it is very difficult to achieve a sharp point, so instead a single stitch is taken across the corner. First, stitch to the corner.

2 Insert the needle into the fabric, then lift the presser foot. Turn the fabric 45 degrees. Put the foot down again and make one stitch.

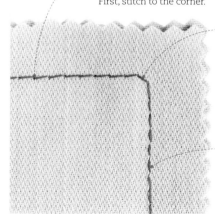

3 With the needle in the fabric, lift the foot and turn the fabric 45 degrees again. Lower the foot and continue stitching along the other side.

SEWING-MACHINE ACCESSORIES pp.32–33 • **STITCHES MADE WITH A MACHINE pp.92–93** • **HOW TO MAKE A PLAIN SEAM p.94**

▶ STITCHING A REINFORCED CORNER

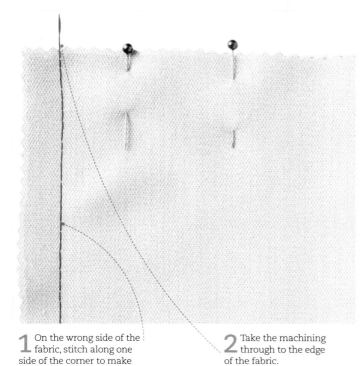

3 Stitch the other side of the corner at a 1.5cm (⅝in) seam allowance, again machining through the edge of the fabric.

4 The two stitching lines will overlap at the corner.

5 Stitch exactly over the first two stitching lines, this time pivoting at the corner (see Stitching a corner, steps 3–5, opposite).

1 On the wrong side of the fabric, stitch along one side of the corner to make a 1.5cm (⅝in) seam.

2 Take the machining through to the edge of the fabric.

6 Remove the surplus stitches in the seam allowance by unpicking.

▶ STITCHING AN INNER CORNER

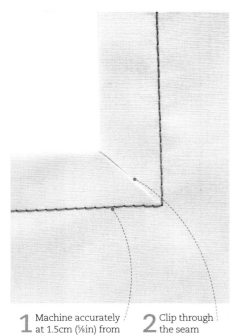

1 Machine accurately at 1.5cm (⅝in) from the edge, pivoting at the corner (see Stitching a corner, steps 3–5, opposite page).

2 Clip through the seam allowance into the corner.

▶ STITCHING AN INNER CURVE

1 Place the right sides of the fabric together.

2 Stitch a seam at 1.5cm (⅝in) from the edge. Be sure the stitching line follows the curve (use the stitching guides on the plate of the machine to help).

▶ STITCHING AN OUTER CURVE

1 Put the right sides of the fabric together and stitch a 1.5cm (⅝in) seam.

2 Follow the curve and keep the stitching line at a uniform distance from the edge.

REDUCING SEAM BULK **pp.108—109**

TWO-TONE **TOTE BAG**

Difficulty level ✱✱✱✱✱

At the beginning of your sewing career, the best projects are those that are easy to make and look anything but! This tote bag certainly meets the challenge of an ideal beginner project being made up of simple rectangles, brought together with straightforward seam and top-stitching techniques.

TECHNIQUES USED How to apply a fusible interfacing **p.54**, Stitching a corner **p.100**, Top-stitching **p.109**

YOU WILL NEED

- 50 x 110cm (36 x 43in) medium-weight cotton for outer fabric A
- 25 x 110cm (36 x 43in) medium-weight cotton for outer fabric B
- 50 x 110cm (36 x 43in) quilting-weight cotton for the lining
- 2 pieces 43 x 43cm (17 x 17in) light- to medium-weight fusible woven interfacing for outer pieces
- 2 pieces 66 x 9cm (26 x 3½in) light- to medium-weight fusible woven interfacing for handles
- 2 pieces 40 x 39cm (16 x 15½in) medium-loft fusible fleece batting for outer pieces
- Matching thread

PIECES TO CUT

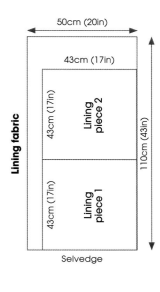

▶ MAKE THE HANDLES

WRONG SIDE OF HANDLE

1 Apply the woven interfacing for each handle piece, positioning it 6mm (¼in) from the sides and 1.2cm (½in) from the ends. Allow to cool for 20 minutes.

2 Fold each handle in half along the length and press the fold.

3 Open out and fold again at each side, bringing each edge into the centre fold. Press.

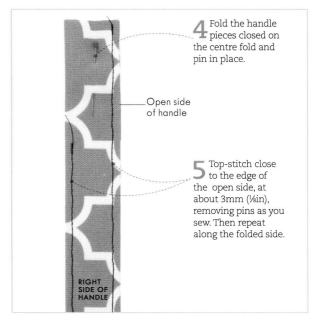

RIGHT SIDE OF HANDLE

Open side of handle

4 Fold the handle pieces closed on the centre fold and pin in place.

5 Top-stitch close to the edge of the open side, at about 3mm (⅛in), removing pins as you sew. Then repeat along the folded side.

PRESSING AIDS **pp.28–29**

▶ **MAKE THE LINING**

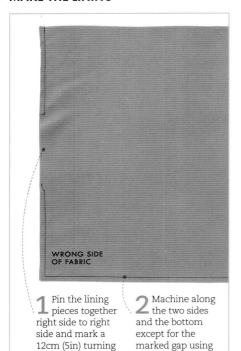

WRONG SIDE
OF FABRIC

1 Pin the lining pieces together right side to right side and mark a 12cm (5in) turning gap on one side.

2 Machine along the two sides and the bottom except for the marked gap using a 1cm (⅜in) seam allowance.

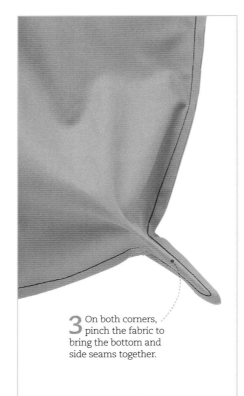

3 On both corners, pinch the fabric to bring the bottom and side seams together.

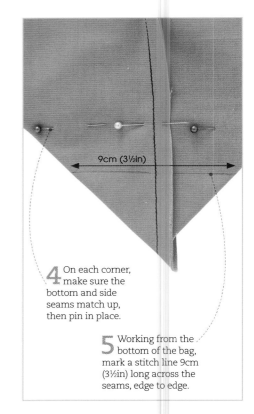

9cm (3½in)

4 On each corner, make sure the bottom and side seams match up, then pin in place.

5 Working from the bottom of the bag, mark a stitch line 9cm (3½in) long across the seams, edge to edge.

6 Still working from the bottom of the bag, create boxed corners by stitching across the marked lines. Reverse stitch across the central bag seam to reinforce.

7 Trim the corner seams to 1cm (⅜in).

▶ **MAKE THE OUTER LAYER**

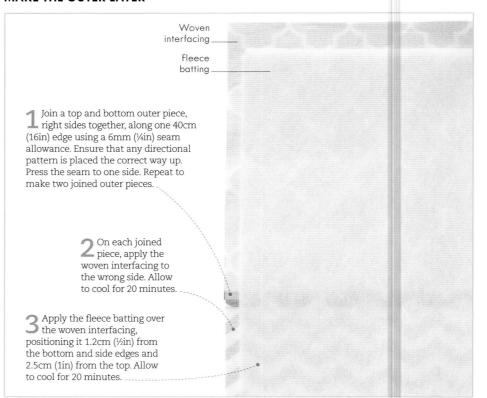

Woven interfacing

Fleece batting

1 Join a top and bottom outer piece, right sides together, along one 40cm (16in) edge using a 6mm (¼in) seam allowance. Ensure that any directional pattern is placed the correct way up. Press the seam to one side. Repeat to make two joined outer pieces.

2 On each joined piece, apply the woven interfacing to the wrong side. Allow to cool for 20 minutes.

3 Apply the fleece batting over the woven interfacing, positioning it 1.2cm (½in) from the bottom and side edges and 2.5cm (1in) from the top. Allow to cool for 20 minutes.

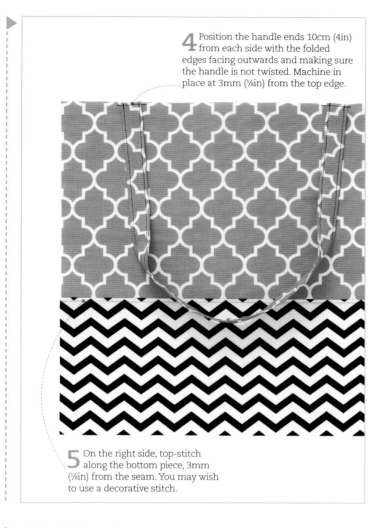

4 Position the handle ends 10cm (4in) from each side with the folded edges facing outwards and making sure the handle is not twisted. Machine in place at 3mm (⅛in) from the top edge.

5 On the right side, top-stitch along the bottom piece, 3mm (⅛in) from the seam. You may wish to use a decorative stitch.

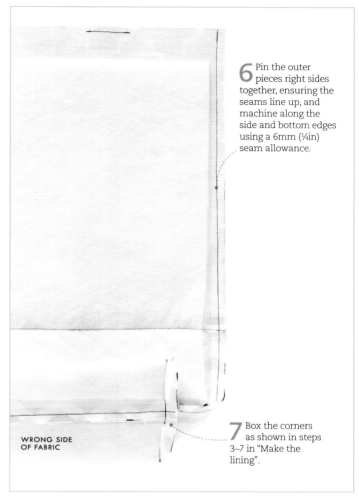

6 Pin the outer pieces right sides together, ensuring the seams line up, and machine along the side and bottom edges using a 6mm (¼in) seam allowance.

WRONG SIDE OF FABRIC

7 Box the corners as shown in steps 3–7 in "Make the lining".

▶ SEW LAYERS TOGETHER

1 Turn the outer layer right side out and place inside the lining, which is wrong side out, so the right sides face each other with the handles tucked inside. Line up the side seams on the two layers and pin in place. Tack together along the top edge.

2 Machine along the top edge using a 1cm (⅜in) seam allowance, reversing over the four handle ends, to reinforce.

3 Turn the bag right side out through the turning gap in the lining. Press the top edge well. Top-stitch around the top at 3mm (⅛in).

4 Close the gap in the lining by hand using a ladder stitch and press the whole bag well.

RIGHT SIDE OF FABRIC

HAND STITCHES **pp.90–91** • STITCHES MADE WITH A MACHINE **pp.92–93** • DECORATIVE STITCHES **p.93**

REDUCING **SEAM BULK**

It is important that the seams used for construction do not cause bulk on the right side. To make sure this does not happen, the seam allowances need to be reduced in size by a technique known as layering a seam. They may also require V shapes to be removed, which is known as notching, or the seam allowance may be clipped.

LAYERING A SEAM

Difficulty level ✳✳✳✳✳

On the majority of fabrics, if the seam is on the edge of the work, the fabric in the seam needs reducing. The seam allowance closest to the outside of the garment or item stays full width, while the seam allowance closest to the body or inside is reduced.

Cut along one side of the seam to reduce the fabric in the seam allowance by half to one-third of its original width.

REDUCING SEAM BULK ON AN INNER CURVE

Difficulty level ✳✳✳✳✳

For an inner curve to lie flat, the seam will need to be layered and notched, then understitched to hold it in place (see opposite page).

1 Stitch the seam on the inner curve.

3 Turn to the right side and press.

RIGHT SIDE OF FABRIC

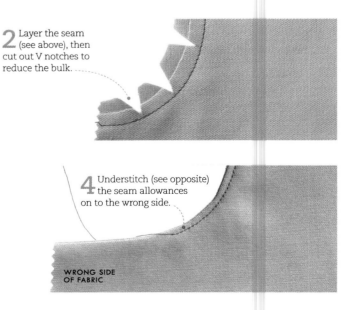

2 Layer the seam (see above), then cut out V notches to reduce the bulk.

4 Understitch (see opposite) the seam allowances on to the wrong side.

WRONG SIDE OF FABRIC

HOW TO MAKE A PLAIN SEAM p.94 ● STITCHING CORNERS AND CURVES **pp.102—103**

REDUCING SEAM BULK ON AN OUTER CURVE

Difficulty level ✶✶✶✶✶

An outer curve also needs layering and notching or clipping to allow the fabric to turn to the right side, after which it is understitched.

1 Make the seam, stitching along the outer curve.

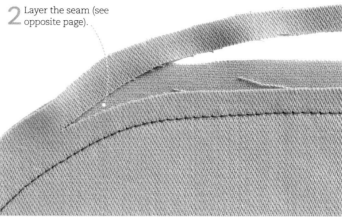

2 Layer the seam (see opposite page).

3 Clip through the seam allowances to reduce bulk.

RIGHT SIDE OF FABRIC

4 Turn through to the right side and press.

WRONG SIDE OF FABRIC

5 Understitch the seam (see below) to finish.

STITCH FINISHES

Difficulty level ✶✶✶✶✶

Top-stitching and understitching are two methods to finish edges. Top-stitching is meant to be seen on the right side of the work, whereas understitching is not visible from the right side.

▶ **TOP-STITCHING**

A top-stitch is a decorative, sharp finish to an edge. Use a longer stitch length, of 3.0 or 3.5, and machine on the right side of the work, using the edge of the machine foot as a guide.

▶ **UNDERSTITCHING**

WRONG SIDE OF FABRIC

Understitching is used to secure a seam that is on the edge of a piece of fabric. It helps to stop the seam from rolling to the right side. First make the seam, then layer, turn, and press on to the right side. Open the seam flat again and push the seam allowance to the wrong side. Machine the seam allowance down.

COMBINATION NECK AND ARMHOLE FACING **p.159** · INSERTING A SET-IN SLEEVE **p.211**

DARTS, TUCKS, PLEATS, AND GATHERS

Shape is put into a piece of flat fabric by means of a dart, a tuck, a pleat, or a gather. It may be to shape the fabric around the body or create shape for crafts or soft furnishings.

DARTS

A dart is used to give shape to a piece of fabric so that it can fit around the contours of the body. Some darts are stitched using straight stitching lines and other darts are stitched using a slightly curved line. Always stitch a dart from the point to the wide end because you are able to sink the machine needle into the point accurately and securely.

DIRECTORY OF DARTS

PLAIN DART ON
BUST (p.113)

PLAIN DART ON
WAIST (p.113)

CONTOUR OR DOUBLE-
POINTED DART (p.115)

BALANCED DART (p.116)

FRENCH DART (p.117)

PLAIN DART

This is the most common type of dart and is used to give shaping to the bust in the bodice. It is also found at the waist in skirts and trousers to give shape from the waist to the hip.

Difficulty level ✱✱✱✱✱

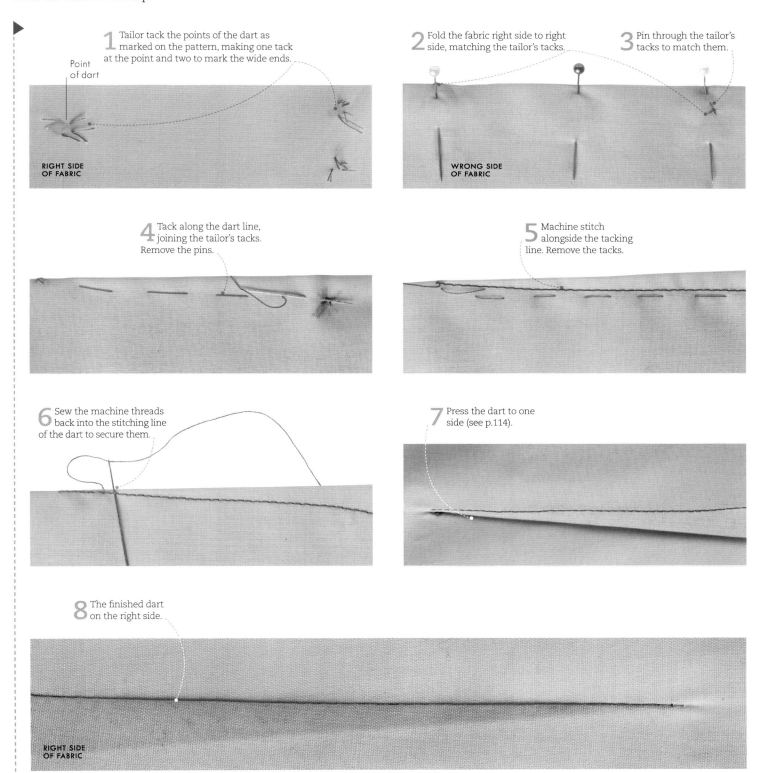

1 Tailor tack the points of the dart as marked on the pattern, making one tack at the point and two to mark the wide ends.

Point of dart

RIGHT SIDE OF FABRIC

2 Fold the fabric right side to right side, matching the tailor's tacks.

3 Pin through the tailor's tacks to match them.

WRONG SIDE OF FABRIC

4 Tack along the dart line, joining the tailor's tacks. Remove the pins.

5 Machine stitch alongside the tacking line. Remove the tacks.

6 Sew the machine threads back into the stitching line of the dart to secure them.

7 Press the dart to one side (see p.114).

8 The finished dart on the right side.

RIGHT SIDE OF FABRIC

MAKING A TOILE **pp.74–75** • PATTERN MARKING **pp.82–83**

SHAPING DARTS TO FIT

Difficulty level **★★**✷✷✷

Due to the curve of our bodies, the straight line of the dart may not sit closely enough to our own personal shape. The dart can be stitched slightly concave or convex so it follows our contours. Do not move the curve out by more than 3mm (⅛in).

▶ **CONVEX DART**

Use this for fuller shapes. Stitch the dart slightly inside the normal stitching line, to make a smooth convex curve.

▶ **CONCAVE DART**

This is for thinner bodies as it takes up more fabric. Stitch the dart slightly outside the normal stitching line, in a smooth concave curve.

PRESSING A DART

If a dart is pressed incorrectly, this can spoil the look of a garment. For successful pressing you will need a tailor's ham and a steam iron on a steam setting. A pressing cloth may be required for delicate fabrics such as silk, satin, and chiffon, and for lining fabrics.

▶ **1** Place the fabric piece, right side down, on the tailor's ham. The point of the dart should be over the end of the ham.

2 Press the fabric around the point of the dart.

3 Move the iron from the point towards the wide end of the dart to press the dart flat, open, or to one side, depending on the type of dart.

CONTOUR OR DOUBLE-POINTED DART

Difficulty level ✹✹✹✹✹

This type of dart is like two darts joined together at the fat end. It is used to give shape at the waist of a garment. It will contour the fabric from the bust into the waist and then out again for the hip.

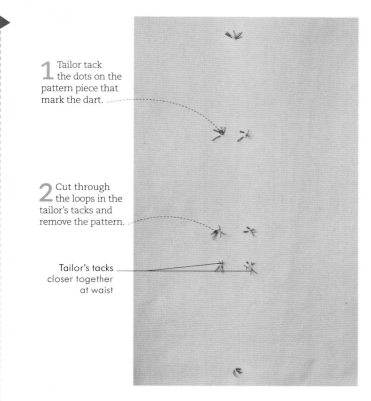

1 Tailor tack the dots on the pattern piece that mark the dart.

2 Cut through the loops in the tailor's tacks and remove the pattern.

Tailor's tacks closer together at waist

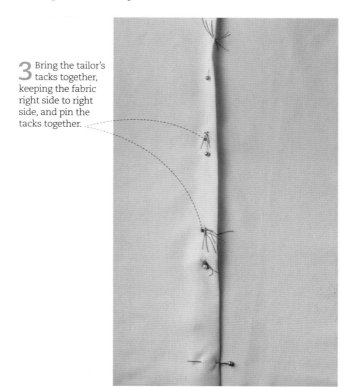

3 Bring the tailor's tacks together, keeping the fabric right side to right side, and pin the tacks together.

4 Make a row of tacking stitches just outside the pin line.

5 Machine stitch following the tailor-tack line, starting at one end and curving out to the widest point, then back to the other point, securing the machine stitching at both ends.

6 Remove the tacking.

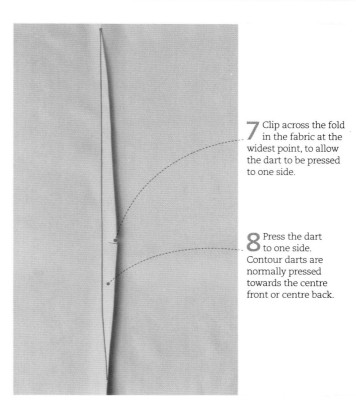

7 Clip across the fold in the fabric at the widest point, to allow the dart to be pressed to one side.

8 Press the dart to one side. Contour darts are normally pressed towards the centre front or centre back.

TECHNIQUES

BALANCED DART

Difficulty level **★★★**✱✱

This dart is used on thicker fabrics such as wool crepe or tweed, as well as on fabrics that mark when pressed. The addition of a balancing strip helps distrubute the fabric on either side of the dart on the wrong side, making it less conspicuous on the worn garment.

1 Mark the position of the dart with tailor's tacks.

2 Cut a strip of straight grain fabric. This should be 4cm (1½in) longer than the dart, and twice the width of the dart at its widest point.

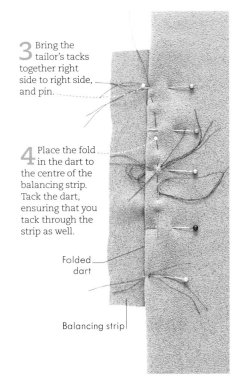

3 Bring the tailor's tacks together right side to right side, and pin.

4 Place the fold in the dart to the centre of the balancing strip. Tack the dart, ensuring that you tack through the strip as well.

Folded dart

Balancing strip

5 Machine the dart through all the layers and from tack to tack.

6 Knot off the machine threads.

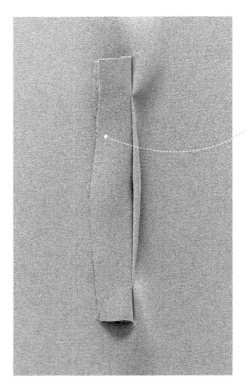

7 Open out the folded dart so the fabric lies flat.

8 Press the dart to one side and the balancing strip to the other.

9 If the fabric is tight, clip the centre of the dart and the centre of the balancing strip at their widest points. This will release tension.

10 Trim back the strip to a neat rectangle shape to reflect the shape of the dart.

FRENCH DART

Difficulty level ✹✹✹✹✹

A French dart is used on the front of a garment only. It is a curved dart that extends from the side seam at the waist to the bust point. As this is a long dart that is shaped, it will need to be slashed prior to construction, in order for it to fit together and then lie flat when pressed.

1 Mark all the dots on the pattern piece using tailor's tacks.

2 Mark the slash line with trace tacking and a different colour thread.

3 Cut through the loops in the tailor's tacks and remove the pattern.

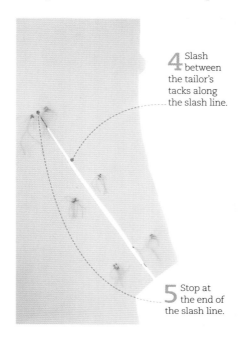

4 Slash between the tailor's tacks along the slash line.

5 Stop at the end of the slash line.

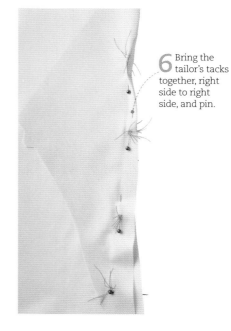

6 Bring the tailor's tacks together, right side to right side, and pin.

7 Machine stitch the dart, starting at the point and securing the stitching, then continue stitching to the fat end.

8 Press the slashed part of the dart open and the non-slashed part of the dart to the one side.

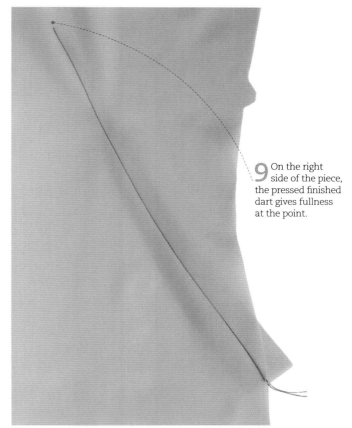

9 On the right side of the piece, the pressed finished dart gives fullness at the point.

TACKING STITCHES p.89 ● **STITCHES MADE WITH A MACHINE pp.92–93**

TUCKS

A tuck is a decorative addition to any piece of fabric, and can be big and bold or very delicate. Tucks are made by stitching evenly spaced folds into the fabric on the right side, normally on the straight grain of the fabric. As the tucks take up additional fabric, it is advisable to make them prior to cutting out.

DIRECTORY OF TUCKS

PLAIN TUCKS (p.119)

SPACED TUCKS (p.119)

PIN TUCKS (p.119)

TWIN NEEDLE TUCKS (p.119)

BLIND TUCKS (p.119)

SHELL TUCKS (p.120)

CORDED OR PIPED TUCKS (p.121)

DARTED TUCKS (p.121)

CROSS TUCKS (p.121)

MARKING AIDS **p.19** ● *PRESSING AIDS* **pp.28–29** ● *SEWING-MACHINE ACCESSORIES* **pp.32–33**

PLAIN TUCKS

A plain tuck is made by marking and creasing the fabric at regular intervals. A row of machine stitches are then worked adjacent to the fold.

1 Mark the position of the tucks lightly with chalk on the right side of the fabric. Make sure the lines are parallel.

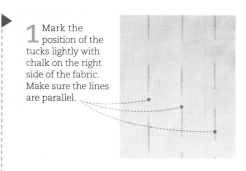

2 Fold along the chalk lines, making sure the folds are straight, and press in place.

3 Machine close to the foldline, using the edge of the machine foot as a guide, or as indicated on your pattern.

4 Repeat along the next fold, and continue until all the folds are stitched.

5 Press the tucks all in the same direction.

OTHER SIMPLE TUCKS

These tucks are also made by marking and creasing the fabric. The positioning of the machine stitching determines the type of tuck.

▶ SPACED TUCKS

These are similar to a plain tuck but with wider regular spacing. Press the tucks in place along the foldlines and pin. Machine 1cm (⅜in) from the foldline. Press all the tucks in one direction.

▶ PIN TUCKS

These narrow, regularly spaced tucks are stitched very close to the foldline, which may require moving the machine needle closer to the fold. Use the pintuck foot on the sewing machine.

▶ TWIN NEEDLE TUCKS

For these regularly spaced tucks, stitch along the foldlines using the twin needle on the sewing machine. The twin needle produces a shallow tuck that looks very effective when multiple rows are stitched.

▶ BLIND TUCKS

These are wide tucks that are stitched so that no machining shows – the fold of each tuck covers the machine stitching of the previous tuck.

STITCHES MADE WITH A MACHINE **pp.92–93**

SHELL TUCKS

A shell tuck is very decorative as it has a scalloped edge. Shell tucks can be easily stitched using the sewing machine. On heavy fabric and delicate fabrics it may be preferable to make the tucks by hand.

Difficulty level ★★☆☆☆

▶ MACHINE SHELL TUCKS

1 Mark the foldlines on the fabric, then fold and press.

2 Tack the folds in place.

3 Use the embroidery foot on the sewing machine and set the sewing machine to a shell hem stitch.

4 Stitch along the fold, keeping the fold close to the right-hand side of the machine foot.

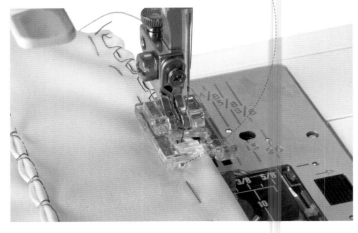

5 The finished tucks should be stitched at regular intervals.

SHELL TUCKS BY HAND

1 Tack the foldlines for the tucks in place.

2 Using a double thread in the needle, make two or three running stitches.

3 Every 1.25cm (½in), make an over-stitch through the fold to produce a scallop.

CORDED OR PIPED TUCKS

These are very substantial tucks that stand proud of the fabric. This type of tuck is best used in soft furnishings.

1 Mark the folds on the fabric and press. Place piping cord into the folds.

2 Tack to hold the cord in place.

3 Using the zip foot on the sewing machine, stitch close to the cord.

4 The finished corded tucks are spaced neatly at regular intervals.

DARTED TUCKS

A tuck that stops to release the fullness is known as a darted tuck. It can be used to give fullness at the bust or hip. The shaped darted tuck is stitched at an angle to release less fabric, while the plain darted tuck is stitched straight on the grainline.

▶ SHAPED DARTED TUCKS

1 Transfer any pattern markings to the fabric.

2 Fold the fabric right side to right side. On the wrong side of the fabric, stitch at an angle to the folded edge.

3 Stop at the point indicated on your pattern.

4 Secure the machining.

▶ PLAIN DARTED TUCKS

1 Make in the same way as a shaped darted tuck (see left), but stitch parallel to the folded edge.

2 Stop as indicated on the pattern.

3 The tuck as seen from the right side.

CROSS TUCKS

These are tucks that cross over each other by being stitched in opposite directions.

1 Press the crease lines into the fabric, both vertically and horizontally.

2 Stitch all the vertical tucks first: fold the fabric wrong side to wrong side along the crease lines. Stitch 5mm (³⁄₁₆in) from the folded edge and press in one direction.

3 Stitch all the horizontal tucks in the same way.

4 Press all the vertical or horizontal tucks in the same direction.

PLEATS

A pleat is a fold or series of folds in fabric. Pleats are most commonly found in skirts where the pleats are made to fit around the waist and hip and then left to fall in crisply pressed folds, giving fullness at the hemline. It is important that pleats are made accurately, otherwise they will not fit the body and will look uneven. Foldlines and placement lines, or foldlines and crease lines, are marked on the fabric from the pattern. It is by using a combination of these lines and the spaces between them that the pleats are made.

DIRECTORY OF PLEATS

KNIFE PLEATS (p.123 and pp.126–128)

BOX PLEATS (pp.124–128)

INVERTED PLEATS (p.124 and pp.126–128)

KICK PLEAT (p.126)

GODET IN A SEAM (p.130)

GODET NOT IN A SEAM (p.131)

PENCIL PLEATS (p.133)

PINCH PLEATS (p.133)

PLEATS ON THE RIGHT SIDE

Knife pleats are normally formed on the right side of fabric. They can all face the same direction or may face opposite directions from opposite sides of the garment. Knife pleats have foldlines and placement lines.

Difficulty level ★★☆☆☆

1 Mark the placement lines and foldlines with trace tacks. Use one colour thread, such as light blue, for placement lines.

2 Use a contrasting colour thread, such as yellow, to mark foldlines.

3 Cut through the thread loops and remove the pattern pieces carefully.

Placement line

Foldline

4 Fold the fabric along the foldline, creasing accurately along the trace tacks.

5 Bring the creased line on to the placement line. Pin to secure.

6 Tack along the foldlines about 2mm (1⁄16in) from the folded edge, through all the layers.

7 Remove the pins and the trace tacking on this part of the pleat.

8 With the right side of the fabric uppermost, cover with a silk organza pressing cloth.

9 Using a steam iron on a steam setting, press the pleats in place. Keep the iron still as opposed to moving it around, and eject a shot of steam each time you lift it to a new position. Repeat this action across all of the pleats.

10 Turn the fabric to the wrong side and insert thin strips of manila card or brown paper under the pleat fabric.

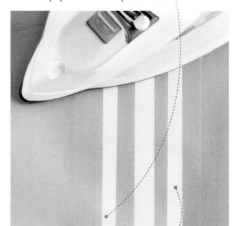

11 Press again with the steam iron and a silk organza cloth. The card or paper will prevent the fabric from leaving an imprint on the right side.

PATTERN MARKING **pp.82–83** • TACKING STITCHES **p.89**

PLEATS ON THE WRONG SIDE

Difficulty level ✹✹✹✹✹

Some pleats, including box (shown below) and inverted pleats, are formed on the wrong side of the fabric. As the pleats are made on the wrong side, you can mark the crease lines and foldlines with a tracing wheel and dressmaker's carbon paper. Use a ruler to guide the tracing wheel, because these pleats need to be straight lines.

1 Mark the crease lines and foldlines on the wrong side of the fabric, using different colours for the different lines. The lines must be marked down the full length of the fabric.

2 Also mark the stop line that shows where to stop stitching. Remove the pattern pieces.

Crease line

Foldline

Stop line

3 Bring the two crease lines that are either side of the foldline together and pin in place.

4 Be sure the foldline is along the fold in the fabric.

5 Tack through the two layers of fabric where the crease lines have been pinned together, along the entire length of the pleat.

Foldline

6 Machine along the crease lines.

7 Stop at the stop marking. Secure the machine stitching.

8 Flatten the pleat on the wrong side so that the foldline is lying on top of the machine stitching. Make sure that the fabric on either side of this foldline to the crease line is equal on both sides.

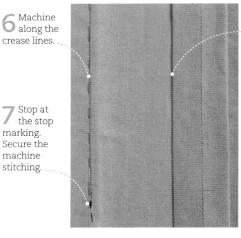

9 Cover the pleats on the wrong side with a silk organza pressing cloth and press, using a steam iron with a shot of steam.

10 Press each section of the pleat in turn, lifting the iron rather than moving it on the fabric.

11 If the fabric is in danger of being marked on the right side with the pleats, place some strips of manila card or brown paper under the pleats on the wrong side, then press again on the wrong side.

PLEATS WITH A SEPARATE UNDERLAY

Sometimes a box pleat is constructed with a separate piece of fabric or underlay. This technique is usually done on large, single box pleats or on a pleat made using thicker fabric, because it reduces the bulk. The seam to make this pleat is much wider than normal, as it is the width of the pleat.

▶

1 Mark the stitching line with trace tacks. Cut through the thread loops and carefully pull away the pattern piece.

2 Place the two pieces of fabric together, right side to right side. Match the notches and trace tacking.

3 Tack along the trace tacks that mark the stitching line, removing the trace tacking as you do so.

4 Machine the seam to the stop point.

5 Press the seam open along its full length.

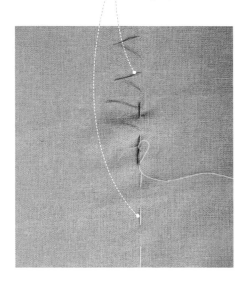

WRONG SIDE OF FABRIC

Trace tacks

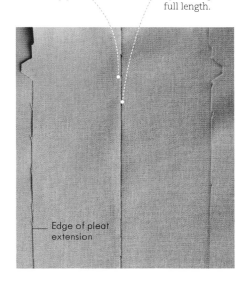

Edge of pleat extension

6 Take the underlay and place carefully on to the pressed seam, matching the notches. The wrong side of the underlay should be uppermost.

7 Pin the underlay in place, being careful to pin it just to the edge of the seam and not through to the main fabric.

8 On this type of pleat, the hem has to be constructed before all the pleats can be made. Stitch either side of the underlay to the edge of the pleat, stopping at least 10cm (4in) above the raw hem edge.

9 Remove the tacking stitches that are holding the pleat together.

10 Turn up the hem including the pleat. Separately turn up the underlay to match.

11 Pin the underlay and the pleat back together from where the machine stitching stopped, down through the hem. Make sure that on the right side the hem is even through this area.

WRONG SIDE OF UNDERLAY

12 Neaten the seams using your preferred method.

13 Remove the lower corner of the underlay/pleat seam, then blanket stitch or whip stitch. Finish by pressing.

TOP-STITCHING AND EDGE-STITCHING PLEATS

Difficulty level ★★☆☆☆

If a pleat is top-stitched or edge-stitched, it will hang correctly and always look crisp. It will also help the pleats on the skirt to stay in shape when you are sitting.

▶ **TOP-STITCHING KNIFE PLEATS**

1 Once the knife pleats have been pressed and all tacks and markings removed, place some pins across the pleat to stop it from moving.

2 Machine stitch from the right side approx 2mm (¹⁄₁₆in) from the fold.

3 Start the stitching at the lower end of the pleat and stitch to the waist.

▶ **TOP-STITCHING BOX PLEATS WITH A SQUARE END**

1 This requires stitching down on either side of the foldline. Stitch down one side about 5mm (³⁄₁₆in) from the foldline.

2 Pivot and stitch horizontally across the end of the stitching of the pleat.

3 Pivot again and stitch up the other side of the foldline about 5mm (³⁄₁₆in) from the foldline.

▶ **TOP-STITCHING BOX PLEATS WITH A POINTED END**

1 Stitch down one side 5mm (³⁄₁₆in) from the foldline, then pivot and stitch diagonally to the centre.

2 Pivot again and stitch diagonally the other side and back to the waist 5mm (³⁄₁₆in) from the foldline.

▶ **EDGE-STITCHING KNIFE PLEATS**

1 After pressing the pleats into shape, stitch 2mm (¹⁄₁₆in) from the fold.

2 Stitch along the entire length of the fold.

▶ **EDGE-STITCHING AND TOP-STITCHING PLEATS**

1 Edge-stitch first the edge of the pleat about 2mm (¹⁄₁₆in) from the folded edge.

2 Stop the edge-stitching just above the point where the pleat is to be top-stitched.

3 Place the machine needle into the pleat, through all layers, four or five stitches below where the edge-stitching stops.

4 Top-stitch through all the layers, continuing at 2mm (¹⁄₁₆in) from the fold, to the waist.

▶ **TOP-STITCHING KICK PLEATS OR INVERTED PLEATS**

1 This pleat is pressed to the right. Just below the stitching line that makes the pleat, stitch a line diagonally, to secure the pleat fabric at the back.

2 Make sure the stitching line finishes exactly on the foldline.

3 Pull the ends of the machine stitching through to the reverse.

HAND STITCHES **pp.90–91** ● STITCHING CORNERS AND CURVES **pp.102–103** ● REDUCING SEAM BULK **pp.108–109** ● STITCH FINISHES **p.109**

STAYING PLEATS

Staying a pleat is a technique used to reduce the bulk of the pleat, especially in the hip area. There are various ways of doing this and the method chosen will depend on the type of pleat, the fabric used, and your personal preference.

▶ SELF-STAYING BOX PLEATS OR INVERTED PLEATS

1 Make the pleat and press into place.

2 Stitch across the underfold of the pleat. Stitch one side at a time, from the crease line to the foldline.

WRONG SIDE OF FABRIC

RIGHT SIDE OF FABRIC

3 Cut down the crease line to within 1.5cm (⅝in) of the horizontal stitching. Do not cut this fabric off.

4 Trim down the fabric that is revealed to 1.5cm (⅝in).

5 Flip the underfold back into place and secure at the waist edge.

▶ STAYING KNIFE PLEATS ON THICKER FABRIC

1 On the wrong side, stitch across the underfold.

Fold of pleat

2 Remove the bulk of the underfold fabric with a curve.

3 Cut a piece of lining large enough to cover the pleated section.

4 Clean finish the lower edge.

5 Tack to secure along the waist edge (to make this fabric fit at the waist, tuck the lining at the waist).

WRONG SIDE OF PLEATS

6 Using a flat fell stitch, hand stitch the edge of the lining to the stitching on the underfold only.

Underfold

TECHNIQUES

HEMMING PLEATS

Most pleated garments or soft furnishings are hemmed after the pleats have been constructed; however, in some cases pleats can be hemmed first. This technique is only used for garments with all-around pleats or that have to follow a check or stripe.

Difficulty level ✸✸✸✸✸

▶ HEMMING KNIFE PLEATS OR INVERTED PLEATS

1 Make sure the pleat has been well pressed. Press the hem up into place, then open the pleat out to reveal the crease lines.

2 Reduce the bulk in the seam area of the hem, from the raw edge to the top edge of the hem when folded into place.

5 Turn up the hem.

6 Press the pleat back into position.

3 Clip through the seam allowance.

4 Press this part of the seam allowance in the opposite direction to the seam.

7 Machine through the crease line in the hem.

▶ HEMMING BOX PLEATS BEFORE THE GARMENT IS FINISHED

1 Turn up the hem.

2 Make the seam and press open.

3 Remove the lower edges of the seam by trimming diagonally.

4 Blanket stitch or whip stitch across these corners.

▶ HEMMING BOX PLEATS AFTER THE GARMENT IS FINISHED

1 Press the pleat into position and press the hem into position.

2 Reduce the seam allowance below the crease line of the hem.

3 Turn up the hem.

4 Match the stitching lines and press the pleat for the final time.

▶ SECURING PLEATS AT THE HEM

The bottom of every pleat on a garment can be secured temporarily with two or three cross stitches.

ADJUSTING PLEATS TO FIT

Difficulty level ✱✱✱✱✱

If a pleated skirt is either too big or too tight at the waist or hip, a small adjustment on each pleat can make a huge difference. Simply take the amount to be added or removed and divide it by the number of pleats. If the adjustment is not the same on all the pleats, they will look unbalanced.

▶ LETTING OUT PLEATS FORMED ON THE RIGHT SIDE

1 Mark the crease lines and foldlines.

2 Take the foldline and place it slightly to the left of the placement line.

3 Taper back on to the placement line at the end of the adjustment. Machine into place.

▶ TAKING IN PLEATS FORMED ON THE RIGHT SIDE

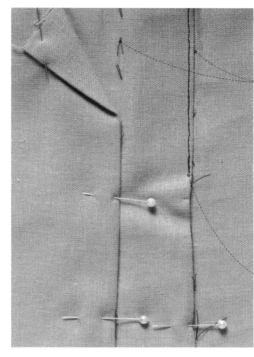

1 Mark the crease lines and foldlines.

2 Take the foldline and, instead of placing it on top of the placement line, overlap it by the small amount required.

3 Taper back on to the placement line at the end of the adjustment, then machine in place.

▶ LETTING OUT PLEATS FORMED ON THE WRONG SIDE

1 The yellow stitching indicates the original stitching line for the pleat. Let the pleat out, stitching closer to the foldline.

2 The purple stitching line indicates the adjustment.

▶ TAKING IN PLEATS FORMED ON THE WRONG SIDE

1 The yellow stitching line indicates the original stitching line for the pleat. Take the pleat in, stitching further from the foldline.

2 The purple stitching line indicates this adjustment.

HEMS pp.262—267

TECHNIQUES

GODET IN A SEAM

Difficulty level ★★★★★

A godet is a type of pleat that is inserted into a garment to give fullness at the hem edge. It is a segment of a circle, usually triangular in shape but also sometimes a half circle – the size of the godet depends on the fullness required. The godet may go from hem to knee or even hem to thigh, according to the style of the skirt. The easiest way to insert a godet is in a seam.

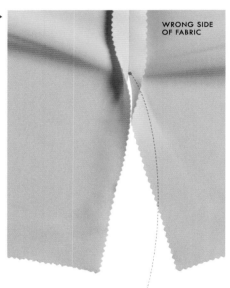

WRONG SIDE OF FABRIC

1 Stitch a 1.5cm (⅝in) seam in the skirt to the given point. Press the seam open.

2 Cut out the godet. Tailor tack to mark where the stitching in the skirt stops.

WRONG SIDE OF GODET

3 Place the godet to the split in the skirt seam, right side to right side.

4 Join one side of the godet to the skirt, machining along the edge, from the hem to the tailor's tack.

5 Stitch the other side of the godet to the skirt, from hem to tailor's tack.

All three stitching lines meet at tailor's tack

6 Snip through the skirt seam to release tension and allow the godet-to-skirt seam to be pressed open.

RIGHT SIDE OF FABRIC

7 Finish the godet by pressing carefully on the right side.

GODET NOT IN A SEAM

Sometimes there are not enough seams in a garment for the number of godets that you would like to insert. If that is the case, a split must be made in the fabric at the hemline to accommodate each godet. A piece of silk organza is sewn on to the point of the split to strengthen it.

1 Mark the split on the skirt. Place a small square of silk organza at the top of the marked split, on the right side of the fabric.

RIGHT SIDE OF FABRIC

2 Stay stitch around the marked split, pivoting at the top through the organza.

3 Slash the split open from the hem to the given point.

4 Pull the organza square to the wrong side.

5 Cut out the godet and mark the stitching stop point.

WRONG SIDE OF FABRIC

6 Pin the godet along one side of the split, right side to right side. Allow a 1.5cm (⅝in) seam allowance on the godet and the minimum seam allowance on the split.

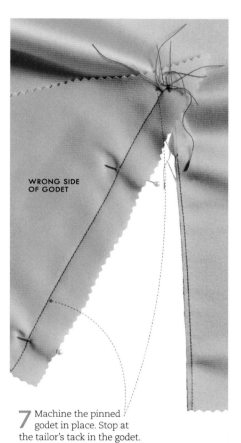

WRONG SIDE OF GODET

7 Machine the pinned godet in place. Stop at the tailor's tack in the godet.

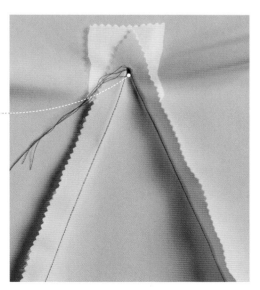

8 Machine the other side of the godet to the split. Make sure the stitching lines meet exactly at the point of the split.

9 On the right side, there should be no creases at the top of the godet. Press gently to finish, using just the toe of the iron.

STITCHES MADE WITH A MACHINE pp.92–93 • **HOW TO MAKE A PLAIN SEAM p.94**

PLEATS ON CURTAINS

Pleats are used in soft furnishings, particularly at the top of curtains, to reduce the fabric so that the curtain will fit on to its track and fit the window. The easiest way to pleat the upper edge of a curtain is to apply a curtain tape. Tapes are available in various depths and will pull the curtain into pencil pleats or goblet pleats. The most common tape used for pencil pleating is 8cm (3¼in) deep. A curtain is normally cut two-and-a-half to three times the width of the window. The curtain tape will reduce the fabric by this much as it pleats up.

Difficulty level ✶✶✶✶✶

▶ PREPARING THE CURTAIN TO TAKE THE TAPE

WRONG SIDE OF FABRIC

1 Turn under the two side edges of the curtain by using a double hem of 2.5cm (1in), i.e. turn the fabric 2.5cm (1in) once and then the same again.

2 Pin the hem edges on the sides of the curtains, then machine stitch.

3 Turn the top of the curtain down by 2.5cm (1in) and pin.

Side edge of curtain

4 Reduce the bulk at the top edge on the corners by trimming away the side hem.

5 Tack the upper edge of the curtain down into place.

▶ MAKING A POCKET FOR THE STRINGS

1 Before the tape is applied, a small pocket needs to be made to take the strings that are used to pull up the tape. Cut a rectangle of spare fabric 15 x 8cm (6 x 3¼in).

2 Turn one short edge wrong side to wrong side and machine to make a single hem.

3 Fold the rectangle right side to right side with a 2cm (¾in) seam at the upper edge free.

4 Stitch down the sides and clip the corners.

5 Turn through to the right side and press.

TECHNIQUES

▶ PENCIL PLEATS

1 Take the curtain tape and release the strings at the one end, making sure they are all visible on the same side.

2 Place the top of the tape 5mm (³⁄₁₆in) down from the folded edge of the curtain. Pin in place, stretching the tape as you do so. Turn under the short end, avoiding the strings and pin.

3 Machine the upper edge of the tape to the curtain fabric. Make sure the strings stay free.

4 Before stitching the lower edge of the tape, place the pocket you made under the end of the tape.

5 Pin the tape and the pocket in place. Machine stitch the tape and pocket.

6 At the opposite end of the tape, stitch across each string individually to prevent it from being pulled out.

7 Pull up the strings in the tape from the end with the pocket to make the pleats.

8 Tie the strings together and place in the pocket.

9 Turn the curtain over to check that the pencil pleats are evenly spaced and will fit the window. Adjust if necessary.

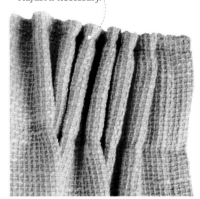

▶ PINCH PLEATS

1 Pinch pleats are three pleats together at regular intervals. When the tape is pulled up, the pleats are close together at the base and fan out at the top. Prepare the curtain to take the tape and make the pocket (see opposite page).

2 Attach the tape in the same way as for pencil pleats (above).

3 After pulling up the tape, secure it by hand on the right side at the base of the tape.

4 Hand stitch the upper edge of the pleats at the back.

UNLINED PATCH POCKET p.239 ● **MACHINED CURTAIN HEMS p.268**

GATHERS

Gathers are an easy way to draw up a piece of larger fabric so that it will fit on to a smaller piece of fabric. They often appear at waistlines or yoke lines. The gather stitch is inserted after the major seams have been constructed, and it is best worked on the sewing machine using the longest stitch length that is available. On the majority of fabrics two rows of gather stitches are required, but for very heavy fabrics it is advisable to make three rows. Try to stitch the rows so that the stitches line up under one another.

TECHNIQUES

DIRECTORY OF GATHERS

GATHERS (p.135)

CORDED GATHERS (p.136)

SHIRRING (p.138)

WAFFLE SHIRRING (p.138)

CORDED SHIRRING (p.139)

SMOCKING (p.140)

HOW TO MAKE AND FIT GATHERS

Difficulty level ✱✱✱✱✱

Once all the main seams have been sewn, stitch the two rows of gathers so that the stitches are inside the seam allowance. This should avoid the need to remove them because removing gathers after they have been pulled up can damage the fabric.

▶ **1** Stitch one row of gathers at 1cm (⅜in) and the second row at 1.2cm (½in) from the raw edge. Leave long tails of thread for gathering. Break the stitching lines at the seams.

2 Place the piece to be gathered to the other garment section, right side to right side.

Other garment section

3 Match the notches and seams, and pin these first.

Section to be gathered

4 Gently pull on the two ends of the thread on the wrong side – the fabric will gather along the thread.

5 Secure the threads at one end to prevent the stitches from pulling out.

6 Even out the gathers and pin.

7 When all the gathers are in place, use a standard machine stitch to stitch a 1.5cm (⅝in) wide seam.

8 Stitch with the gathers uppermost and keep pulling them to the side to stop them creasing up.

9 Turn the other garment section inside. Using a mini iron or the tip of a regular iron, press the seam very carefully to avoid creasing the gathers.

10 Neaten the seam by stitching both edges together. Use either a zigzag stitch or a 3-thread overlock stitch.

11 Press the seam up.

12 Press the gathers using a mini iron or the tip of a regular iron.

Seam pressed up

STITCHES MADE WITH A MACHINE **pp.92–93** • HOW TO MAKE A PLAIN SEAM **p.94**

CORDED GATHERS

Corded gathers are gathers that are pulled up over a narrow cord or thick thread. This technique is used for thicker fabrics, such as for soft furnishings, where machine gathers may not be strong enough.

1 Lay a cord on the wrong side of the fabric in the seam allowance.

2 Zigzag stitch over the cord without catching the cord in the stitching.

3 Make a knot in the cord at one end, then gather the fabric along the cord.

WRONG SIDE OF FABRIC

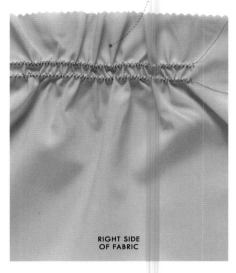

4 Turn to the right side to check that the gathers are even. Knot the other end of the cord.

RIGHT SIDE OF FABRIC

STAYING A GATHERED SEAM

A gathered seam is often stayed by stitching on cotton stay tape, to ensure the gathers remain in place and also to help strengthen the seam.

1 Machine the stay tape in place adjacent to the seam stitching line.

Seamline

Gathers in the seam allowance

2 Using a zigzag stitch, machine the top of the stay tape to the raw edge of the seam.

JOINING TWO GATHERED EDGES TOGETHER

Difficulty level ✳✳✳✳✳

On some garments it may be necessary to join together two gathered edges. This usually happens when gathering a skirt on to a gathered bodice. The one side, usually the skirt, is gathered first on to a stay tape and the second side is gathered to fit, then stitched in place.

1 Stitch two rows of gathers at the waist edge.

2 Pull up the gathers to fit a stay tape that fits the waist. Pin and tack the gathers to the tape.

WRONG SIDE OF GATHERED SKIRT

3 Stitch two rows of gathers at the waist edge of the bodice.

4 Place the bodice waist, right side to right side, to the skirt waist, matching seams and notches.

5 Pull up the bodice gathers to fit the skirt.

6 Pin the two layers together.

Ungathered bodice

WRONG SIDE OF GATHERED SKIRT

7 Machine the two sets of gathers together through the tape.

8 Make a second row of stitching for strength.

WRONG SIDE OF GATHERED SKIRT

9 The waist of the bodice is now gathered to fit the skirt waist.

WRONG SIDE OF BODICE

INTERLININGS **p.324**

SHIRRING

Shirring is the name given to multiple rows of gathers. It is an excellent way to give fullness in a garment. If made using shirring elastic in the bobbin, gathers can stretch. On heavier fabrics, such as for soft furnishings, static shirring is more suitable.

Difficulty level ✶✶✶✶✶

▶ MACHINE SHIRRING

1 Hand wind shirring elastic on to the bobbin.

2 Insert the bobbin into the sewing machine and pull the elastic through the tension on the bobbin case. Use all-purpose thread on the top.

3 Set the machine to a stitch length of 5.0. Stitch a row of machining across the fabric.

4 Stitch a second row of machining. Make sure the rows of stitching are parallel.

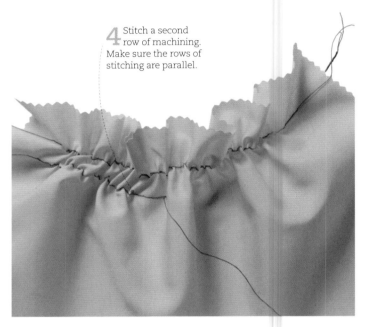

5 Continue stitching as many rows of shirring as required.

6 Knot the ends of the elastic together.

▶ WAFFLE SHIRRING

1 For this, two rows of shirring cross each other at right angles. Machine horizontal rows of shirring using shirring elastic in the bobbin (see above).

2 Cross these with vertical rows of shirring.

▶ CORDED SHIRRING

WRONG SIDE
OF FABRIC

1 This is a way of shirring that is static.
Fold the fabric right side to right side
and stitch a piece of piping cord into the
fold made. Use the zip foot and stitch
2mm (1⁄16in) from the cord.

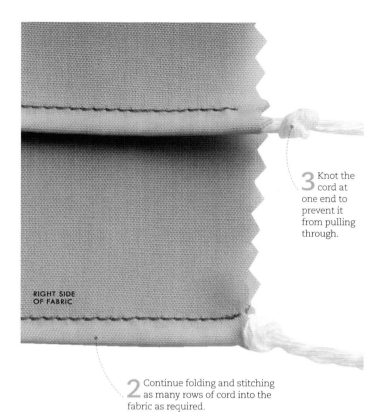

RIGHT SIDE
OF FABRIC

3 Knot the
cord at
one end to
prevent it
from pulling
through.

2 Continue folding and stitching
as many rows of cord into the
fabric as required.

4 Push the fabric along
the cord to create the
shirred gathers.

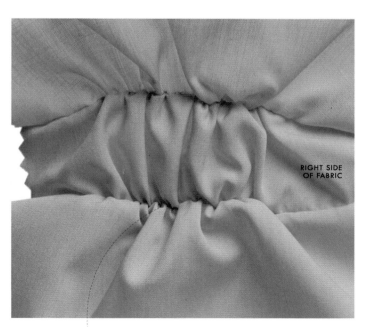

RIGHT SIDE
OF FABRIC

5 Turn to the right side
of the fabric and even
out the gathers.

6 Knot the other end of
the cord to secure.

SMOCKING

Smocking is one of the oldest ways of gathering fabric. It is very decorative and can add interest to a garment. Smocking involves pulling up multiple rows of gathers that have been stitched in by hand, in line with each other, to produce fine tubes in the fabric. These tubes are then stitched over. Smocking dots that can be heat-transferred to the fabric are used as a guide for the hand gathers. Dots can be purchased with different spaces between them.

Difficulty level ★★★★★

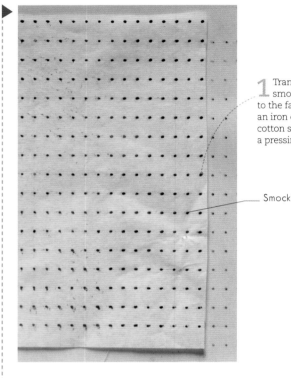

1 Transfer the smocking dots to the fabric using an iron on a cotton setting and a pressing cloth.

Smocking dots

2 Using double sewing thread and a knot in the end, take a stitch between each dot.

3 Repeat the stitches in the same order on the remaining rows.

4 Pull up the threads to produce gathers. Even the gathers out.

5 Stitch across each tube using a backstitch. Work left to right, stitching through one tube and then moving to the right and repeating the process.

6 Using the same stitch, patterns can be created across the tubes.

SMOCKING FOR CUSHIONS

Difficulty level ✸✸✷✷

Smocking can be used in a much larger format to produce a decorative effect on cushions.
Patterns and templates can be purchased for this effect.

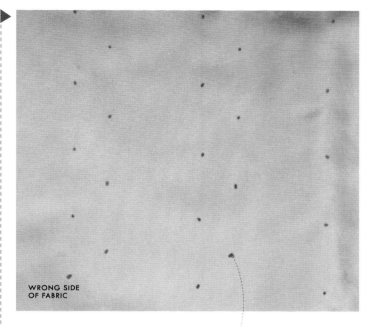

WRONG SIDE
OF FABRIC

1 Mark the dots on the wrong side of the fabric
with chalk. Use two different colours to
distinguish the different kinds of dots.

2 Stitch adjacent purple dots to purple
dots and green to green using an
over-sewing stitch or a close whip stitch.

3 Continue working across the fabric,
joining the green dots to green dots
and purple dots to purple dots.

RIGHT SIDE
OF FABRIC

4 On the right side of the
fabric, a chevron smocking
effect will be produced.

RUFFLES

Ruffles can be single layer or double layer and are used to give a decorative gathered effect to a garment. The amount of fullness in a ruffle depends on the fabric used – to achieve a similar result, a fine, thin fabric will need twice the fullness of a thicker fabric.

DIRECTORY OF RUFFLES

PLAIN RUFFLE
(p.143)

RUFFLE WITH A HEADING
(p.143)

DOUBLE RUFFLE 1
(p.144)

DOUBLE RUFFLE 2
(p.144)

DOUBLE RUFFLE 3
(p.144)

CIRCULAR RUFFLE
(pp.148–149)

PLAIN RUFFLE

A plain ruffle is normally made from a single layer of fabric cut on the straight of the grain. The length of the fabric needs to be at least two-and-a-half times the length of the seam into which it is to be inserted or of the edge to which it is to be attached. The width of the ruffle depends on where it is to be used.

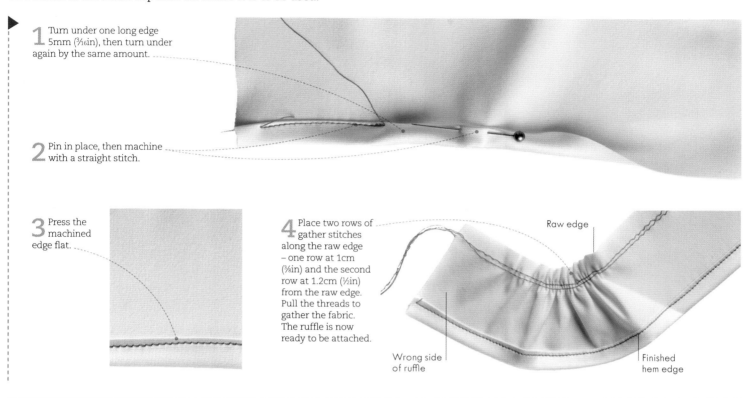

1 Turn under one long edge 5mm (³⁄₁₆in), then turn under again by the same amount.

2 Pin in place, then machine with a straight stitch.

3 Press the machined edge flat.

4 Place two rows of gather stitches along the raw edge – one row at 1cm (³⁄₈in) and the second row at 1.2cm (½in) from the raw edge. Pull the threads to gather the fabric. The ruffle is now ready to be attached.

Raw edge

Wrong side of ruffle

Finished hem edge

RUFFLE WITH A HEADING

This type of ruffle can give a decorative effect on clothing and soft furnishings.

1 Neaten one long edge as for a plain ruffle (see steps 1–3 above).

2 Turn down the other long edge – the amount of the turn down is the depth of the required heading plus a seam allowance of 1.5cm (⁵⁄₈in).

3 Tack the heading in place.

Thread to pull up gathers

Tacking stitches

4 Insert the two rows of gather stitches.

5 Pull up the stitches to make the gathers.

6 After gathering, there will be gathers with a ruffle on one side of the stitch line and a short gathered heading on the other. Pull out the tacking stitches.

HOW TO MAKE AND FIT GATHERS p.135

DOUBLE RUFFLE VERSION 1

Difficulty level ✱✱✱✱✱

This is a great ruffle on fine fabrics as it can be highly decorative. Attach to the garment by stitching through the centre of the gather lines.

1 Neaten both long edges by turning the fabric once and then again, and machining (see Plain ruffle, steps 1–3, p.143).

WRONG SIDE OF FABRIC

2 Work two rows of gather stitches lengthways down the centre of the fabric.

3 Pull up the gather stitches to create a ruffle to fit.

4 Turn the ruffle over to the right side to check that the gathers are equally spaced. Adjust if necessary, then attach to the garment.

DOUBLE RUFFLE VERSION 2

Difficulty level ✱✱✱✱✱

This ruffle has one side longer than the other and is fashioned from two plain ruffles.

1 Cut two pieces of fabric for the ruffle, one wider than the other. Neaten one long edge of each piece (see Plain ruffle, steps 1–3, p.143).

2 Pin the pieces of fabric together along the raw edges, right sides up, making sure the narrower piece is on the top.

3 Insert two rows of gather stitches through the two layers.

4 Pull the threads to gather the double ruffle to fit.

DOUBLE RUFFLE VERSION 3

Difficulty level ✱✱✱✱✱

This is a useful ruffle on a fabric that is prone to fraying.

1 Cut the fabric for the ruffle twice the required depth.

2 Fold the fabric lengthways, wrong side to wrong side.

3 Pin the raw edges together.

4 Insert gathers along the raw edge.

5 Pull up the gathers to fit.

STITCHING INTO A SEAM

Difficulty level ✷✷✷✷✷

Once the ruffle has been constructed it can either be inserted into a seam or attached to the edge of the fabric (see p.146). The two techniques below apply to both single and double ruffles.

1 Insert two rows of gathers at the edge of the ruffle.

2 Pull up the gathers to fit along one side of the fabric seam and pin.

3 Even out the gathers and pin again.

4 Tack to secure.

RIGHT SIDE OF FABRIC

5 Place the other piece of fabric over the ruffle, right side to right side.

6 Pin all the layers together.

7 Machine through all the layers using a 1.5cm (⅝in) seam allowance.

8 Layer the seam to reduce bulk.

9 Turn the fabric and ruffle through to the right side.

WRONG SIDE OF FABRIC

WRONG SIDE OF FABRIC

RIGHT SIDE OF FABRIC

STITCHING AROUND A CORNER

Difficulty level ✷✷✷✷✷

It can be difficult to stitch a ruffle to a corner and achieve a sharp point. It is easier to fit the gathers into a tight curve, which can be done as the ruffle is being applied to the corner.

1 Pull up the gathers to fit along one side of the fabric seam and pin in place.

2 Fit the gathers into a tight curve at the corner.

3 Machine the ruffle in place.

4 Attach the other piece of fabric and machine in place. Layer the seam.

5 Turn the fabric and ruffle through to the right side. The corner will have a tight curve.

LAYERING A SEAM **p.108** ● HOW TO MAKE AND FIT GATHERS **p.135**

STITCHING A RUFFLE TO AN EDGE

Difficulty level ✶✶✶✶✶

If a ruffle is not in a seam then it will be attached to an edge. The edge of the seam will require neatening, which is often best done by using a binding method as it is more discreet. A self-bound edge, where the seam is wrapped on to itself, is suitable for fine, delicate fabrics. For thicker fabrics, use a bias binding to finish the edge.

▶ SELF-BOUND FINISH

1 Place the gathered ruffle to the edge of the fabric, right side to right side. Pin in place.

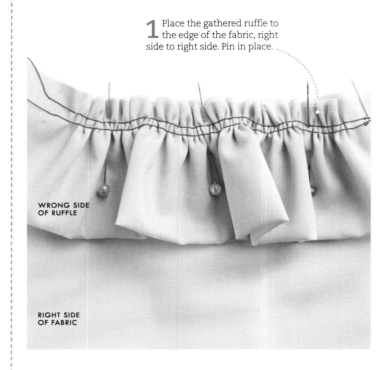

WRONG SIDE OF RUFFLE

RIGHT SIDE OF FABRIC

2 Machine the ruffle to the fabric using a 1.5cm (⅝in) seam allowance.

3 Trim the gathered side of the seam allowance down to half.

4 Wrap the longer, fabric side of the seam over the gathered seam, tucking under the raw edge. Pin in place.

Raw edge

WRONG SIDE OF FABRIC

5 Machine the wrapped seam to secure. Make sure it is attached to the seam only.

▶ **BIAS-BOUND FINISH**

1 Machine the gathered ruffle to the edge of the fabric, right side to right side, using a 1.5cm (⅝in) seam allowance (see steps 1 and 2, opposite).

2 Use a 2cm (¾in) wide bias binding. Stitch the crease in the bias over the machine stitching.

3 Trim back both sides of the seam allowance.

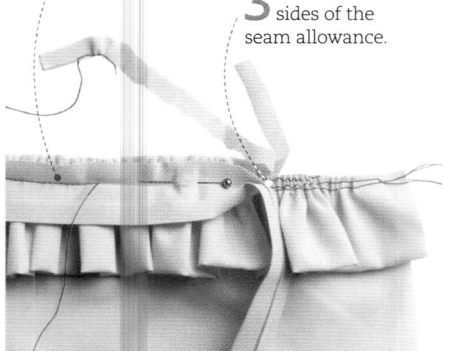

4 Wrap the bias over to the wrong side of the seam. Pin in place.

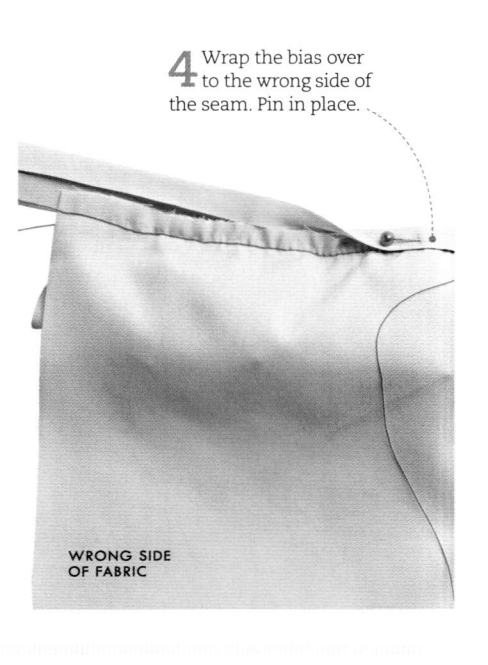

WRONG SIDE OF FABRIC

5 Machine stitch the other side of the bias close to the fold.

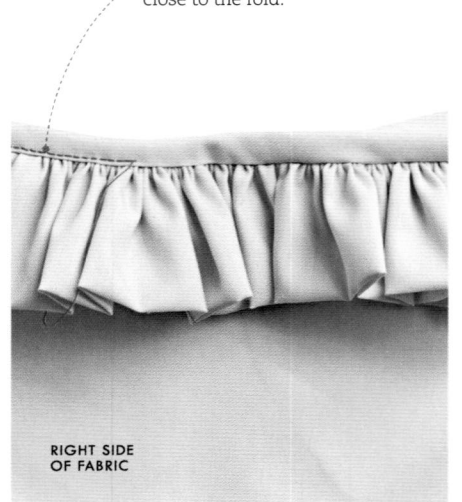

RIGHT SIDE OF FABRIC

ATTACHING A DOUBLE FRILL TO AN EDGE

Difficulty level ✶✶✶✶✶

This is a very neat way to attach a double ruffle to an edge as the seam is hidden. The ruffle is stitched first to the wrong side of the work and then folded on to the right side.

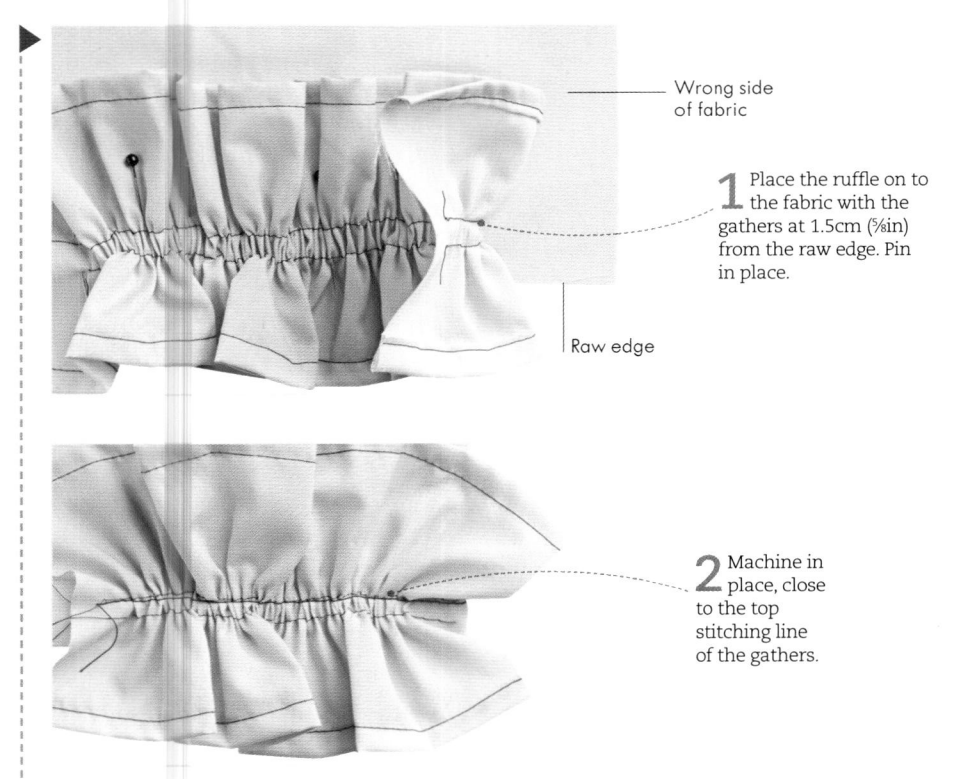

Wrong side of fabric

1 Place the ruffle on to the fabric with the gathers at 1.5cm (⅝in) from the raw edge. Pin in place.

Raw edge

2 Machine in place, close to the top stitching line of the gathers.

3 Turn the frill to the right side of the fabric. Trim away half the seam allowance behind the frill.

4 Machine stitch along the second row of gathering stitches.

BIAS-BOUND HEMS p.272

CIRCULAR RUFFLE

Difficulty level ★★★★★

A ruffle can be cut using a circular shape. The advantage is that there are no gathers because the centre part of the circle is cut out to make a seam. The fullness occurs as the inner edge of the circle is stretched and attached. For a circular ruffle you will need a pattern.

MAKING THE PATTERN FOR A CIRCULAR RUFFLE

1 **Get some pattern paper** to cut your circle and a compass or a pencil with a piece of string tied on to it.

2 **Draw an inner circle,** the circumference of which is the length of the seam into which the ruffle is to be attached plus 3cm (1¼in) for the seam allowances at each end of the ruffle. You can join several ruffles together to achieve a longer measurement.

3 **Draw a smaller circle** 1.5 cm (⅝in) inside the inner circle. This is the seam allowance for the edge where the ruffle will be attached.

4 **From the seamline** measure out the depth of the ruffle, then draw to make a large outer circle.

5 **Cut out the larger circle,** then cut out the seam allowance circle. Cut through the pattern, from the outer edge to the inner edge.

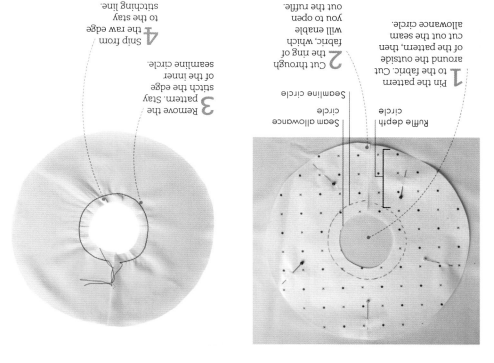

Ruffle depth circle

Seam allowance circle

Seamline circle

1 Pin the pattern to the fabric. Cut around the outside of the pattern, then cut out the seam allowance circle.

2 Cut through the ring of fabric, which will enable you to open out the ruffle.

3 Remove the pattern. Stay stitch the edge of the inner seamline circle.

4 Snip from the raw edge to the stay stitching line.

5 If necessary, join rings of fabric together using a plain seam until the required length of ruffle is achieved. Press the seam open.

6 Neaten the outer edge with an overlock stitch, or with a rolled hem (see opposite page).

7 Turn the neatened edge to the wrong side. Straight stitch to secure, to make a hem about 4mm (³⁄₁₆in) deep.

TECHNIQUES

DOUBLE CIRCULAR RUFFLE

Difficulty level ★★★★★

On very lightweight fabrics such as chiffon or silk, it is advisable to make a double-layer ruffle as it will hang better. With this method there is no edge to neaten.

1 Cut two circular ruffles (see opposite) and join them together, right side to right side. Pin to secure.

2 Machine the outer edges together with a 1.5cm (⅝in) seam allowance. Leave one short end unstitched, to turn through later.

Turning gap left at short end

3 Trim down one half of the seam allowance.

4 Cut out V shapes to reduce the bulk.

5 Turn through to the right side, pushing out the corners. Press.

6 Stay stitch the inner edge through both layers. The ruffle is now ready to be attached (see steps 8 and 9, above).

▶ NEATENING THE RUFFLE EDGE WITH A ROLLED HEM

An alternative way to neaten the outer edge is to use the sewing machine with the rolled hem foot and a straight stitch.

Another alternative is a rolled hem on the sewing machine using the rolled hem foot and a zigzag stitch.

8 Place the ruffle to the edge where it is to be attached, right side to right side. Pin in place.

Snips open out

9 Machine in place just below the stay stitching.

FACINGS AND NECKLINES

Edges on garments are often neatened by means of a facing. This is a shaped piece of fabric, which may be stiffened with interfacing, attached to a neckline – or to an armhole or at a waist edge – for a strong finish.

FACINGS AND NECKLINES

The simplest way to finish the neck or armhole of a garment is to apply a facing. The neckline can be any shape to have a facing applied, from a curve to a square to a V, and many more. Some facings and necklines can add interest to the centre back or centre front of a garment.

TECHNIQUES

DIRECTORY OF NECKLINES

ROUND NECKLINE
(p.156)

SQUARE NECKLINE
(p.156)

V-NECK
(p.156)

SWEETHEART NECKLINE (p.156)

SLASHED NECKLINE
(p.157)

BOUND NECK EDGE
(p.160)

PIPED NECKLINE
(p.154)

SLASHED NECKLINE WITH PLACKETS (p.163)

V-NECK WITH BANDING (p.165)

HOW TO APPLY A FUSIBLE INTERFACING **p.54** ● TACKING STITCHES **p.89**

APPLYING INTERFACING TO A FACING

Difficulty level ✱✱✱✱✱

All facings require interfacing. The interfacing is to give structure to the facing and to hold it in shape. A fusible interfacing is the best choice and it should be cut on the same grain as the facing. Choose an interfacing that is lighter in weight than the main fabric.

▶ INTERFACING FOR HEAVY FABRIC

For a heavy-weight fabric use a medium-weight fusible interfacing. Remove the seam allowance on the interfacing on the inner curve to reduce bulk.

Right side of facing

▶ INTERFACING FOR LIGHT FABRIC

For a light to medium-weight fabric, choose a lightweight interfacing and fuse it over the complete facing.

Right side of facing

CONSTRUCTION OF A FACING

Difficulty level ✱✱✱✱✱

The facing may be in two or three pieces in order to fit around a neck or armhole edge. The facing sections need to be joined together prior to being attached. The photographs here show an interfaced neck facing in three pieces.

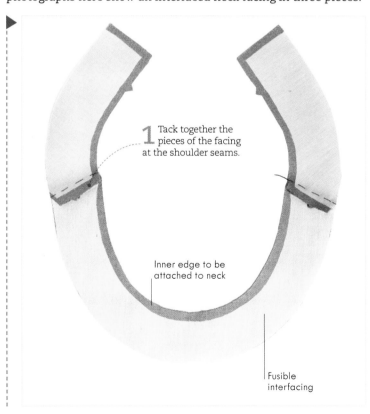

1 Tack together the pieces of the facing at the shoulder seams.

Inner edge to be attached to neck

Fusible interfacing

3 Stay stitch around the edge of the inner curve, to prevent stretch.

2 Stitch the shoulder seams and press open.

4 Trim off the outer corners on the shoulder seams.

5 The right side of the facing, ready to attach to the neckline.

STITCHES MADE WITH A MACHINE pp.92—93

NEATENING THE EDGE OF A FACING

Difficulty level ✱✱✱✱✱

The outer edge of a facing will require neatening to prevent it from fraying, and there are several ways to do this. Binding the lower edge of a facing with a bias strip makes the garment a little more luxurious and can add a designer touch inside the garment. You can make your own bias strip or buy one ready-made. Alternatively, the edge can be stitched or pinked (see opposite page).

▶ **HOW TO CUT BIAS STRIPS**

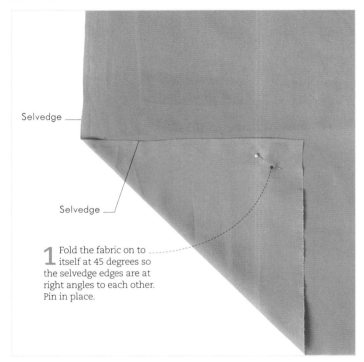

Selvedge

Selvedge

1 Fold the fabric on to itself at 45 degrees so the selvedge edges are at right angles to each other. Pin in place.

2 Using tailor's chalk and a ruler, mark lines 4cm (1½in) apart.

3 Cut along these lines to make bias strips.

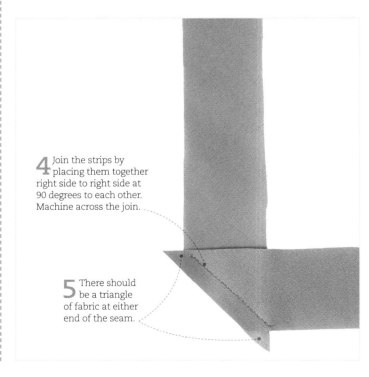

4 Join the strips by placing them together right side to right side at 90 degrees to each other. Machine across the join.

5 There should be a triangle of fabric at either end of the seam.

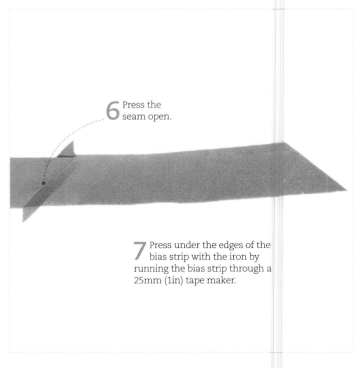

6 Press the seam open.

7 Press under the edges of the bias strip with the iron by running the bias strip through a 25mm (1in) tape maker.

MARKING AIDS **p.19** • USEFUL EXTRAS **pp.20—21** • OVERLOCKER **pp.34—35**

▶ NEATENING AN EDGE WITH A BIAS STRIP

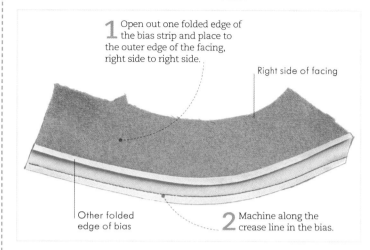

1 Open out one folded edge of the bias strip and place to the outer edge of the facing, right side to right side.

Right side of facing

Other folded edge of bias

2 Machine along the crease line in the bias.

3 Press the other folded edge flat.

Fusible interfacing

4 Wrap the bias around to the wrong side of the work. Tack to hold in place.

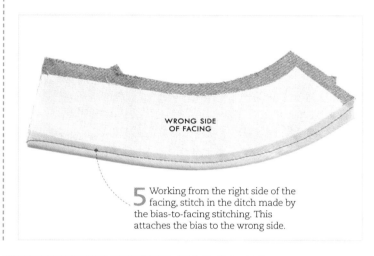

WRONG SIDE OF FACING

5 Working from the right side of the facing, stitch in the ditch made by the bias-to-facing stitching. This attaches the bias to the wrong side.

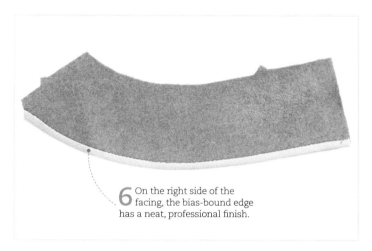

6 On the right side of the facing, the bias-bound edge has a neat, professional finish.

OTHER NEATENING METHODS

Difficulty level

The following techniques are alternative popular ways to neaten the edge of a facing. The one you choose depends upon the garment being made and the fabric used.

▶ OVERLOCKED

Neaten the outer edge with a 3-thread overlock stitch.

▶ PINKED

Machine stitch 1cm (⅜in) from the edge and trim the raw edge with pinking shears.

▶ ZIGZAGGED

Neaten the outer edge with a zigzag stitch.

TACKING STITCHES **p.89** • STITCHES MADE WITH A MACHINE **pp.92–93**

ATTACHING A NECK FACING

This technique applies to all shapes of neckline, whether round, square, V neck, or sweetheart.

Difficulty level ★★★★★

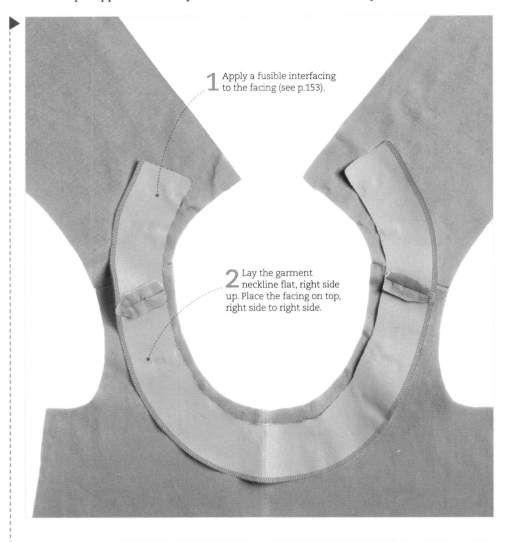

1 Apply a fusible interfacing to the facing (see p.153).

2 Lay the garment neckline flat, right side up. Place the facing on top, right side to right side.

3 Pin the facing in place, matching around the neck edge.

4 Match the shoulder seams on the facing and the bodice.

Facing and garment match at centre back

5 Machine in place using a 1.5cm (⅝in) seam allowance.

6 Trim the facing side of the seam down to half its width.

Shoulders still matching

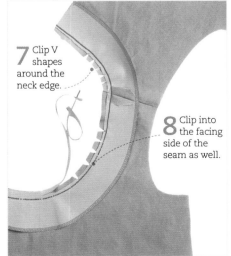

7 Clip V shapes around the neck edge.

8 Clip into the facing side of the seam as well.

9 Press the seam allowance towards the facing.

10 Understitch by stitching the seam allowance down on to the facing about 5mm (³⁄₁₆in) from the stitching line.

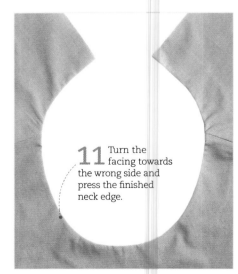

11 Turn the facing towards the wrong side and press the finished neck edge.

FACING A SLASHED NECKLINE

Difficulty level ✶✶✶✶✶

A slashed neckline occurs at either the centre front or the centre back neck edge.
It enables a close-fitting neckline to open sufficiently to go over the head.

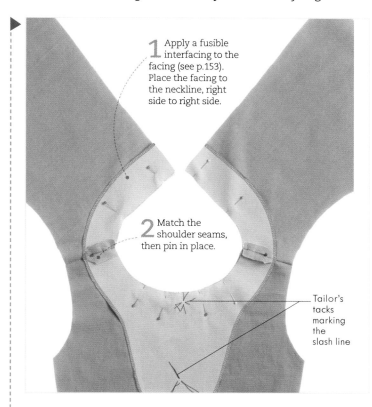

1 Apply a fusible interfacing to the facing (see p.153). Place the facing to the neckline, right side to right side.

2 Match the shoulder seams, then pin in place.

Tailor's tacks marking the slash line

3 Stitch the facing at the neck edge, pivoting to stitch along both sides of the slash between the tailor's tacks. Take one stitch horizontally at the bottom edge of the slash line.

4 Trim the facing side of the seam down to half.

5 Clip V shapes at the neck edge to reduce the bulk.

6 Cut straight down the slash line between the stitching lines.

7 Snip off the upper corners.

8 Clip into the corners at the bottom edge of the slash.

9 Turn the facing to the inside of the neckline and press.

STITCHING CORNERS AND CURVES pp.102–103 ● **REDUCING SEAM BULK pp.108–109** ● **APPLYING INTERFACING TO A FACING p.153**

ARMHOLE FACING

On sleeveless garments, a facing is an excellent way of neatening an armhole because it is not bulky. Also, as the facing is made in the same fabric as the garment, it does not show.

 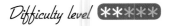

1 Construct the interfaced armhole facing (see p.153) and neaten the edge by your preferred method.

Armhole

2 Place the facing to the armhole, right side to right side. Match at the shoulder seams and at the underarm seam.

3 Match the notches, one at the front and two at the back. Pin the facing in place.

4 Machine around the armhole to attach the facing, taking a 1.5cm (⅝in) seam allowance.

5 Trim the facing side of the seam allowance down to half.

6 Clip out some V shapes in the seam allowance to reduce bulk.

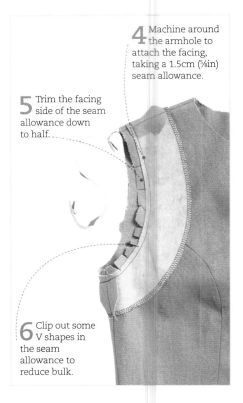

7 Turn the facing into position on the wrong side. Understitch by pressing the seam allowance on to the facing and machining down.

8 On the underarm and shoulder seams, secure the facing to the seam allowance with cross stitches.

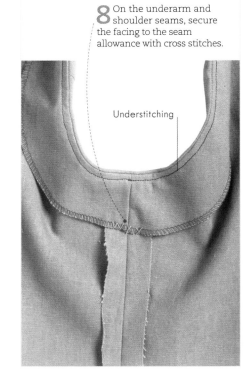

Understitching

9 Press the stitched edge. On the right side, the armhole will have a neat finish.

HOW TO APPLY A FUSIBLE INTERFACING p.54

COMBINATION NECK AND ARMHOLE FACING

Difficulty level ✶✶✶✶✶

This type of facing neatens the neck and the armhole edge at the same time. It needs to be stitched in place before the centre back seam or the side seams are constructed.

1 Put the facing in position on the fabric, right side to right side. Match the shoulder seams.

GARMENT BACK

GARMENT FRONT

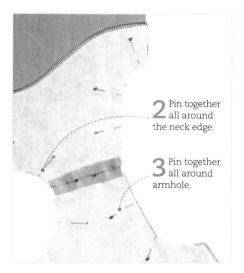

2 Pin together all around the neck edge.

3 Pin together all around armhole.

4 Before machining on the garment side, pin out a tiny pleat of fabric – this is known as a tailor's blister. It will make the shoulder slightly bigger on the right side when finished, which will prevent the seams from showing.

5 Re-pin the shoulder at the armhole edge.

6 Machine around the neck and armhole edges, taking a 1.5cm (⅝in) seam allowance.

7 Trim down the facing side of the seam by half.

8 Clip the seam allowances as required.

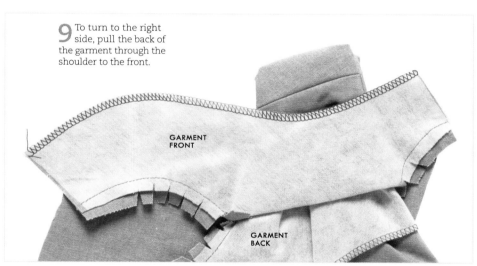

9 To turn to the right side, pull the back of the garment through the shoulder to the front.

GARMENT FRONT

GARMENT BACK

10 Press the completed neck and armhole facing on the right side.

11 To join the side seams, place the facing and sides together, right side to right side. Match the seam at the underarm.

12 Stitch the facing and side together in one continuous seam. Press the seam open.

13 The faced neckline and armholes as seen from the right side.

TECHNIQUES

GROWN-ON FACING

Difficulty level ✶✶✶✶✶

A facing is not always a separate unit. Many garments, especially blouses, feature what is known as a grown-on facing, which is where the facing is an extension of the front of the garment, cut out at the same time.

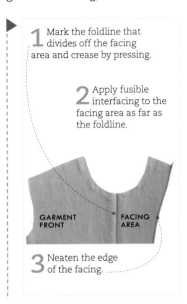

1 Mark the foldline that divides off the facing area and crease by pressing.

2 Apply fusible interfacing to the facing area as far as the foldline.

GARMENT FRONT   FACING AREA

3 Neaten the edge of the facing.

4 Fold the facing back, right side to right side. Match around the neck and pin.

RIGHT SIDE OF GARMENT

5 Machine around the neck edge to join the facing to the garment.

6 Trim the facing side of the seam and clip the seam allowance.

7 Turn through to the right side and press.

BOUND NECK EDGE

Difficulty level ✶✶✶✶✶

Binding is an excellent way to finish a raw neck edge. It has the added advantage of being a method that can be used if you are short of fabric or you would like a contrast or decorative finish. You can use bought bias binding or a bias strip cut from the same or a contrasting fabric (see p.154). A double bias strip is used on fine fabrics.

▶ **BIAS-BOUND NECK EDGE VERSION 1**

1 Open out one edge of the bias strip and place the crease line on the 1.5cm (⅝in) stitching line. Pin in place.

RIGHT SIDE OF GARMENT

2 Machine in place along the crease line.

3 Trim away the surplus fabric from the seam allowance.

4 Clip the neck seam if required.

5 Wrap the bias strip over the neck to the wrong side of the garment.

6 Machine the bias strip on the inside of the garment. Press.

HOW TO APPLY A FUSIBLE INTERFACING p.54 ● **HAND STITCHES pp.90—91**

▶ BIAS-BOUND NECK EDGE VERSION 2

1 This technique is used on bulkier fabrics. Cut a bias strip 7cm (2¾in) wide.

2 Pin to the neck edge.

RIGHT SIDE OF GARMENT

3 Machine along the neck edge using a 1.5cm (⅝in) seam allowance.

4 Turn to the wrong side and trim the seam allowance to half on the garment side.

5 Clip the seam allowance on the bias strip.

WRONG SIDE OF GARMENT

6 Fold the raw edge of the bias to the wrong side, to touch the machine stitches.

7 Fold again to bring the folded edge of the bias to the same place, and pin.

WRONG SIDE OF GARMENT

8 Stitch permanently in position using a flat fell stitch.

RIGHT SIDE OF GARMENT

▶ DOUBLE BIAS-BOUND NECK EDGE

1 Cut a bias strip 6cm (2⅜in) wide. Press in half.

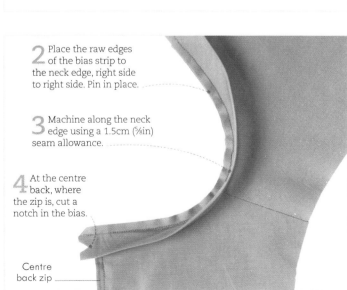

2 Place the raw edges of the bias strip to the neck edge, right side to right side. Pin in place.

3 Machine along the neck edge using a 1.5cm (⅝in) seam allowance.

4 At the centre back, where the zip is, cut a notch in the bias.

Centre back zip

5 Turn the folded edge of the bias to the wrong side. Pin the fold on to the machine stitching.

6 Stitch in place with a flat fell stitch.

STITCHES MADE WITH A MACHINE **pp.92–93** ● REDUCING SEAM BULK **pp.108–109** ● HOW TO CUT BIAS STRIPS **p.154**

PIPED NECK EDGE

Difficulty level ✶✶✶✶✶

This technique features a piping around the neck as well as a facing. A piped neckline looks very good on special-occasion wear.

1 Cut a strip of bias 4cm (1½in) wide and as long as the required neck measurement plus 3cm (1¼in). Press in half lengthways, wrong side to wrong side. Open out.

2 Turn under 1.5cm (⅝in) at each end of the bias to neaten, and secure a length of piping cord in the centre using a machine stitch across it.

3 Fold the bias strip in half.

Neatened end

4 Machine close to the piping cord using a zip foot.

5 Place the bias around the neck, right side to right side. Position the neatened ends at the centre back. Pin in place.

6 Machine around the neck using the zip foot.

7 Attach the neck facing over the piped bias and machine in place.

8 Trim the seam allowance on the facing side of the seam.

9 Clip the seam allowance on the bias and neck of the garment.

Piping

Facing

10 Turn the facing to the wrong side.

11 Turn under the edge of the facing to the edge of the zip.

12 The finished neckline with piped edge.

PLACKETS

Difficulty level ✱✱✱✱✱

A placket is an opening that stops partway down a bodice. It is made by applying two separate bands of fabric to the bodice. Care must be taken to ensure that the pattern pieces are accurately marked. A placket opening is popular on sportswear.

1 Cut two placket bands and apply fusible interfacing.

2 On the centre front of the bodice, use trace tacking to mark the stitching lines on either side of the opening.

3 Stay stitch along the lines.

4 Slash the seam allowance into the corners. Mark the stop points with tailor's tacks.

RIGHT SIDE OF FABRIC

5 Stitch one placket to one side of the opening, right side to right side. Stop stitching at the given point.

Neck edge

Tailor's tacks to mark stop points

WRONG SIDE OF FABRIC

Right side of fabric

WRONG SIDE OF FABRIC

6 Repeat with the other placket, stitching it on to the other side of the opening.

7 Trim the placket side of the seam down on both plackets.

WRONG SIDE OF FABRIC

8 Fold each placket in half on to itself. Turn under the raw edge and pin to the stitching line.

9 At the bottom edge, the right-hand placket is under the left-hand placket.

WRONG SIDE OF FABRIC

10 Hand stitch the turned-under edge of each placket.

11 Stitch the plackets together at the bottom edge. Pink or zigzag the raw edge, if you like.

RIGHT SIDE OF FABRIC

12 Turn to the right side and press.

NECKLINES IN STRETCH KNITS

Difficulty level ✱✱✱✱✱

When working with a stretch knit fabric, the neckline can be finished with a single banding or a more decorative double banding. The banding is usually attached with a 4-thread overlock stitch, which enables the neck to stretch over the head. If you do not have an overlocker you can use a 3-step zigzag stitch on the sewing machine.

▶ SINGLE BANDING WITH OVERLOCKER

1 This round neck banding is made from a single piece of fabric. Pin the folded neck banding to the neck edge right side to right side. Stretch to fit.

RIGHT SIDE OF FABRIC

2 Tack along the stitching line. The banding will require stretching.

3 Overlock along the raw neck edge using a 4-thread overlock stitch.

4 When the garment is constructed, this is how the neckline will look on the right side.

▶ DOUBLE BANDING WITH OVERLOCKER

1 This round neck banding is constructed with two bands attached together. Cut the two bands, making one wider than the other.

2 Fold the two bands lengthways in half and tack together.

3 Attach to the neckline as for a single band (see above), with the wider banding against the neck.

▶ ATTACHING BANDING WITH A SEWING MACHINE

1 Using a slight zigzag stitch, with stitch length 0.5 and stitch width 3.0, machine the single or double banding to the neckline.

2 Neaten the raw edge with a 3-step zigzag stitch.

▶ BANDING FOR A V NECK

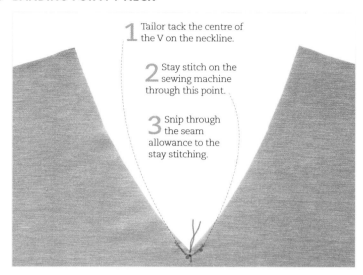

1 Tailor tack the centre of the V on the neckline.

2 Stay stitch on the sewing machine through this point.

3 Snip through the seam allowance to the stay stitching.

4 Cut the band as a straight strip, not as a V shape.

5 Pin the band to the V neckline, straightening out the garment front as you do so. Tack in place.

WRONG SIDE OF FABRIC

6 Straighten out the band and stitch to the neckline using a 4-thread overlock stitch. (If you do not have access to an overlocker, use a zigzag stitch as described on the opposite page.)

7 Snip the seam allowance in the centre.

8 Turn to the wrong side and place a pin in line with the centre front of the garment.

9 Stitch through the band in line with the centre front. Press flat.

10 When turned to the right side, there will be a sharp V.

A-LINE **SHIFT DRESS**

Difficulty level ✱✱✱✱✱

With its simple, easy silhouette, this dress will suit all figures. This is a great project for practising garment construction – you'll use lots of key techniques such as making darts, pockets, and attaching a zip and facings. Use a wool fabric for a winter dress, or a light cotton or linen fabric for a summer one.

TECHNIQUES USED Attaching a neck facing **p.156**, Inserting a set-in sleeve **p.211**, Separate in-seam pocket **p.248**, Concealed or invisible zip **p.290**

YOU WILL NEED

- Pattern templates on pp.370–373. Choose your size using the Women's Sizing chart on p.368.
- 250cm x 150cm (100 x 60in) light- to medium-weight dressmaking fabric, such as cotton, linen, crepe, silk, fine wool suitings, scuba, or medium-weight polyester
- 50cm (20in) lightweight fusible interfacing
- 56cm (22in) concealed zip
- Concealed zip foot

Front   Back

PIECES TO CUT

Single layer fabric

Double layer fabric

MAKE THE DARTS

1 Cut out the fabric pieces and, with the paper pattern still in place, mark the position of all the darts and pockets using tailor's tacks.

2 Cut through the loops in the tacks then gently remove the paper and separate the layers of fabric.

3 You should have two bust darts on the front and a contour dart on each back piece.

WRONG SIDE OF FRONT

4 On each back piece, bring the tailor's tacks together and pin in place. Use tacking stitches to mark the stitching line between the tailor's tacks.

5 Machine along the tacked line, then press the contour darts towards the centre back seam on each piece. Remove the tacks.

WRONG SIDE OF LEFT-HAND BACK

6 Neaten the centre back seam, side seam, and shoulder seam edges on each back piece using a 3-thread overlock stitch or a small zigzag stitch.

Shoulder seam edge

Side seam edge

Centre back seam edge

WRONG SIDE OF LEFT-HAND BACK

PROJECT

7 On the front piece, bring the tailor's tacks for the bust darts together and pin in place. Tack to mark the stitching line, then machine. Remove the tacks.

8 Press both bust darts towards the waist.

9 Neaten the side seams and shoulder seams using a 3-thread overlock stitch or a small zigzag stitch.

Pocket positions marked

WRONG SIDE OF FRONT

INSERT THE CONCEALED ZIP

1 Fuse a 2 x 60cm (¾ x 24in) strip of interfacing on the wrong side of both centre back seam allowances to match the zip placement.

2 Tack the centre back seam allowance on the right-hand back piece. Pin the zip in place on the right side.

3 Undo the zip and stitch it to the seam allowance along the tacked line using a concealed zip foot.

Open the zip fully before stitching

Tacked line

RIGHT SIDE OF RIGHT-HAND BACK

4 Do the zip up. Tack the centre back seam allowance on the left-hand back. Pin the other side of the zip in place on the right side.

Zip attached to right side of left-hand back

5 Undo the zip and machine in place along the tacked line using a concealed zip foot.

WRONG SIDE OF RIGHT-HAND BACK

6 Using a normal machine foot, machine the seam below the zip with a 1.5cm (⅝cm) seam allowance.

7 Stitch the ends of the zip tape to the seam allowances to secure. Press the seam open below the zip.

Centre back seam

▷ **INSERT THE IN-SEAM POCKETS**

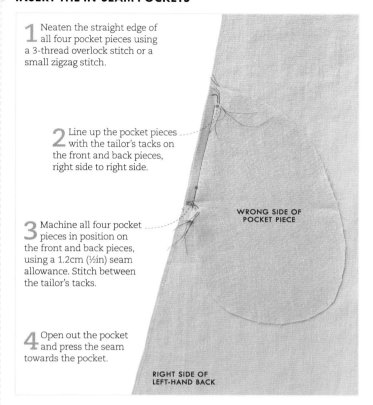

1 Neaten the straight edge of all four pocket pieces using a 3-thread overlock stitch or a small zigzag stitch.

2 Line up the pocket pieces with the tailor's tacks on the front and back pieces, right side to right side.

3 Machine all four pocket pieces in position on the front and back pieces, using a 1.2cm (½in) seam allowance. Stitch between the tailor's tacks.

4 Open out the pocket and press the seam towards the pocket.

WRONG SIDE OF POCKET PIECE

RIGHT SIDE OF LEFT-HAND BACK

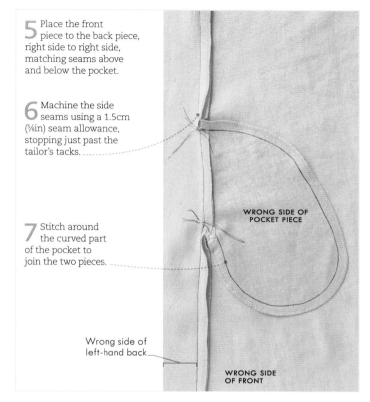

5 Place the front piece to the back piece, right side to right side, matching seams above and below the pocket.

6 Machine the side seams using a 1.5cm (⅝in) seam allowance, stopping just past the tailor's tacks.

7 Stitch around the curved part of the pocket to join the two pieces.

WRONG SIDE OF POCKET PIECE

Wrong side of left-hand back

WRONG SIDE OF FRONT

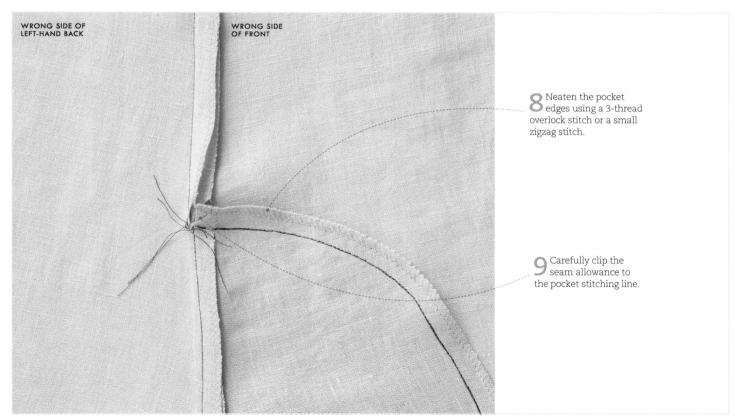

WRONG SIDE OF LEFT-HAND BACK

WRONG SIDE OF FRONT

8 Neaten the pocket edges using a 3-thread overlock stitch or a small zigzag stitch.

9 Carefully clip the seam allowance to the pocket stitching line.

SEPARATE IN-SEAM POCKET p.248 ● **CONCEALED OR INVISIBLE ZIP p.290**

PROJECT

ATTACH THE NECK FACING

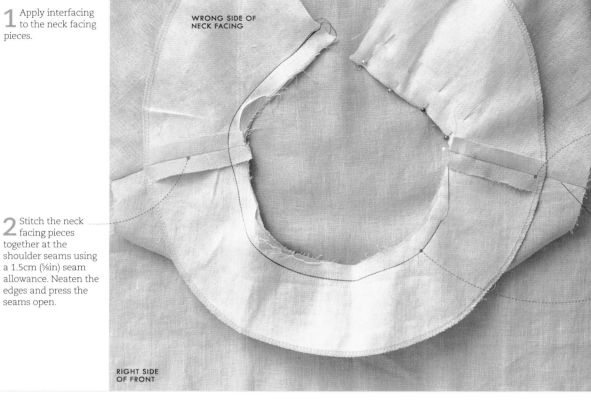

1 Apply interfacing to the neck facing pieces.

2 Stitch the neck facing pieces together at the shoulder seams using a 1.5cm (⅝in) seam allowance. Neaten the edges and press the seams open.

WRONG SIDE OF NECK FACING

3 Place the facing to the neck of the dress, right side to right side, matching the shoulder seams. Pin in place.

Shoulder seam

4 Machine stitch the neck facing in place using a 1.5cm (⅝in) seam allowance.

RIGHT SIDE OF FRONT

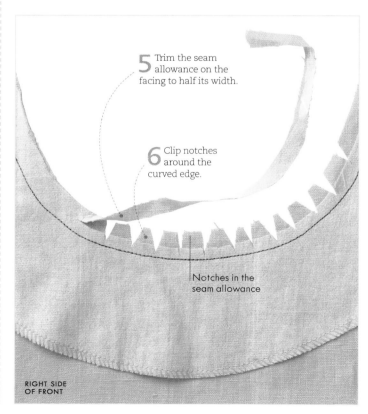

5 Trim the seam allowance on the facing to half its width.

6 Clip notches around the curved edge.

Notches in the seam allowance

RIGHT SIDE OF FRONT

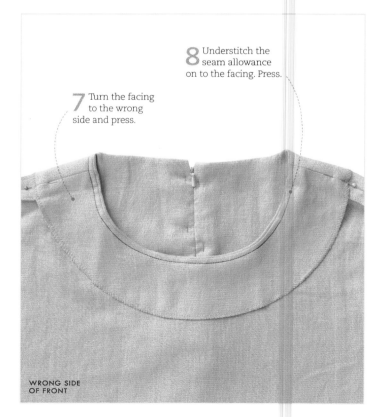

8 Understitch the seam allowance on to the facing. Press.

7 Turn the facing to the wrong side and press.

WRONG SIDE OF FRONT

▶ ATTACH THE SLEEVES

1 Machine the sleeve seam using a 1.5cm (⅝in) seam allowance. Press the seam open.

2 Stitch two rows of ease stitches around the sleeve head.

WRONG SIDE OF SLEEVE

3 Place the sleeve into the armhole, right side to right side, matching the underarm seam.

4 Match the top of the sleeve to the shoulder seam. Match the double notches at the back and the single notches at the front.

Overlock or zigzag seams

5 Pull up the ease stitches so that the sleeve fits into the armhole. Pin.

6 Machine the sleeve using a 1.5cm (⅝in) seam allowance, starting at the underarm seam. Neaten the seams.

▶ STITCH THE HEM

1 Neaten the raw hem edge with a 3-thread overlock stitch or a small zigzag stitch. Turn up the hem by 4cm (1½in) and pin. Shrink any fullness out by hovering a steamy iron over it.

2 Hand stitch the hem using a slip hem stitch to the wrong side of the fabric along the overlocked edge.

INSERTING A SET-IN SLEEVE p.211 ● **CURVED HEM FINISH p.265**

COLLARS

Collars frame the face and neck, and are always a focal point on any garment. There are three main types: flat, stand, and rolled. To construct a symmetrical collar, careful and accurate marking and stitching are essential.

TECHNIQUES

COLLARS

All collars consist of a minimum of two pieces, the upper collar (which will be on the outside) and the under collar. Interfacing, which is required to give the collar shape and structure, is often applied to the upper collar to give a smoother appearance to the fabric.

DIRECTORY OF COLLARS

FLAT COLLAR (see p.175 and pp.176–177)

STAND COLLAR (p.178)

SHAWL COLLAR (p.179)

BLOUSE COLLAR WITH REVERS (p.180)

TWO-PIECE SHIRT COLLAR (pp.180–181)

FLAT COLLAR

Difficulty level ✱✱✱✱✱

A flat collar is the easiest of all the collars to construct, and the techniques used are the same for most other shapes of flat collar and facings.

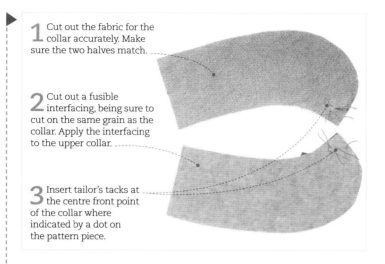

1 Cut out the fabric for the collar accurately. Make sure the two halves match.

2 Cut out a fusible interfacing, being sure to cut on the same grain as the collar. Apply the interfacing to the upper collar.

3 Insert tailor's tacks at the centre front point of the collar where indicated by a dot on the pattern piece.

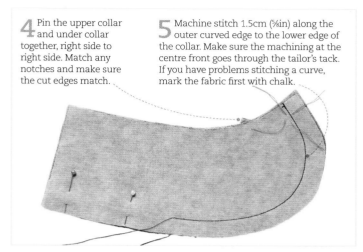

4 Pin the upper collar and under collar together, right side to right side. Match any notches and make sure the cut edges match.

5 Machine stitch 1.5cm (⅝in) along the outer curved edge to the lower edge of the collar. Make sure the machining at the centre front goes through the tailor's tack. If you have problems stitching a curve, mark the fabric first with chalk.

6 Trim the under collar seam allowance to half of its width, which will reduce the bulk.

7 Trim around the curve with pinking shears, reducing both layers. This will allow the fabric to turn.

8 Press the seam allowance of the upper collar on to the collar.

9 While the collar is still warm from the steam iron, turn to the right side.

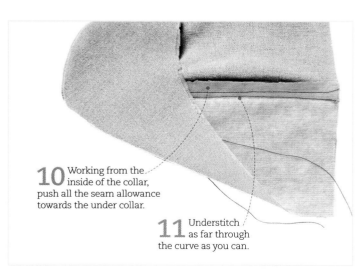

10 Working from the inside of the collar, push all the seam allowance towards the under collar.

11 Understitch as far through the curve as you can.

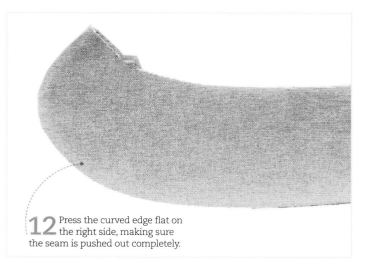

12 Press the curved edge flat on the right side, making sure the seam is pushed out completely.

TECHNIQUES

ATTACHING A FLAT COLLAR

Difficulty level ✲✲✲✲✲

A flat collar can be attached to the neckline by means of a facing. Depending upon the style of the garment, the facing may go all around the neck, which is usually found on garments with centre back openings, or just be at the front. The collar with no back facing has to be attached to the garment in stages.

▶ **FLAT ROUND COLLAR WITH NO BACK FACING**

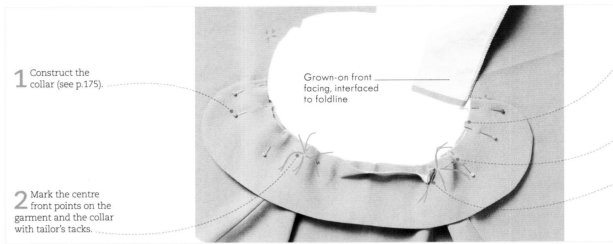

1 Construct the collar (see p.175).

Grown-on front facing, interfaced to foldline

2 Mark the centre front points on the garment and the collar with tailor's tacks.

3 Place the collar to the neckline, right side to right side. Match the notches.

4 Pin in place, pinning just to the tailor's tacks.

5 Snip the collar at the tailor's tacks on the shoulders. The collar should be loose across the back neck.

6 Machine the under collar across the back of the neck first, stitching from tailor's tack to tailor's tack. Keep the upper collar clear of stitching.

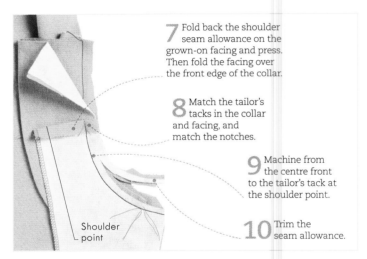

7 Fold back the shoulder seam allowance on the grown-on facing and press. Then fold the facing over the front edge of the collar.

8 Match the tailor's tacks in the collar and facing, and match the notches.

9 Machine from the centre front to the tailor's tack at the shoulder point.

10 Trim the seam allowance.

Shoulder point

11 Turn through to the right side and press.

12 At the centre back, turn under the seam allowance on the upper collar and hand stitch across the back neck with a flat fell or blind hem stitch.

▶ **FLAT ROUND COLLAR WITH A FULL FACING**

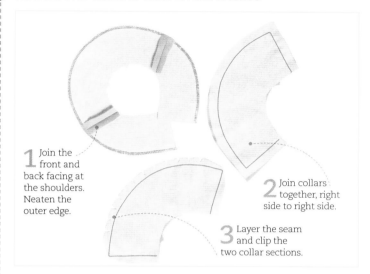

1 Join the front and back facing at the shoulders. Neaten the outer edge.

2 Join collars together, right side to right side.

3 Layer the seam and clip the two collar sections.

4 Pin the collar to the neck edge, matching notches.

5 At the centre back, fold the back facing over the collar.

6 Pin the facing over the collar. Match notches and shoulder seams.

7 Layer the facing side of the seam.

8 Layer a small amount off the collar.

9 Clip V shapes.

10 Turn to the wrong side and understitch.

WRONG SIDE OF GARMENT

11 Turn to the right side and press.

SEAM NEATENING **p.95** ◆ REDUCING SEAM BULK **pp.108–109** ◆ STITCH FINISHES **p.109** ◆ GROWN-ON FACING **p.160**

TECHNIQUES

STAND COLLAR

Difficulty level ★★★★★

Also called a mandarin collar, this collar stands upright around the neck. It is normally cut from a straight piece of fabric, with shaping at the centre front edges. For a very close-fitting stand collar, the collar is cut with a slight curve.

1 Apply a fusible interfacing to the upper collar (see p.175). Insert any tailor's tacks as indicated on the pattern.

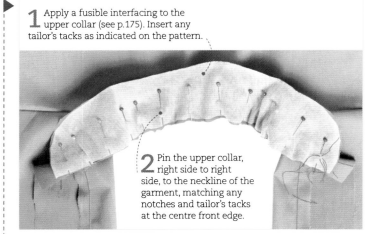

2 Pin the upper collar, right side to right side, to the neckline of the garment, matching any notches and tailor's tacks at the centre front edge.

3 Machine the upper collar to the neckline using a 1.5cm (⅝in) seam allowance. Make sure the stitching stops at the tailor's tack at the front edge.

4 Reduce the seam allowance on the upper collar by half.

5 Clip though the seam allowances – this will allow the fabric to relax into shape when pressed later.

6 Working from the wrong side of the garment, turn in the centre front edge as indicated by the pattern. This will leave the front edge of the collar proud of the garment.

WRONG SIDE OF COLLAR

7 Pin the under collar to the upper collar, right side to right side, along the top edge.

8 Machine the two pieces together using a 1.5cm (⅝in) seam allowance.

9 At the centre front, the reduced neck seam allowance needs to be pointing up into the collar, so that the machining attaching the two collar sections together goes over it. Be sure the machining is in line with the centre front of the garment.

10 Reduce the seam allowance to half its width on the under collar side of the seam (the non-interfaced side).

11 Clip V shapes out of the seam allowance to reduce the bulk. Be careful not to cut through the stitching.

12 Press the seam as it has been stitched, and while warm turn to the right side.

13 Turn under the lower edge seam allowance on the under collar and tack in place around the neck edge.

Wrong side of the garment

14 Make sure the two leading front edges of the collar are symmetrical.

15 Use a flat fell stitch to secure the under collar at the neck edge.

SHAWL COLLAR

A shawl collar, which is a deep V-neck shape that combines both collar and rever in one, gives a flattering neckline that is often found on blouses and jackets. Although the collar looks complicated, it is straightforward to make. The under collar is usually part of the front of the garment.

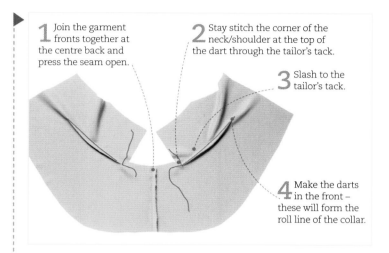

1 Join the garment fronts together at the centre back and press the seam open.

2 Stay stitch the corner of the neck/shoulder at the top of the dart through the tailor's tack.

3 Slash to the tailor's tack.

4 Make the darts in the front – these will form the roll line of the collar.

5 Join the back sections of the garment together at the centre back and press the seam open.

6 Join the front to the back across the shoulder seams, stopping at the slash.

7 Join the front of the garment to the back across the back neck, working from slash line to slash line. Press open.

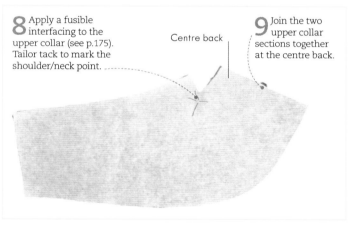

8 Apply a fusible interfacing to the upper collar (see p.175). Tailor tack to mark the shoulder/neck point.

Centre back

9 Join the two upper collar sections together at the centre back.

10 Pin the upper collar to the garment, matching the centre back seams and any notches. Machine in place using a 1.5cm (⅝in) seam.

11 Trim the seam allowance on the under collar side (the non-interfaced side) by half. Clip V shapes into the seam to reduce the bulk.

12 Press the seam as it has been stitched and turn to the right side while still warm.

13 Press on the right side so the seam falls slightly to the wrong side, to avoid it showing on the right side.

14 At the back neck, turn under the raw edge and hand stitch in place with a flat fell stitch. Neaten the other raw edges of the upper collar by your preferred technique.

HAND STITCHES **pp.90–91** • REDUCING SEAM BULK **pp.108–109**

TECHNIQUES

BLOUSE COLLAR WITH REVERS

Difficulty level ★★★★★

A blouse collar can have rounded or pointed centre front edges, depending on the style of blouse chosen. A blouse collar forms a V neckline with revers. When constructing the collar, before fusing the interfacing to the upper collar, trim the corners of the interfacing to reduce bulk.

1 Mark any pattern markings with tailor's tacks. Construct the collar by placing the fabric right side to right side. Machine using a 1.5cm (⅝in) seam allowance.

2 Trim away the under collar side of the seam.

3 Clip across the interfacing at the corners.

Back neck

4 At the centre back neck, snip through the seam allowance of just the upper collar at the tailor's tacks. Press this part of the seam open.

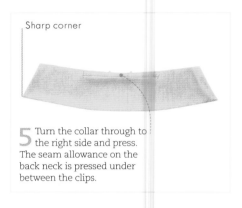

Sharp corner

5 Turn the collar through to the right side and press. The seam allowance on the back neck is pressed under between the clips.

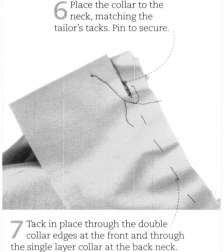

6 Place the collar to the neck, matching the tailor's tacks. Pin to secure.

7 Tack in place through the double collar edges at the front and through the single layer collar at the back neck.

8 Place the front facing over the front part of the collar, matching notches and tailor's tacks.

9 Machine in place, stitching across the back neck at the same time. Match at the shoulder seams.

Sharp point in stitching at centre front

10 Trim and layer the seam. Turn to the right side and press.

11 Turn under the raw edge of the upper collar at the back neck and tack in place, then hand stitch with a flat fell or blind hem stitch.

Rever

12 Press the collar and revers.

TWO-PIECE SHIRT COLLAR

Difficulty level ★★★★★

A traditional-style shirt has a collar that consists of two pieces: a collar and a stand, both of which require interfacing. The stand fits close around the neck and the collar is attached to the stand. This type of collar is found on men's and ladies' shirts. On a man's shirt, the stand accommodates the tie.

1 Apply interfacing to the upper collar.

2 Machine the upper and under collar together, right side to right side, stitching around the sides and the outside edge. Stitch a sharp point by pivoting at the corners.

3 Trim the seam allowance from the under collar.

4 Remove surplus fabric at the point.

5 Press the seam open, pressing the upper collar seam allowance down on to the collar. Clip as required.

6 The fabric at the point should not be bulky. If it is, remove more.

HOW TO APPLY A FUSIBLE INTERFACING p.54 • **PATTERN MARKING pp.82–83** • **HAND STITCHES pp.90–91**

7 Turn the collar to the right side and press.

8 Top-stitch the sides and outside edge using the edge of the machine foot as a guide.

9 Apply interfacing to one side of the stand.

Collar fits between the tailor's tacks

10 Place the non-interfaced side of the collar to the interfaced side of the stand. Match the notches, then pin in place.

11 Machine the collar to the stand.

12 Place the stand to the shirt neck, matching the notches, and pin in place.

13 Tack the stand to the neckline. The seam allowance on the stand extends at the centre front.

14 Pin the non-interfaced side of the collar stand to the neck edge, so that there is a collar stand on either side of the shirt.

15 Tack the collar stand to the neckline.

16 Reposition the stand so that the front edges come together right side to right side.

17 Machine along the neck edge and around the centre front curve to the collar.

18 Trim away the non-interfaced side of the stand.

19 Remove surplus fabric from the corner.

20 Turn and press.

21 Bring the raw edge of the stand to the collar and turn under. Pin in place. Secure this edge with a flat fell stitch.

22 Top-stitch the stand, if required. The stand fits snugly under the collar at the centre front.

STITCHES MADE WITH A MACHINE **pp.92–93** • STITCHING CORNERS AND CURVES **pp.102–103** • REDUCING SEAM BULK **pp.108–109**

WAISTLINES, BELTS, AND TIE-BACKS

Bodice and skirt sections are often joined together at the waist. However, on some garments a "waist" needs to be created to take a piece of elastic. A waist may be enhanced by making a matching belt. Curtain tie-backs are also covered in this section.

WAISTLINES

Waistlines can be formed where a bodice and skirt join together or at the waist edge of a skirt or pair of trousers. Some waistlines are attached to the garment to create a feature and others are more discreet. They may be shaped to follow the contours of the body.

DIRECTORY OF WAISTLINES

FITTED WAISTLINE
(p.185)

GATHERED WAISTLINE
(p.185)

WAISTLINE WITH A CASING (p.186–187)

APPLIED CASING
(p.187)

MOCK CASING USING ELASTIC (p.188)

ALTERNATIVE CASING USING A SEAM ALLOWANCE (p.189)

PARTIAL CASING
(p.189)

WAISTLINE WITH A FACING
(p.190)

STRAIGHT WAISTBAND
(p.192–193)

JOINING A FITTED SKIRT TO A BODICE

Difficulty level ✱✱✱✱✱

Many dresses feature a straight fitted skirt attached to a fitted dress bodice. When joining them together, it is important that the darts or seamlines on the bodice line up with those on the skirt.

1 Be sure the darts on the skirt section are pressed towards the centre. Stay stitch the waistline.

WRONG SIDE OF SKIRT

2 Press the seam allowances on the bodice open.

3 Place the skirt to the bodice, matching up the darts and the bodice seams. Pin the bodice and skirt together.

4 Machine the bodice to the skirt using a 1.5cm (⅝in) seam allowance. Press.

5 Neaten the skirt/ bodice seam using either a 3-thread overlock stitch or a zigzag stitch.

6 Press the seam up towards the bodice.

WRONG SIDE OF GARMENT

7 On the right side, the seams and darts match at the waist.

RIGHT SIDE OF GARMENT

JOINING A GATHERED SKIRT TO A BODICE

Difficulty level ✱✱✱✱✱

When attaching a gathered skirt to a fitted bodice, the gathers must be distributed evenly around the waist. If there are seams on the gathered skirt these must be matched to the bodice seams and darts.

1 Machine a double row of gather stitches around the waistline of a half circle skirt.

2 Pull up the gathers to fit the bodice waist.

3 Pin the gathered skirt to the bodice, making sure the bodice darts face towards the centre.

4 Machine the gathered skirt to the bodice using a 1.5cm (⅝in) seam allowance. Neaten the seam using either a 3-thread overlock stitch or a zigzag stitch.

WRONG SIDE OF GARMENT

5 Press the seam up towards the bodice. On the right side the skirt seam is gathered into a smooth bodice seam.

RIGHT SIDE OF GARMENT

PLAIN DART **p.113** ● HOW TO MAKE AND FIT GATHERS **p.135**

MAKING A CASING AT THE WAIST EDGE

Difficulty level ✱✱✱✱✱

An elasticated waist edge can be featured on both skirts and trousers and also at the waist edge on casual jackets. A casing can be made by using a deep waist seam or by attaching a facing.

▶ **USING A DEEP WAIST SEAM AS A CASING**

1 Turn under a 1.5cm (⅝in) seam allowance to the wrong side and press.

2 Turn again by 3cm (1¼in). Pin in place.

WRONG SIDE OF FABRIC

3 Stitch 2mm (⅟₁₆in) from the top folded edge.

WRONG SIDE OF FABRIC

4 Machine the lower edge of the fold 2mm (⅟₁₆in) from the edge. Leave a gap of about 3cm (1¼in) to insert the elastic through.

5 Cut a piece of non-roll elastic the length required to go around the waist comfortably.

6 Pin one end of the elastic to the fabric just below the opening.

7 Pin a safety pin to the other end and thread through the casing.

8 Pull the two ends of the elastic together and machine to join in a square shape with an X for strength.

9 Push the elastic into the casing and stitch across the gap.

▶ USING A FACING AS A CASING

1 Cut the facing, and join the facing sections together at the side seams. Press open. Do not join the centre back seam but press back the seam allowances.

2 Pin the facing to the raw edge of the garment right side to right side.

3 Stitch the facing to the edge of the garment.

4 Layer the seam and press as stitched.

Gap where centre back seam has been left open

5 Press the facing on to the wrong side of the garment.

6 Turn under the lower edge of the facing by 1.5cm (⅝in).

RIGHT SIDE OF FACING

WRONG SIDE OF FABRIC

7 Machine stitch down the facing at the folded edge, leaving a gap for the elastic to be inserted.

8 Insert the elastic into the facing and secure the ends.

Open seam on facing

Seam on garment

APPLIED CASINGS

Difficulty level ✱✱✱✱✱

Some elasticated waist edges will require the application of extra fabric to make a casing into which the elastic can be inserted. The casing may be applied to the inside or the outside of the garment. A quick way is to make the casing with bias binding. The casing can also be made from the same fabric as the garment or from a facing.

▶ INTERNAL CASING

1 This type of casing is often used on a shirt-waisted dress or on a blouson-style jacket. Cut a strip of fabric on the straight of grain wide enough to accommodate your elastic and turnings.

2 Turn under the edge at one end by 1.5cm (⅝in) and then the same along the sides.

3 Mark the waist with a row of tacks.

4 Place the casing over the tacks with the finished short end towards the centre front. Pin in place.

5 Machine to attach the casing to the waist.

6 Insert the elastic into the casing. Secure the elastic at both ends.

▶ INTERNAL CASING USING BIAS BINDING

1 Be sure to use bias binding that will be wide enough to insert an elastic through after it has been stitched down. Apply the bias to the waistline and stitch at 2mm (1/16in) from either edge.

2 Insert the elastic and knot the ends.

2cm (¾in) wide bias binding

▶ EXTERNAL CASING

1 Cut a strip of straight grain fabric 3.5cm (1⅜in) wide x the waist measurement on the garment. Turn under all raw edges by 5mm (³/₁₆in) and press.

2 Place this casing over the garment waistline, with the short ends to the centre front.

3 Machine in place along the long edges. Insert elastic to fit the waist.

CONSTRUCTION OF A FACING **p.153**   ●   HOW TO CUT BIAS STRIPS **p.154**

TECHNIQUES

MOCK CASINGS

Difficulty level ★★★★★

There are several ways to construct mock casings. The simplest is to stitch on elastic at the waist. An alternative, if a bodice and skirt have a waist seam joining them together, is to insert elastic between the seam allowances. On many garments, there is elastic at the back only, in a partial casing, and a waistband interfacing at the front.

▶ STITCHING ON ELASTIC TO MAKE A WAISTLINE

1 Cut a piece of elastic to the required length. Mark the waistline on the garment with a row of tacking stitches.

2 Secure the elastic at one end with a pin.

3 Stretch the elastic across the fabric, pinning at regular intervals. The fabric will be loose under the elastic.

4 Secure the elastic at one end with a few machine stitches.

5 Place under the sewing machine and join the elastic to the fabric using a 3-step zigzag stitch, stretching the fabric and elastic together as you do so.

6 The elastic stitched in place.

7 On the right side there is a neat elasticated waistline.

▶ CASING IN A WAIST SEAM ALLOWANCE

1 Join the fabric together using a 2cm (¾in) seam allowance.

2 Stitch again 1.5cm (⅝in) from this stitching line, 5mm (³⁄₁₆in) from the raw edge.

3 Neaten the edge of the seam using a 3-thread overlock stitch or a zigzag stitch.

4 Insert elastic into the casing that you have made, with the help of a safety pin.

▶ ALTERNATIVE CASING USING A SEAM ALLOWANCE

1 Press the waist seam allowances open.

WRONG SIDE OF GARMENT

2 Top-stitch the seam allowances open, stitching 1cm (⅜in) from the seam, to make a channel on either side of the seam.

WRONG SIDE OF GARMENT

3 Using a cord elastic and a bodkin, insert a length of elastic through each channel.

4 Knot the elastic together, then gather the fabric along the elastic to the required measurement.

RIGHT SIDE OF GARMENT

5 Knot the elastic together at the other end and cut off any excess.

▶ PARTIAL CASING

1 The front waist is made by using a grown-on waistband. This means the waistband has been cut in one piece together with the garment front. Apply a fusible interfacing to the front waistband allowance.

2 Neaten the raw edge with the overlocker or a zigzag stitch.

3 Fold the waistband down on to the skirt, and machine at the lower edge to secure.

FRONT PIECE OF GARMENT

4 On the back of the skirt, fold down the waist allowance.

5 Top-stitch close to the fold at the upper edge.

6 Turn under the lower edge and machine to make a casing.

7 Insert the elastic. Pull up the elastic to the required length and secure with a row of machining.

BACK PIECE OF GARMENT

8 Join the skirt front to the back, right side to right side, at the side seams.

9 Press the seam open.

Gathered back

Front waist with waist stiffening

10 On the right side, the stitching line securing the front waist should be in line with the back elastic casing.

STITCHES MADE WITH A MACHINE **pp.92–93** • HOW TO MAKE A PLAIN SEAM **p.94** • STITCH FINISHES **p.109**

TECHNIQUES

A WAIST WITH A FACING

Difficulty level ✲✲✲✲✲

Many waistlines on skirts and trousers are finished with a facing, which will follow the contours of the waist but will have had the dart shaping removed to make it smooth. A faced waistline always sits comfortably to the body. The facing is attached after all the main sections of the skirt or trousers have been constructed.

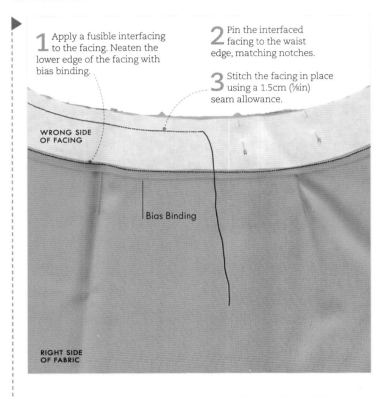

1 Apply a fusible interfacing to the facing. Neaten the lower edge of the facing with bias binding.

2 Pin the interfaced facing to the waist edge, matching notches.

3 Stitch the facing in place using a 1.5cm (⅝in) seam allowance.

WRONG SIDE OF FACING

Bias Binding

RIGHT SIDE OF FABRIC

4 Layer the seam allowance on the facing side of the seam to reduce it by half.

5 Clip the seam allowance by using straight cuts at 90 degrees to the stitching line.

6 Press the waist seam up into the facing.

7 Stitch the seam allowance down on to the facing at a distance of about 3mm (⅛in) from the original stitching (this is called understitching).

8 Turn the facing to the inside of the garment and press.

9 Reduce the bulk from the top of the dart.

WRONG SIDE OF FABRIC

Right side of waistline

PETERSHAM-FACED WAIST

Difficulty level ★★★★★

Petersham is an alternative finish to a facing if you do not have enough fabric to cut a facing. Available in black and white, it is a stiff, ridged tape that is 2.5cm (1in) wide and curved – the tighter curve is the top edge. Like a facing, petersham is attached to the waist after the skirt or trousers have been constructed.

1 Stay stitch around the waist 1.2cm (½in) from the raw edge.

2 Trim back the raw edge to 6mm (¼in).

3 Pin the top edge of the petersham (the tighter curve) to the waist so that it overlaps the stay stitching by 2mm (¹⁄₁₆in).

4 Tack in place.

RIGHT SIDE OF FABRIC

5 Machine the petersham in place, stitching about 2mm (¹⁄₁₆in) from the edge of the petersham. Do not worry if the other edge looks wavy.

WRONG SIDE OF FABRIC

6 Turn over and roll the petersham to the inside of the waist.

7 Press the petersham flat to the fabric, making a neat pressed edge along the top of the seam.

FINISHING THE EDGE OF A WAISTBAND

Difficulty level ★★★★★

One long edge of the waistband will be stitched to the garment waist. The other edge will need to be finished, to prevent fraying and reduce bulk inside.

▶ **TURNING UNDER**

This method is suitable for fine fabrics only. Turn under 1.5cm (⅝in) along the edge of the waistband and press in place. After the waistband has been attached to the garment, hand stitch the pressed-under edge in place.

▶ **OVERLOCK STITCHING**

This method is suitable for heavier fabrics as it is left flat inside the garment after construction. Neaten one long edge of the waistband with a 3-thread overlock stitch.

▶ **BIAS BINDING**

This method is ideal for fabrics that fray badly and can add a feature inside the garment. It is left flat inside the garment after construction. Apply a 2cm (¾in) bias binding to one long edge of the waistband.

STITCHES MADE WITH A MACHINE pp.92–93 ● **LAYERING A SEAM p.108** ● **STITCH FINISHES p.109** ● **NEATENING THE EDGE OF A FACING p.154**

ATTACHING A STRAIGHT WAISTBAND

Difficulty level ★★★★★

A waistband is designed to fit snugly but not tight to the waist. Whether it is straight or slightly curved, it will be constructed and attached in a similar way. Every waistband will require a fusible interfacing to give it structure and support. Special waistband interfacings are available, usually featuring slot lines that will guide you where to fold the fabric. Make sure the slots on the outer edge correspond to a 1.5cm (⅝in) seam allowance. If a specialist waistband fusible interfacing is not available you can use a medium-weight fusible interfacing.

1 Cut the waistband and apply the interfacing. Neaten one long edge.

2 Pin the waistband to the skirt waist edge, right side to right side. Match the notches.

3 Stitch the waistband to the waist edge using a 1.5cm (⅝in) seam allowance. The waistband will extend beyond the zip by 1.5cm (⅝in) on the left and 5cm (2in) on the right.

4 Press the waistband away from the skirt.

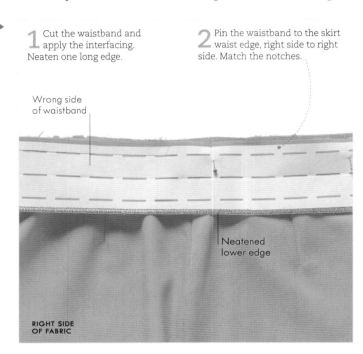

Wrong side of waistband

Neatened lower edge

RIGHT SIDE OF FABRIC

Waistband extension to be finished

Centre slot line on interfacing

Neatened lower edge

5 Fold the waistband along the centre slot line on the interfacing, right side to right side. The neatened edge of the waistband should extend 1.5cm (⅝in) below the stitching line.

6 Pin the left-hand end of the waistband in line with the centre back seam. Machine stitch together.

7 On the right-hand end of the waistband, extend the waist to skirt stitching line into the waistband and along the short end.

8 Clip the corners and turn the ends of the waistband to the right side. The extension on the waistband should be on the right-hand back.

9 Add your chosen fasteners.

10 To complete the waistband, stitch through the band to the skirt seam. This is known as stitching in the ditch.

11 The finished straight waistband.

RIBBON-FACED WAISTBAND

Difficulty level ✱✱✱✱✱

On a bulky fabric, you can replace the inner side of the waistband with a ribbon. This will not affect the structure and stability of the waistband, but will produce a less bulky finish. Use a grosgrain ribbon that is 2.5cm (1in) wide. Grosgrain ribbon looks like petersham (see p.191) but is ribbed and much softer.

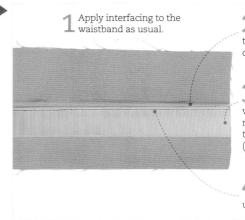

1 Apply interfacing to the waistband as usual.

2 Press the waistband in half, wrong side to wrong side, to give a defined crease.

3 Working from the right side of the waistband, place the ribbon along one side of the crease about 3mm (⅛in) from the crease.

4 Machine in place along the upper edge only.

Grosgrain ribbon

Interfacing

5 Using pinking shears, remove surplus waistband from behind the ribbon. (Pinking shears will give a softer line on bulky fabrics.)

6 Attach the waistband to the skirt as for a normal waistband (see opposite page).

7 Fold the ribbon side to the inside of the waistband and press.

Ribbon

8 To finish the lower edge, stitch in the ditch from the right side.

WRAP **SKIRT**

Difficulty level ✱✱✱✱✱

This modern take on the classic wrap skirt is every bit as chic as it is utility with its stylish, contemporary tabs. For year-round style, you could make it in linen, denim, or corduroy – but allow extra fabric and cut on a nap layout for fabrics with pile, such as corduroy or suedette.

TECHNIQUES USED Layering a seam **p.108**, Understitching **p.109**, Attaching a straight waistband **pp.192–93**, Machined hems **p.266**

YOU WILL NEED

- Pattern templates on pp.374–377. Choose your size using the Women's Sizing chart on p.368.
- 275 x 115cm (110 x 45in) or 175 x 150cm (70 x 60in) medium-weight dressmaking fabric, such as denim, linen, corduroy, heavy cupro, or suedette. (Requirements for sizes 6–16; see pp.374–77 for other sizes).
- 50cm (20in) lightweight fusible interfacing
- 6 snap fasteners
- 1 button
- Matching thread

Front

Back

PIECES TO CUT

Single layer fabric

Right-hand front (cut 1)

Left-hand front (cut 1)

75cm (30in)

150cm (60in)

Right front facing (cut 1)

Double layer fabric

Fold

Left waistband (cut 2)

Right waistband (cut 2)

Back waistband (cut 2)

Back (cut 1 on fold)

Tab (cut 2)

150cm (60in) folded

100cm (40in)

▶ APPLY THE INTERFACING

Interfacing

Inner tab

Back inner waistband

Right inner waistband

Left inner waistband

1 Apply fusible interfacing to one tab and three waistband pieces (these are the inner pieces). Cut out all the fabric pieces.

▶ ADD THE DARTS

1 Transfer all notches, fastener placements, and darts from the pattern onto your fabric.

2 With the paper pattern still in place, mark the position of the darts on the wrong side of the back piece using tailor's tacks. Cut through the loops in the tacks and remove the paper.

Wrong side of back

PROJECT

3 Fold the fabric so that the top tacks meet, right side to right side, and pin.

4 Machine from the point of the dart to the waistline.

5 Press the darts towards the centre back.

Wrong side of back

Wrong side of right-hand front

3 Machine the side seams using a 1.5cm (⅝in) seam allowance. Press the seams open.

Wrong side of back

▶ PREPARE THE TAB

1 Using a 1.5cm (⅝in) seam allowance, machine the tab pieces, right sides together, on three sides, leaving a short end open.

2 Trim the interfaced seam allowance to half its width and the other down to 1.2cm (½in).

3 Clip the corners on the stitched end.

Open end

▶ SEW THE SIDE SEAMS

1 Neaten the edges using a 3-thread overlock stitch or a small zigzag stitch.

2 Place the front pieces right side to right side on the back piece, with the left-hand piece (as worn) overlapping the right. Align the side seams and pin in place.

Wrong side of left-hand front

▶ HEM THE LEFT FRONT EDGE

1 Neaten the raw edge of the left-hand front piece with a 3-thread overlock stitch or a small zigzag stitch. Fold the edge over by 1.5cm (⅝in) and pin in place.

2 Machine the hem in place.

Folded raw edge of left-hand front

4 Turn the tab right side out. Press.

5 Mark the position of the fasteners, following the pattern markings.

▶ **ATTACH THE TAB AND FACING**

Wrong side of tab

1 Pin the tab to the right-hand front piece, right side to right side, at the point indicated by the double notch.

Right side of right-hand front

2 Prepare the right front facing by neatening the outer edge with a 3-thread overlock stitch or a small zigzag stitch.

3 Pin the facing in place on the right-hand front piece, right side to right side, with the tab in between, aligning the raw edges.

Wrong side of facing

4 Machine stitch the seam along the front edge using a 1.5cm (⅝in) seam allowance.

5 Trim the seam allowance to half its width. Understitch the seam allowance to the facing.

Wrong side of right-hand front

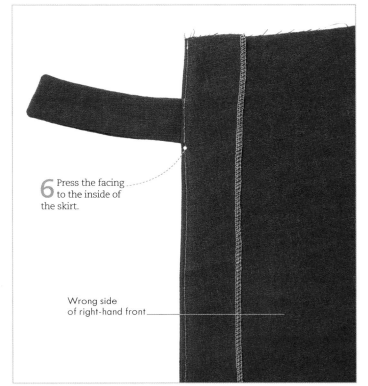

6 Press the facing to the inside of the skirt.

Wrong side of right-hand front

MACHINED HEMS p.226

▶ **ASSEMBLE THE WAISTBAND**

1 Pin the outer waistband pieces together at the side seams, right side to right side.

2 Stitch together using a 1.5cm (⅝in) seam allowance.

Right side of outer waistband piece

Right side of outer waistband piece

Right side of outer waistband piece

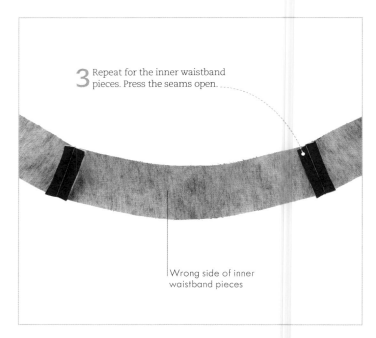

3 Repeat for the inner waistband pieces. Press the seams open.

Wrong side of inner waistband pieces

4 Pin the inner and outer waistband pieces together, right side to right side, along the top concave curve, around the right front flap, and down the left front end.

5 Mark the notch on the right front flap with a pin.

Pin marks stop point

Right front flap

Wrong side of outer waistband

6 Stitch in place using a 1.5cm (⅝in) seam allowance, starting at the left front end and ending after rounding the flap, stopping at the first notch.

7 Make small snips along the seam allowance to help release tension along the concave seam.

Right side of outer waistband

8 Turn the waistband right side out. Press.

Fastener placement marks

HAND STITCHES **pp.90–91** ● SEAM NEATENING **p.95** ● REDUCING SEAM BULK **pp.108–109** ● ATTACHING A STRAIGHT WAISTBAND **pp.192–193**

▶ **FINISH THE SKIRT**

1 Lay the skirt out flat, right side facing. Pin the waistband to the skirt's waistline, right side of the outer waistband facing the right side of the skirt, raw edges aligned, and matching side seams.

Raw edges aligned

2 Machine in place, clip into the curves of the seam allowance, and press the seam up into the waistband.

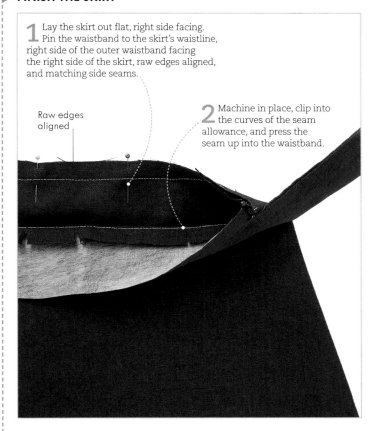

3 Press the unstitched waistline edge of the inner waistband in by 1.5cm (⅝in) and pin in place at the inside of the waistline. Blind hem stitch to secure.

4 Make a buttonhole on the left front waistband at the point indicated by the pattern markings.

Wrong side of left front

5 Attach a button to the inner waistband on the right front piece at the point indicated on the pattern markings.

6 Attach snap fasteners to the tab and to the extended end of the outer right waistband, and to the corresponding positions on the left underskirt.

▶ **STITCH THE HEM**

1 Using a 3-thread overlock stitch or a small zigzag stitch, neaten the raw edge of the hem.

2 Turn up the hem by 2.5cm (1in), or the amount required for your desired length. Press and pin.

3 Hand stitch the hem using a blind hem stitch to the wrong side of the fabric along the overlocked edge. Alternatively, machine in place.

HAND-STITCHED HEMS **pp.264–265** ● MACHINED HEMS **p.266** ● MACHINE-MADE BUTTONHOLES **p.306**

BELTS

A belt in a fabric that matches the garment can add the perfect finishing touch. Whether it be a soft tie belt or a stiff structured belt, it will be best if it has an interfacing of some kind – the firmer and more structured the belt, the firmer the interfacing should be. A belt will also need belt carriers to support it and prevent it from drooping.

DIRECTORY OF BELTS AND TIE-BACKS

STRAIGHT BELT (pp.202–203)

TIE BELT (p.204)

OBI SASH (pp.204–205)

STRUCTURED CURTAIN TIE-BACK (p.206)

RUCHED CURTAIN TIE-BACK (p.207)

BELT CARRIERS

Belt carriers can be made from fabric strips and machined to the garment, or they can be made more simply from thread loops fashioned by hand stitching. Fabric carriers are designed to support a heavier belt.

Difficulty level ✳✳✳✳✳

▶ HAND-STITCHED BELT LOOPS

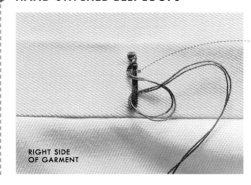

RIGHT SIDE OF GARMENT

1 Work the belt loop prior to the waistband being finished on the inside. Using double bold machine thread, work several strands of thread long enough to slot a belt through.

2 Use a buttonhole stitch and work the stitches across the loops.

3 When the loops are covered with buttonhole stitches, take the thread to the reverse and finish securely.

▶ MACHINE-STITCHED BELT CARRIERS

1 Cut the fabric strips 3cm (1¼in) wide and long enough to allow for the depth of the belt plus turnings of 1.5cm (⅝in) at each end.

2 Press the long edges of the fabric carriers to the centre, wrong side to wrong side.

3 Press the carriers in half lengthways.

4 Machine along the open edge of each carrier to secure the fold.

5 Press again to be sure the stitch line runs down the side edge of the carrier.

6 Starting at each side seam and then at regular intervals between, place the carriers to the waist of the garment, on the right side. Stitch to secure at the waist inside the seam allowance.

7 Apply the waistband to the garment, stitching across the carriers as you do so.

8 Press the waistband in half lengthways to give a centre crease.

9 Bring the carriers up on to the waistband.

10 Secure the end of each carrier to the inner edge of the waistband using a small, close zigzag stitch.

11 When the waistband is completed, the carrier will sit on it with no visible stitching.

STITCHES MADE WITH A MACHINE **pp.92—93**

REINFORCED STRAIGHT BELT

Difficulty level ★★★★★

This is a straightforward way to make a belt to match a garment. It can be of any width as it is reinforced with a very firm fusible interfacing, such as a craft interfacing. If one layer of interfacing is not firm enough, try adding another layer. The interfacing should be cut along its length to avoid joins. To ensure that it is cut straight, use a rotary cutter on a self-healing mat.

1 Cut the interfacing to the dimensions of the finished belt. Cut the fabric to twice the width of the interfacing plus seam allowances.

2 Fold the fabric in half lengthways and press to mark the centre line. Place the interfacing along the crease, leaving the fabric longer at the pointed end of the interfacing.

3 Fuse the cut interfacing to the fabric.

4 At the centre line on the pointed end, cut through to the side of the interfacing point.

5 Press the fabric edges over the interfacing. Press the point carefully.

6 Fold one long raw edge of the belt under and press.

7 Press under the remaining edge to match and pin in place.

8 Tack along the pressed-under edges to sew them together.

9 Use short tacking stitches around the point.

10 Machine stitch along both long sides of the belt, stitching on the right side of the fabric. Keep the machine stitching close to the edge – 2mm (¹⁄₁₆in) from it. Make sure the stitching is accurate through the point.

11 Measure the positioning of the eyelets towards the pointed end of the belt.

Right side of belt

12 Punch the hole for each eyelet with pliers.

13 Insert a 4mm (³⁄₁₆in) eyelet into the hole, working from the right side of the belt.

14 Change the heads in the pliers and squeeze the eyelets around the hole.

15 Insert one eyelet at the other end of the belt about 5cm (2in) from the end, placing it centrally on the right side of the belt.

Wrong side of belt

16 Push the buckle prong through the eyelet.

17 Fold the surplus fabric over on itself under the buckle and pin.

18 Secure the surplus on the wrong side with a machine or hand stitch, then turn the belt over.

Right side of belt

19 When the belt is placed around the waist, check that the fit is correct. Add extra eyelets if required.

EYELETS **p.321**

TIE BELT

Difficulty level ✳✳✳✳✳

A tie belt is the easiest of all the belts to make. It can be any width and made of most fabrics, from cottons for summer dresses to satin and silks for bridal wear. Most tie belts will require a light- to medium-weight interfacing for support. A fusible interfacing is the best choice as it will stay in place when tied repeatedly. If a very long tie belt is required, the belt can be joined at the centre back.

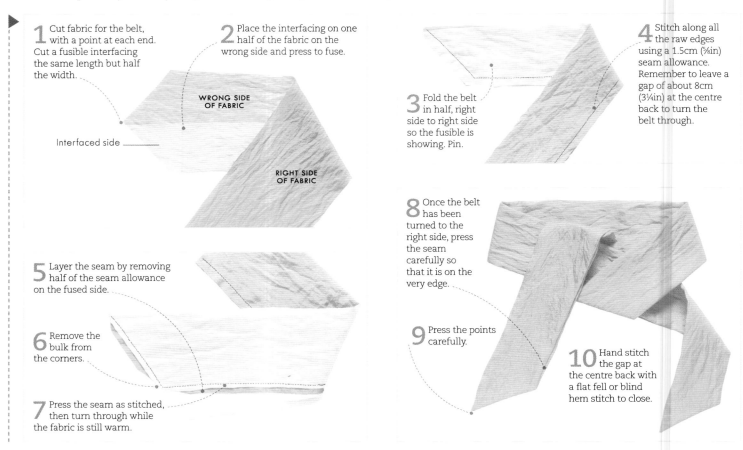

1 Cut fabric for the belt, with a point at each end. Cut a fusible interfacing the same length but half the width.

Interfaced side

WRONG SIDE OF FABRIC

RIGHT SIDE OF FABRIC

2 Place the interfacing on one half of the fabric on the wrong side and press to fuse.

3 Fold the belt in half, right side to right side so the fusible is showing. Pin.

4 Stitch along all the raw edges using a 1.5cm (⅝in) seam allowance. Remember to leave a gap of about 8cm (3¼in) at the centre back to turn the belt through.

5 Layer the seam by removing half of the seam allowance on the fused side.

6 Remove the bulk from the corners.

7 Press the seam as stitched, then turn through while the fabric is still warm.

8 Once the belt has been turned to the right side, press the seam carefully so that it is on the very edge.

9 Press the points carefully.

10 Hand stitch the gap at the centre back with a flat fell or blind hem stitch to close.

OBI SASH

Difficulty level ✳✳✳✳✳

An obi sash is a variation of the traditional sash that is worn with a kimono. This type of sash has a stiffened centre piece with softer ties that cross at the back and then wrap to the front and tie. If you are using a firm fabric, such as silk dupion or heavy cotton, interfacing will not be required for the ties.

1 Make the ties first. Cut long strips of fabric of the required length and width.

2 Fold the ties lengthways in half, right side to right side, and pin.

3 Stitch the long raw edges together. Stitch across the angled end.

4 Trim the pointed corners.

5 Turn the tie ends to the right side and press.

6 Next make the centre section. Cut out two shaped pieces of fabric and a matching piece of very firm fusible interfacing.

Interfacing

RIGHT SIDE OF FABRIC

7 Fuse the interfacing to the wrong side of one piece of fabric. If one layer of interfacing does not make the fabric stiff enough, add another layer.

8 Centre the tie ends to the short ends of the stiffened centre piece on the right side. Machine stitch to secure, using a 1cm (⅜in) seam allowance.

RIGHT SIDE OF FABRIC

WRONG SIDE OF FABRIC

9 Place the non-stiffened fabric centre piece on top, right side to right side, and pin around the edge.

10 Fold up and tuck the tie ends inside, between the two layers of fabric.

11 Machine stitch around the centre section, leaving a gap at the lower edge for turning through.

13 Clip the curved edges of the centre section in the seam allowance.

12 Remove the surplus fabric from the corners.

14 Pull the tie ends through the gap at the lower edge.

15 Turn the centre section through to the right side and press.

16 Hand stitch the gap at the lower edge with a flat fell or blind hem stitch.

17 The finished obi sash.

STITCHES MADE WITH A MACHINE **pp.92—93** • HOW TO MAKE A PLAIN SEAM **p.94** • REDUCING SEAM BULK **pp.108—109**

CURTAIN TIE-BACKS

Difficulty level ★★★★★

Tie-backs are used to hold the drape of a curtain in position. Some are structured, with an interfacing, and follow a predetermined shape, while others are softer and more decorative. The construction of a tie-back is similar to that of a tie belt.

TECHNIQUES

▶ **STRUCTURED TIE-BACK**

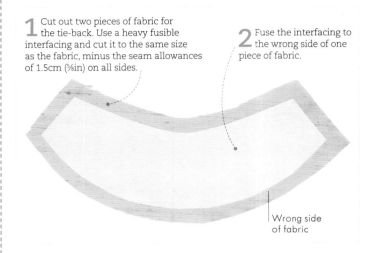

1 Cut out two pieces of fabric for the tie-back. Use a heavy fusible interfacing and cut it to the same size as the fabric, minus the seam allowances of 1.5cm (⅝in) on all sides.

2 Fuse the interfacing to the wrong side of one piece of fabric.

Wrong side of fabric

3 Pin the non-interfaced piece of fabric to the interfaced piece, right side to right side.

4 Stitch around the two pieces, taking a 1.5cm (⅝in) seam allowance. Leave a gap of about 8cm (3¼in) at the lower edge to turn through.

5 The machining should follow the edge of the interfacing, but not go through it.

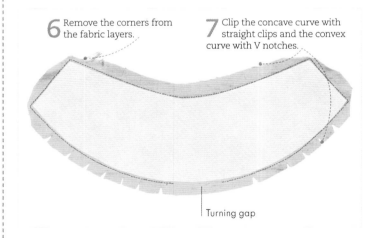

6 Remove the corners from the fabric layers.

7 Clip the concave curve with straight clips and the convex curve with V notches.

Turning gap

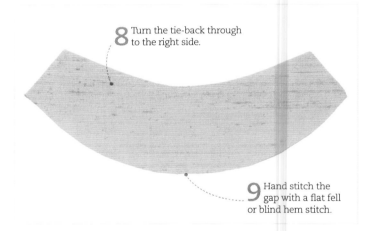

8 Turn the tie-back through to the right side.

9 Hand stitch the gap with a flat fell or blind hem stitch.

10 On the two short ends of the tie-back, sew on a curtain ring. Use a buttonhole stitch to secure it.

▶ **DECORATIVE RUCHED TIE-BACK**

1 Cut a piece of curtain interlining 25cm (10in) wide and to the required tie-back length.

2 Roll up the interlining like a sausage, but not too tight, and pin in place.

3 Using a bold thread, herringbone stitch the raw edge down to hold it in position. Make sure the rolled interlining is the same thickness throughout.

4 For the outer decorative layer, cut a piece of fabric 12cm (5in) wide and three times the required length.

5 Fold lengthways in half, right side to right side.

6 Machine stitch the long raw edges together using a 1cm (⅜in) seam allowance.

7 Stitch again, between the stitching line and the raw edge. The double stitching is for strength.

8 Turn the decorative top layer fabric through to the right side and press.

9 Tie the thread ends from the herringbone stitch on the interlining to a loop turner.

10 Using the loop turner, pull the interlining sausage through the decorative layer. This is difficult as it will stick. Work the decorative fabric gently down the interlining.

11 Ruche the decorative fabric up around the interlining, spreading out the fabric with your fingers. Remove the loop turner.

12 Hand stitch with a small, straight running stitch about every 3cm (1¼in) to secure the ruching on the tie-back.

13 Sew on a curtain ring at each end, using a buttonhole stitch to secure the rings.

INTERLININGS **p.324**

SLEEVES AND SLEEVE FINISHES

Sleeves come in all shapes and lengths. They should always hang properly from the end of the wearer's shoulder, without wrinkles. The lower end of the sleeve is normally finished by means of a cuff or a facing.

SLEEVES

A few sleeves, such as the dolman, are cut as part of the garment, but most sleeves, including set-in and raglan, are made separately and then inserted into the armhole. Whichever type of sleeve is being inserted, always place it to the armhole and not the armhole to the sleeve – in other words, always work with the sleeve facing you.

DIRECTORY OF SLEEVES

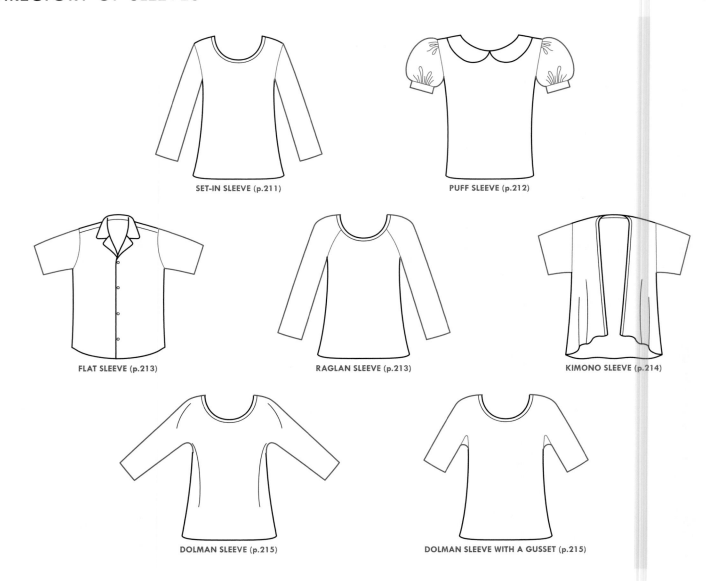

SET-IN SLEEVE (p.211)

PUFF SLEEVE (p.212)

FLAT SLEEVE (p.213)

RAGLAN SLEEVE (p.213)

KIMONO SLEEVE (p.214)

DOLMAN SLEEVE (p.215)

DOLMAN SLEEVE WITH A GUSSET (p.215)

STITCHES MADE WITH A MACHINE pp.92—93 ● **HOW TO MAKE A PLAIN SEAM p.94**

INSERTING A SET-IN SLEEVE

A set-in sleeve should feature a smooth sleeve head that fits on the end of your shoulder accurately. This is achieved by the use of ease stitches, which are long stitches used to tighten the fabric but not gather it.

Difficulty level ❋❋❋❋❋

1 Machine the side seams and the shoulder seams on the garment and press them open.

Armhole with notches

Single notch denotes front of the sleeve

Double notch denotes back of the sleeve

2 Machine the seam of the sleeve and press open. Turn the sleeve to the right side.

3 Around the sleeve head, work two rows of long stitches between the notches – one row at 1cm (⅜in) from the edge and the second row at 1.2cm (½in). These are the ease stitches.

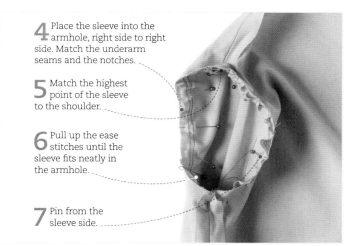

4 Place the sleeve into the armhole, right side to right side. Match the underarm seams and the notches.

5 Match the highest point of the sleeve to the shoulder.

6 Pull up the ease stitches until the sleeve fits neatly in the armhole.

7 Pin from the sleeve side.

8 Machine the sleeve in, starting at the underarm seam, using a 1.5cm (⅝in) seam allowance. Machine so that the sleeve is uppermost and keep the machining straight over the shoulder.

9 Overlap the machining at the underarm to reinforce the stitching.

10 Stitch around the sleeve again inside the seam allowance.

11 Trim the raw edges of the sleeve.

Smooth sleeve head

12 Neaten the seam with a zigzag or overlock stitch, then turn the sleeve through the armhole.

RIGHT SIDE OF GARMENT

PUFF SLEEVE

Difficulty level ✳✳✴✴✴

A sleeve that has a gathered sleeve head is referred to as a puff sleeve or gathered sleeve. It is one of the easiest sleeves to insert because the gathers take up any spare fabric.

1 Machine stitch the sleeve, right side to right side, using a 1.5cm (⅝in) seam allowance. Press the seam open.

2 Between the sleeve notches, insert two rows of gather stitches, one row at 1cm (⅜in) from the raw edge and the second row at 1.2cm (½in).

Notches

RIGHT SIDE OF FABRIC

3 Place the sleeve into the armhole, right side to right side.

4 Match the notches and the underarm seams.

5 Pull up the gathers to make the sleeve head fit the armhole.

6 Pin from the sleeve side.

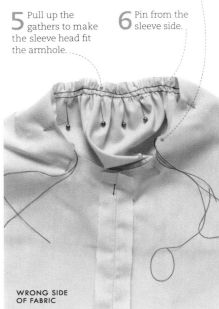

WRONG SIDE OF FABRIC

7 Working with the sleeve uppermost, machine the sleeve to the armhole. Use a 1.5cm (⅝in) seam allowance. Overlap the machining at the underarm.

8 Stitch around the sleeve seam again between the seam stitching and the raw edge.

9 Trim away the surplus fabric by 5mm (³⁄₁₆in).

10 Neaten the seam.

11 Turn right side out – all the gathers will be at the top of the sleeve.

FLAT SLEEVE CONSTRUCTION

Difficulty level ★★☆☆☆

On shirts and children's clothes, sleeves are inserted flat prior to the side seams being constructed. This technique can be difficult on firmly woven fabrics, because ease stitches are not normally used.

1 The shoulder seam on the garment should be stitched and pressed open. Place the sleeve to the armhole of the garment, right side to right side.

2 Match the notches and pin.

3 Stitch the sleeve to the armhole at a 1.5cm (⅝in) seam allowance.

4 Stitch again between the stitching line and the raw edge.

5 Neaten the seam.

6 Press the sleeve seam towards the sleeve.

7 Fold the garment and sleeve right side to right side. Match the underarm seams.

8 Stitch together with a 1.5cm (⅝in) seam allowance. Stitch up the side seam and down the sleeve.

9 Press the seam open, then turn the sleeve through the armhole, right side out.

RAGLAN SLEEVE

Difficulty level ★★★☆☆

A raglan sleeve can be constructed as a one-piece sleeve or a two-piece sleeve. The armhole seam on a raglan sleeve runs diagonally from the armhole to the neck.

1 Join the front and back sleeves together, right side to right side.

2 Press the seam open.

Sleeve front

Sleeve back

3 Pin the sleeve to the front and back of the garment, matching the notches.

4 Stitch together using a 1.5cm (⅝in) seam allowance.

5 Press the seams open.

Sleeve | Back | Sleeve

6 Bring the front and the back of the garment together, right side to right side.

7 Machine the side seam of the garment and continue stitching down the sleeve.

8 Press the seam open, then turn the sleeve through the armhole to the right side.

REDUCING SEAM BULK pp.108–109 ● **HOW TO MAKE AND FIT GATHERS p.135**

KIMONO SLEEVE

Difficulty level ✷✷✷✷

A kimono sleeve is a very large, deep sleeve that is stitched on as the side seams of the garment are made. Some kimono sleeves are cut with a curve and others are cut straight, but they are made in the same way.

1 Make the shoulder seam on the garment and press open.

2 Pin the sleeve to the garment, centring the sleeve to the shoulder. Machine in place, stopping 1.5cm (⅝in) from the end of the sleeve.

3 Neaten the seam allowance by using pinking shears or a zigzag stitch.

4 Machine the side seam of the garment, starting where the sleeve stitching stops.

5 Push the sleeve seam allowance towards the garment and stitch the sleeve seam.

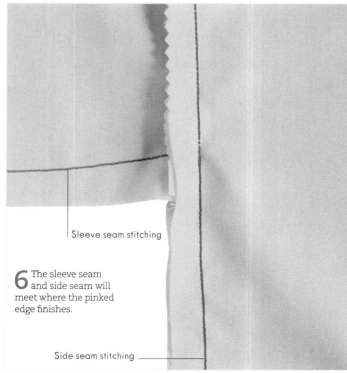

Sleeve seam stitching

6 The sleeve seam and side seam will meet where the pinked edge finishes.

Side seam stitching

7 Turn the sleeve through to the right side. The sleeve to garment side should be square. Finish the sleeve opening with a single hem.

DOLMAN SLEEVE

Difficulty level ✳✳✳✳✳

A dolman sleeve is cut as an extension to a garment. As the armhole is very loose, it is ideal for a coat or jacket. The dolman sleeve often has a raglan shoulder pad to define the shoulder end.

1 The back and the front of the garment feature the same shape from neck to sleeve end. Stitch the back and front together along the shoulder/sleeve seam.

2 Stitch the underarm/side seam.

3 Clip V shapes under the arm.

4 Press the seams open, then turn the sleeve through the armhole to the right side.

DOLMAN SLEEVE WITH A GUSSET

Difficulty level ✳✳✳✳✳

A dolman sleeve can be cut to give a tight sleeve. However a tight dolman sleeve will require an underarm gusset to allow movement. The gusset requires accurate stitching and marking if it is to be inserted correctly.

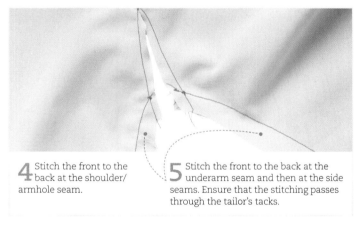

1 Mark the gusset placement on the front of the sleeve with tailor's tacks. Use different colours for the different dots on the pattern.

2 Stay stitch between the dots, then slash open. Repeat this process on the back of the sleeve.

3 Slash between the stay stitching.

4 Stitch the front to the back at the shoulder/armhole seam.

5 Stitch the front to the back at the underarm seam and then at the side seams. Ensure that the stitching passes through the tailor's tacks.

6 Mark the dots on the gusset with tailor's tacks, using different colours for opposite corners.

7 Place the gusset into the opening in the sleeve, matching the coloured tailor's tacks.

8 Stitch from one tailor's tack to the next. Do not pivot at corners.

9 Press, then turn the sleeve through to the right side.

Points of gusset

UNISEX **DRESSING GOWN**

Difficulty level ✴✴✴✴✴

Perfect for him or for her to wear on lazy Sundays, this fabulous gown looks luxurious but is straightforward to make. Optional hem and cuff panels allow you to make long or short variations, and it will drape beautifully in lightweight fabrics such as cotton lawn, silk, or viscose.

TECHNIQUES USED Tie belt **p.204**, Kimono sleeve **p.214**, Attaching a patch pocket **p.242**

YOU WILL NEED

● Pattern templates on pp.378–383. Choose your size using the Unisex Sizing chart on p.368.

● For long version (pictured): 3.3m x 150cm (130 x 60in) main fabric and 2.6m x 150cm (102 x 60in) contrast fabric in lightweight fabrics, such as cotton lawn, cotton silk, woven viscose, silk habutai, or lightweight linen. (See pp.378–383 for full fabric requirements for both long and short versions.)

● Loop turner

Front   Back

PIECES TO CUT

3.3m (130in)
Fold
Sleeve (cut 2)
Front (cut 2)
Back (cut 1 on fold)
150cm (60in) folded
Main fabric

2.6m (102in)
Fold
Cuff (cut 2)
Back hem panel (cut 1 on fold)
Pocket (cut 2)
Loops
Neckband (cut 2)
Front hem panel (cut 2)
Tie belt (cut 1)
150cm (60in) folded
Contrast fabric

► ASSEMBLE AND SEW ON THE POCKETS

1 Fold the top edge of the pocket pieces to the wrong side at the first notch and press.

2 Fold again to the right side at the second notch. Machine stitch the sides of the turned down top in place.

First fold   Second fold

3 Clip the corners to reduce bulk.

RIGHT SIDE OF POCKET

4 Turn the top flap to the wrong side and press. Machine close to the folded edge.

5 Fold and press the side edges to the wrong side by 1.5cm (⅝in).

WRONG SIDE OF POCKET

UNLINED PATCH POCKET **p.239**

6 Mitre the bottom corners of the pocket piece and pin in place.

Diagonal stitch

7 Position the pockets on the right side of the front pieces according to the pattern markings. Top-stitch the sides and along the bottom, as close to the edge as possible.

8 Reinforce the top corners with a diagonal stitch.

JOIN THE EXTENSION PANELS (LONG VERSION)

Wrong side of back

1 For the long version only, join the hem extension panel to the base of the back and two front pieces, right side to right side. Use a 1.5cm (⅝in) seam allowance.

2 Neaten the edges with a 3-thread overlock stitch or a small zigzag stitch. Press the seams towards the hem.

Back hem panel

ASSEMBLE THE HANGING AND BELT LOOPS

1 Fold each belt loop and the hanging loop piece in half lengthways. Press. Open out and fold the side edges in to meet the centre fold. Pin.

2 Top-stitch close to the folded edge.

SEW THE SHOULDER SEAMS

1 Pin the front pieces to the back piece at the shoulder seam, aligning the raw edges.

Wrong side of back

2 Machine the shoulder seams using a 1.5cm (⅝in) seam allowance. Press the seam towards the back, and neaten.

Wrong side of left-hand front

▶ ATTACH THE SLEEVES

Right side of
right-hand front

Wrong side
of sleeve

Right side of back

1 Pin the sleeve, flat,
right side to right
side, to the side seam.
Align the sleeve between
the two notches on the
side seam, and match
the central notch with
the shoulder seam.

2 Machine in place
using a 1.5cm (⅝in)
seam allowance. Press
the seam towards the
sleeve.

3 Repeat steps
1–2 for the
other sleeve.

▶ SEW THE SIDE SEAMS

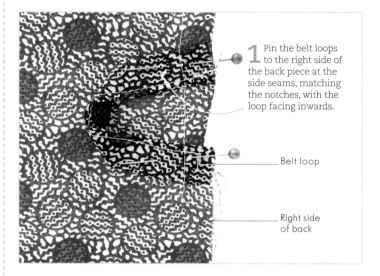

1 Pin the belt loops
to the right side of
the back piece at the
side seams, matching
the notches, with the
loop facing inwards.

Belt loop

Right side
of back

Wrong side of sleeve

2 Fold the sleeve
right side to
right side, so that
the sleeve edges and
side seams align.
Pin, taking care over
the belt loops.

3 Using a 1.5cm
(⅝in) seam
allowance, machine
stitch the sleeve's
underarm seam
and the side seam
in one go.

4 Clip into the right
angle at the
underarm intersection
to release the tension,
being careful not to cut
the stitches.

REINFORCING POCKET CORNERS **p.242** ● MITRED CORNERS **p.269**

▶ **ATTACH THE CUFF**

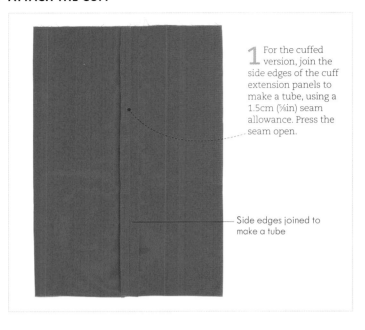

1 For the cuffed version, join the side edges of the cuff extension panels to make a tube, using a 1.5cm (⅝in) seam allowance. Press the seam open.

— Side edges joined to make a tube

2 Fold the cuff piece in half, wrong side to wrong side. Align the raw edge of the cuff to the raw edge of the sleeve, right side to right side. Match the underarm seam to the cuff seam.

Cuff seam aligned with underarm seam

3 Machine stitch, then neaten the seam using a 3-thread overlock stitch or a small zigzag stitch.

4 Fold the cuff out to the right side and press in place.

▶ **ASSEMBLE AND ATTACH THE NECKBAND**

Hanging loop

Wrong side of back

1 First, pin the hanging loop to the top neck edge of the back piece on the wrong side, with the loop facing down.

2 Machine the short ends of the neckband pieces together using a 1.5cm (⅝in) seam allowance.

3 Fold one long edge over by 1.5cm (⅝in) and press.

4 Attach the unfolded raw edge of the neckband along the back and front pieces, right side to right side. Pin, then machine in place using a 1.5cm (⅝in) seam allowance. Press the seam into the neckband.

Raw edge of neckband

USEFUL EXTRAS **p.20** ● HAND STITCHES **pp.90—91** ● SEAM NEATENING **p.95** ● TOP-STITCHING **p.109** ● TIE BELT **p.204**

5 Fold and press the unstitched edge of the neckband in to the wrong side, so that it meets the seamline. Pin in place.

Wrong side of front

Right side of front

6 Top-stitch the neckband from the right side, as close as possible to the edge.

▶ **FINISH THE SLEEVES AND HEM**

1 For the short sleeve version, make a double-turn hem by folding and pressing the hem by 6mm (¼in) and again by 1.2cm (½in) – or the amount required for your desired length. Machine 1cm (⅜in) from the folded edge.

2 To finish the bottom hem, make a double-turn hem by folding and pressing the hem by 6mm (¼in) and again by 1.2cm (½in) – or the amount required for your desired length. Machine 1cm (⅜in) from the folded edge.

▶ **ASSEMBLE THE TIE BELT**

1 Fold the tie belt piece in half lengthways, right side to right side. Machine the long side and one short side. Leave one side open to turn through.

2 Trim the corners.

3 Turn the tie belt right side out through the gap using a loop turner. Hand stitch the gap closed.

SLEEVE EDGE **FINISHES**

The lower edge of a sleeve has to be finished according to the style of the garment being made. Some sleeves are finished tight into the arm or wrist, while others may have a more decorative or functional finish.

DIRECTORY OF SLEEVE EDGE FINISHES

SLEEVE EDGE WITH
SELF HEM (p.223)

SLEEVE EDGE WITH A
BIAS-BOUND HEM (p.223)

ELASTICATED SLEEVE EDGE
WITH A HEADING (p.224)

ELASTICATED SLEEVE
EDGE (p.225)

SLEEVE EDGE WITH
RUFFLE (p.226)

FACED SLEEVE
EDGE (p.227)

SLEEVE HEMS

The simplest way to finish a sleeve is to make a small hem, which can be part of the sleeve or additional fabric that is attached to turn up. A self hem is where the edge of the sleeve is turned up on to itself. If there is insufficient fabric to turn up, a bias binding can be used to create the hem. You can use purchased bias binding or make your own bias strips.

Difficulty level ★★✦✦✦

▶ SELF HEM

1 Mark the final length of the sleeve with a row of tacking stitches.

Hem allowance

Seam pressed open

2 Remove the excess seam allowance in the hem area.

3 Turn up the hem along the tacked line.

4 Match the seams. Pin in place.

5 Turn under the top edge of the hem allowance by 1cm (⅜in) and pin.

6 Tack to secure.

7 Hand stitch the sleeve hem in place using a slip stitch.

Finished hem

▶ BIAS-BOUND HEM

1 Mark the final length of the sleeve with a row of tacking stitches.

2 Trim back the hem allowance to 5mm (³⁄₁₆in).

3 Cut a strip of 2cm (¾in) wide bias binding to the required length. Attach the bias to the sleeve, right side to right side.

4 Turn under the end of the bias, placing the fold of the bias to the sleeve seam.

5 Machine in place using a 5mm (³⁄₁₆in) seam allowance.

6 Press the seam allowance towards the bias.

Bias binding

Turned under end now on the top

7 Turn the bias to the inside of the sleeve and machine in place, stitching along the upper edge of the bias.

A CASING ON A SLEEVE EDGE

Difficulty level ✹✹✹✹✹

A casing is often used on the edge of a sleeve to insert elastic into, which will allow you to gather the sleeve in a specific place. The casing may be grown-on, which means it is part of the sleeve, or it may be applied separately. The photographs below show an applied casing of bias binding.

1 Before the sleeve is constructed, double turn the lower edge, turning to the wrong side, and machine in place.

RIGHT SIDE OF SLEEVE

2 Press the hem that you have made.

WRONG SIDE OF SLEEVE

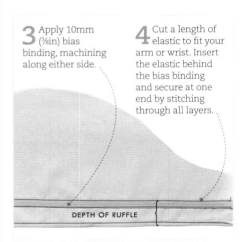

3 Apply 10mm (⅜in) bias binding, machining along either side.

4 Cut a length of elastic to fit your arm or wrist. Insert the elastic behind the bias binding and secure at one end by stitching through all layers.

DEPTH OF RUFFLE

5 Push up the bias binding along the elastic to tighten the edge of the sleeve to fit the arm or wrist. Secure at the other end by machining.

Wrong side of sleeve

6 To complete, join the sleeve seam, matching through the elastic and casing.

7 Press the seam open, then turn the sleeve through the armhole to the right side. You can adjust the ruffles if they are not evenly placed.

ELASTICATED EDGE WITH A HEADING

Difficulty level ✹✹✹✹✹

This is an alternative method for making a ruffle or heading at the end of a sleeve, using a casing that is part of the sleeve.

1 Make up the sleeve and press the seam open.

2 Tack a line 2.5cm (1in) from the raw edge – this will be the casing.

3 From the first tacked line, measure the required depth of the heading and tack along this line.

4 Turn up the raw edge of the fabric to the wrong side of the sleeve along the second line of tacks.

5 Turn the fabric under to make a casing along the first tacking line.

6 Work two rows of machining 1cm (⅜in) apart for the elastic, leaving a gap in the top line of stitching where the elastic will be inserted.

7 Cut a piece of elastic to fit the arm or wrist. Insert it into the gap between the two stitching lines. Secure the ends of the elastic together.

8 Turn the sleeve through to the right side and even out the elasticated gathers.

TACKING STITCHES **p.89** ● SEAM NEATENING **p.95** ● RUFFLES **pp.142–144**

ELASTICATED SLEEVE EDGE

The ends of sleeves on workwear and children's clothes are often elasticated to produce a neat and functional finish. Elastic that is 12mm (½in) or 25mm (1in) wide will be most suitable.

Difficulty level ★★☆☆☆

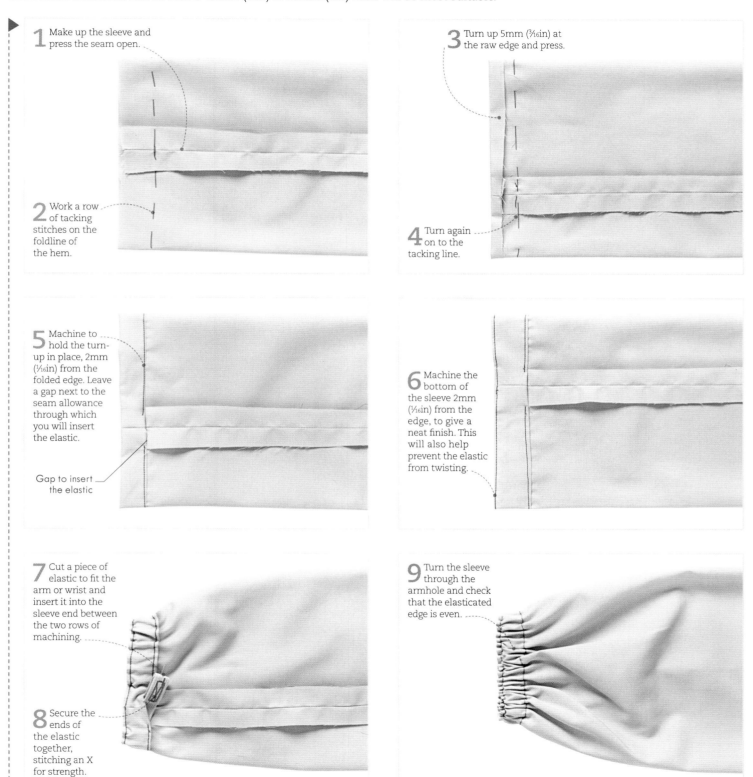

1 Make up the sleeve and press the seam open.

2 Work a row of tacking stitches on the foldline of the hem.

3 Turn up 5mm (³⁄₁₆in) at the raw edge and press.

4 Turn again on to the tacking line.

5 Machine to hold the turn-up in place, 2mm (¹⁄₁₆in) from the folded edge. Leave a gap next to the seam allowance through which you will insert the elastic.

Gap to insert the elastic

6 Machine the bottom of the sleeve 2mm (¹⁄₁₆in) from the edge, to give a neat finish. This will also help prevent the elastic from twisting.

7 Cut a piece of elastic to fit the arm or wrist and insert it into the sleeve end between the two rows of machining.

8 Secure the ends of the elastic together, stitching an X for strength.

9 Turn the sleeve through the armhole and check that the elasticated edge is even.

MACHINED HEMS p.266

SLEEVE EDGE WITH RUFFLE

Difficulty level ✱✱✱✱✱

A ruffle at the end of a sleeve is a very feminine finish. It is used on a set-in sleeve that may or may not have a gathered sleeve head.

1 First, cut out the ruffle according to your pattern.

WRONG SIDE OF FABRIC

2 Neaten the outer edge of the ruffle with a 3-thread overlock stitch or a zigzag stitch.

3 Turn the neatened edge to the wrong side of the ruffle and machine in place.

4 Join the short ends of the ruffle together, right side to right side, using a 1.5cm (⅝in) seam allowance.

5 Neaten the seam edge using your preferred method, then press the seam open.

6 Place the ruffle at the end of the sleeve, right side to right side, matching seams and notches.

7 Stretch the ruffle to fit, then pin in place.

8 Machine the ruffle to the sleeve around the sleeve edge, using a 1.5cm (⅝in) seam allowance.

9 Neaten the seam allowance then press it towards the ruffle.

WRONG SIDE OF FABRIC

10 Turn the sleeve through the armhole to the right side.

PRESSING AIDS **pp.28–29** • HOW TO APPLY A FUSIBLE INTERFACING **p.54** • HOW TO MAKE A PLAIN SEAM **p.94**

FACED SLEEVE EDGE

Difficulty level ✷✷✶✶✶

Adding a facing to the end of a sleeve produces a very clean and bulk-free finish. This technique is particularly suitable for dress sleeves and sleeves on unlined jackets.

1 Apply a fusible interfacing to the facing.

WRONG SIDE OF FABRIC

2 Join the short ends of the facing together, right side to right side, then press the seam open.

3 Turn up one long edge of the facing and pin.

4 Machine the turned-up edge and press the folded edge flat.

RIGHT SIDE OF FABRIC

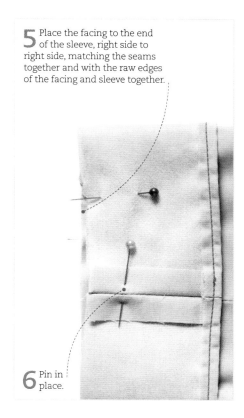

5 Place the facing to the end of the sleeve, right side to right side, matching the seams together and with the raw edges of the facing and sleeve together.

6 Pin in place.

7 Trim the facing seam allowance down to half its width.

8 Press the whole seam allowance towards the facing. Use a seam roll to help the pressing.

9 Understitch the seam allowance to the facing.

10 Turn the facing through to the inside of the sleeve.

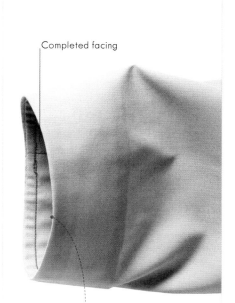

Completed facing

11 Press the sleeve edge on the right side.

SEAM NEATENING **p.95** • REDUCING SEAM BULK **pp.108–109** • STITCH FINISHES **p.109**

TECHNIQUES

CUFFS AND OPENINGS

A cuff and an opening are ways of producing a sleeve finish that will fit neatly around the wrist. The opening enables the hand to fit through the end of the sleeve, and it allows the sleeve to be rolled up. There are various types of cuffs – single or double, and with pointed or curved edges. All cuffs are interfaced, with the interfacing attached to the upper cuff. The upper cuff is sewn to the sleeve.

DIRECTORY OF CUFFS AND OPENINGS

SINGLE CUFF WITH FACED OPENING (p.230)

SINGLE CUFF WITH BOUND OPENING (p.231)

SHIRT CUFF WITH PLACKET OPENING (p.232–233 AND p.235)

LAPPED CUFF (p.234)

DOUBLE CUFF (p.235)

HOW TO APPLY A FUSIBLE INTERFACING **p.54** • TACKING STITCHES **p.89**

ONE-PIECE CUFF

A one-piece cuff is cut out from the fabric in one piece, and in most cases only half of it is interfaced. The exception is the one-piece double cuff (see p.235).

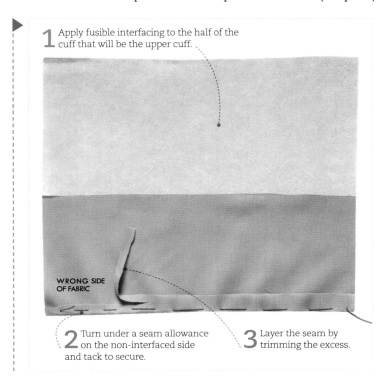

1 Apply fusible interfacing to the half of the cuff that will be the upper cuff.

2 Turn under a seam allowance on the non-interfaced side and tack to secure.

3 Layer the seam by trimming the excess.

WRONG SIDE OF FABRIC

4 Fold the cuff in half, right side to right side.

Seam allowance free on interfaced side of cuff

5 Machine stitch down the two short ends.

6 Layer the seam by trimming one edge, and clip the corners.

WRONG SIDE OF FABRIC

Seam allowance ready to stitch on to sleeve

7 Turn the cuff through to the right side and press.

RIGHT SIDE OF FABRIC

TWO-PIECE CUFF

Some cuffs are cut in two pieces: an upper cuff and an under cuff. The upper cuff piece is interfaced.

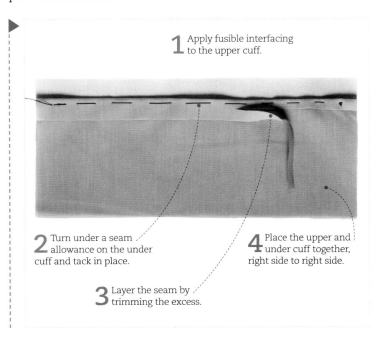

1 Apply fusible interfacing to the upper cuff.

2 Turn under a seam allowance on the under cuff and tack in place.

3 Layer the seam by trimming the excess.

4 Place the upper and under cuff together, right side to right side.

5 Machine stitch the two short ends together. Also machine together along the lower edge.

Seam allowance on upper cuff free

6 Layer the seam and clip the corner.

7 Turn the cuff through to the right side and press. The seam allowance at the top is ready to be stitched to the sleeve.

HOW TO MAKE A PLAIN SEAM p.94 • **REDUCING SEAM BULK pp.108—109**

FACED OPENING

Difficulty level ★★✱✱✱

Adding a facing to the area of the sleeve where the opening is to be is a neat method of finishing. This type of opening is appropriate to use with a one-piece cuff.

1 Turn under the long edges and one short edge on the facing by about 3mm (⅛in). Machine stitch to secure.

2 Place the right side of the facing to the right side of the sleeve at the appropriate sleeve markings.

3 Stitch vertically up the centre of the facing. Take one stitch across the top and then stitch straight down the other side. Keep a distance of about 5mm (³⁄₁₆in) between the stitching lines at the raw edge.

4 Slash between the stitching lines.

5 Snip with small scissors into the corners.

6 Turn the facing to the wrong side of the sleeve and press.

7 The finished opening on the right side.

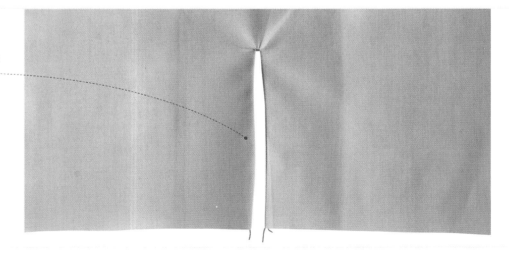

BOUND OPENING

On a fabric that frays badly or a sleeve that may get a great deal of wear, a strong bound opening is a good idea. It involves binding a slash in the sleeve with a matching bias strip.

1 Stay stitch the split in the sleeve.

2 Slash between the stay stitching lines.

The bias strip

WRONG SIDE OF FABRIC

3 Working on the right side of the sleeve, pin the bias strip along the stay stitching lines. To stitch around the top of the split, open the split out into a straight line.

WRONG SIDE OF FABRIC

5 Hand stitch to secure.

4 Wrap the bias strip, edge turned under, to the wrong side and pin in place.

WRONG SIDE OF FABRIC

6 Allow the bias strip to close. One side of the bias strip will fold under and the other will extend.

7 Secure the top fold in the bias with a double stitch.

RIGHT SIDE OF FABRIC

8 Tailor tack to aid the placement of the cuff.

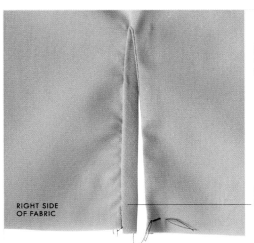

RIGHT SIDE OF FABRIC

9 The finished bias-bound opening.

Bias strip folded and secured at top

MACHINED HEMS p.266

TECHNIQUES

SHIRT SLEEVE PLACKET

Difficulty level ✱✱✱✱✱

This is the opening that is found on the sleeves of men's shirts and tailored ladies' shirts.
It looks complicated but is straightforward if you take it one step at a time.

1 Cut out the placket and mark the pattern dots with tailor's tacks. Only these four tailor's tacks are required.

2 Place the placket to the shirt sleeve, right side of the placket to the wrong side of the sleeve, matching the tailor's tacks.

3 Pin in place.

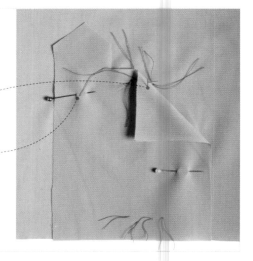

4 Machine a rectangular box, joining the tailor's tacks together. Make sure the rows of stitching are parallel. Remove the tacks.

5 Slash through the placket and sleeve straight down the centre, between the rows of stitching.

6 Slash into the corners of the rectangle.

7 Open up the placket to the right side of the fabric and press. You will have a rectangular gap with sharp corners.

8 Fold back the long edge of the shorter side of the placket.

9 Place the folded edge on top of the machine stitching and pin in place.

10 Machine the folded edge. Stop the machining at the top of the gap.

11 Fold the other side of the placket across the shorter side.

12 Press under the long edge. Fold back so that the pressed-under edge is on the machining line. Pin in place.

13 Fold under the top pointed end, following the cut edge, and press.

14 Machine the long folded edge in place. Make sure the underside of the placket is not caught in the stitching.

15 Continue the machining around the point.

16 Stitch an X through the point.

17 Pull all the ends of the machining threads through to the reverse and tie off.

18 On the right side, the completed placket will be neatly stitched.

MACHINED HEMS p.266

ATTACHING A CUFF

Difficulty level ✳✳✳✳✳

There are various types of cuff that can be attached to sleeve openings. The one-piece lapped cuff works well with a bound or faced opening. A two-piece shirt cuff is usually on a sleeve with a placket opening, but works equally well on a bound opening. The double cuff, or French cuff, is for men's dress shirts and tailored shirts for both ladies and men, and may be cut in one or two sections. It is usually found with a placket or bound opening.

▶ **LAPPED CUFF**

1 Apply fusible interfacing to the upper half of the cuff. Pin the interfaced end of the cuff to the sleeve end, right side to right side.

Seam allowance extending

2 Machine the cuff to the sleeve using a 1.5cm (⅝in) seam allowance.

3 Trim the sleeve side of the seam down by half. Press the seam towards the cuff.

Overlap

4 Fold the non-interfaced edge of the cuff over to the wrong side by 1.5cm (⅝in) and press along the non-attached edge.

5 Fold the cuff to itself, right side to right side, so the folded side of the cuff comes to the sleeve-to-cuff seamline.

6 Stitch one of the short ends in line with the opening.

7 Stitch the other short end along from the sleeve-to-cuff seam and then down the cuff.

8 Remove the corners. Press the seams open.

9 Turn the cuff to the right side. Push the corners out to points.

10 On the inside, hand stitch the folded edge with a flat fell or blind hem stitch.

11 Make a buttonhole on the upper side of the cuff.

12 Sew a button on the underside of the cuff.

HOW TO APPLY A FUSIBLE INTERFACING p.54 ● REDUCING SEAM BULK **pp.108–109** ● STITCH FINISHES **p.109**

▶ SHIRT CUFF

1 Apply fusible interfacing to the upper cuff. Place it to the sleeve end, right side to right side, with a seam allowance extending at either end. Pin in place.

Upper cuff

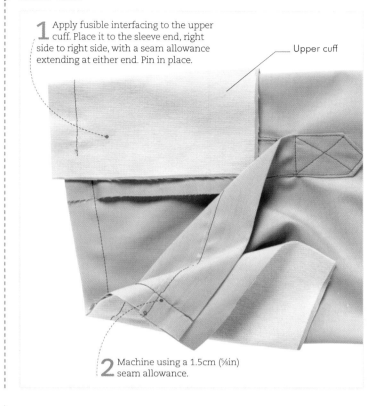

2 Machine using a 1.5cm (⅝in) seam allowance.

3 Place the right side of the under cuff to the right side of the upper cuff. Machine together around three sides, stitching in line with the sleeve opening.

Under cuff

Upper cuff

4 Trim down the under cuff side of the seam.

5 Remove bulk from the corners. Press.

6 Turn the cuff to the right side and press.

7 Turn under the raw edge of the under cuff and place to the end of the sleeve. With this type of cuff, the edge is machined in place.

8 Add buttonholes to the upper cuff and attach buttons to the under cuff.

▶ DOUBLE CUFF

1 Apply interfacing to the whole of the cuff. Attach the cuff to the sleeve end, right side to right side, using a 1.5cm (⅝in) seam allowance.

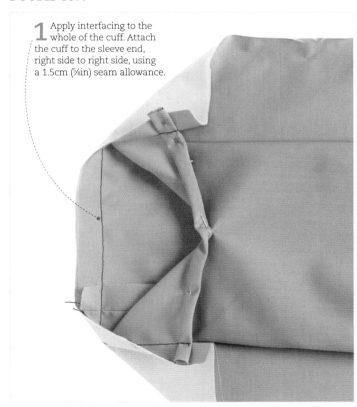

2 Fold the cuff back on to itself, right side to right side.

3 Machine stitch the two sides in line with the sleeve opening.

4 Trim the bulk from the seams and corners.

5 Press, then turn the cuff through to the right side.

6 Fold the cuff up in half so that it is doubled.

7 Hand stitch inside to finish the other edge of the cuff.

8 Insert a buttonhole through the top two layers of the cuff and sew a button on to the under cuff.

BUTTONHOLES **pp.304–311**

POCKETS

Pockets can be functional or just for show, and are essential on some items of clothing. Making a pocket requires a little patience, but the finished result is well worth it.

POCKETS

Pockets come in lots of shapes and formats. Some, such as patch pockets, paper bag pockets, and jetted pockets with a flap, are external and can be decorative, while others, including front hip pockets, are more discreet and hidden from view. They can be made from the same fabric as the garment or from a contrasting fabric. Whether casual or tailored, all pockets are functional.

DIRECTORY OF POCKETS

PATCH POCKET
(pp.239–242)

PAPER BAG POCKET
(p.243)

WELT POCKET
(p.244)

WELT POCKET ON
TROUSER BACK (p.245)

JETTED POCKET
WITH A FLAP (pp.246–247)

IN-SEAM POCKET
(pp.248–249)

FRONT HIP POCKET
(p.250)

CHINO POCKET
(p.251)

KANGAROO POCKET
(p.252)

HOW TO APPLY A FUSIBLE INTERFACING **p.54** • PATTERN MARKING **pp.82—83** • HAND STITCHES **pp.90—91**

UNLINED PATCH POCKET

Difficulty level ★★✳✳✳

An unlined patch pocket is one of the most popular types of pocket. It can be found on garments of all kinds and be made from a wide variety of fabrics. On lightweight fabrics, such as that used for a shirt pocket, interfacing is not required, but on medium and heavier fabrics it is advisable to apply a fusible interfacing.

1 If needed, apply an interfacing to the pocket fabric.

2 Mark the fold lines with tailor's tacks.

WRONG SIDE OF POCKET

3 Overlock or zigzag stitch the edge to neaten.

4 Fold the top of the pocket down, folding where indicated by the tailor's tacks.

5 Stitch down the sides of the turned-down top.

RIGHT SIDE OF POCKET

6 Stitch a long machine stitch through the corners.

8 Remove the top corner.

7 Trim away the fabric in the seam allowance in the curves.

RIGHT SIDE OF POCKET

9 Turn the top edge over to the wrong side.

10 Pull up the stitching in the curves to tighten. Press.

11 Turn under the curved edges.

WRONG SIDE OF POCKET

12 Tack through the bottom edge and curves to secure.

13 Using a herringbone stitch, hand stitch the top edge to the wrong side of the pocket.

14 Press. The pocket is now ready to attach.

RIGHT SIDE OF POCKET

SEAM NEATENING **p.95** ● REDUCING SEAM BULK **pp.108–109**

TECHNIQUES

SELF-LINED PATCH POCKET

Difficulty level ✶✶✶✶✶

If a patch pocket is to be self-lined, it needs to be cut with the top edge of the pocket on a fold. Like an unlined pocket, if you are using a lightweight fabric an interfacing may not be required, whereas for medium-weight fabrics a fusible interfacing is advisable. A self-lined patch pocket is not suitable for heavy fabrics.

1 Cut the pocket fabric and apply a fusible interfacing, if needed.

2 Fold the pocket in half, right side to right side. Pin to secure.

3 Machine around the three open sides of the pocket. Leave a gap of about 3cm (1¼in) for turning through.

4 Remove bulk from the corners by trimming.

5 Trim one side of the seam allowance down to half its width.

6 Use pinking shears to trim the corners.

7 Turn the pocket through the gap to the right side. Press.

8 Hand stitch the gap in the seam using a flat fell or blind hem stitch. The pocket is now ready to be attached.

LINED PATCH POCKET

Difficulty level ✶✶✶✶✶

If a self-lined patch pocket is likely to be too bulky, then a lined pocket is the answer. It is advisable to interface the pocket fabric.

1 Cut the pocket fabric and apply interfacing. Cut the lining fabric. The lining will be shorter than the pocket fabric.

2 Place the lining top edge to the upper edge of the pocket and machine together. Leave a gap of about 3cm (1¼in) in the seam for turning through.

3 Press the pocket-to-lining seam open.

4 Bring the bottom edges of the pocket together.

5 Pin through the corners and sides.

6 Stitch around the other three open sides of the pocket to attach the lining to the pocket fabric.

7 Remove the corners.

8 Use pinking shears to trim the curves.

9 Turn through the gap left in the seam to the right side. Press.

10 Hand stitch the gap with a flat fell or blind hem stitch.

11 The lined patch pocket is ready to be attached.

SQUARE PATCH POCKET

It is possible to have a patch pocket with square corners. This requires mitring the corners to reduce the bulk. Use a fusible interfacing on medium-weight fabrics.

Difficulty level ✱✱✱✱✱

1 Cut the pocket and apply interfacing, if needed. Neaten the upper edge of the pocket with overlock or zigzag stitching.

2 Fold over the upper edge and stitch down the sides.

3 Fold in the other three edges and press to crease.

4 Remove the top corners.

5 Fold in the bottom corners, then fold across these to give creases for the mitres.

6 Stitch the crease lines together in each bottom corner to mitre it.

7 Cut off the surplus fabric, then press the corner seam open with the tip of the iron.

WRONG SIDE OF FABRIC

Flat mitred corners

8 Turn the edges of the pocket to the wrong side.

9 The finished pocket is now ready to be attached.

MITRED CORNERS **p.269**

TECHNIQUES

ATTACHING A PATCH POCKET

Difficulty level ✱✱✱✱✱

To attach a pocket successfully, accurate pattern marking is essential. It is best to do this by means of tailor's tacks or even trace tacking. If you are using a check or stripe fabric, the pocket fabric must align with the checks or stripes on the garment.

1 Mark the pocket placement lines on the garment with tailor's tacks.

2 Take the completed pocket and place it to the fabric, matching the corners with the tailor's tacks. Pin in position.

3 To make sure the pocket remains in the correct position, tack around the edge along the sides and bottom. Keep the tacking stitches close to the finished edge of the pocket.

4 Machine stitch about 1mm (¹⁄₃₂in) from the edge of the pocket.

5 Remove the tacking stitches. Press.

6 Alternatively, the pocket can be hand stitched in place, using a slip hem stitch into the underside of the pocket seam. Do not pull on the thread too tightly or the pocket will wrinkle.

REINFORCING POCKET CORNERS

Difficulty level ✱✱✱✱✱

On any patch pocket it is essential to reinforce the upper corners as these take all the strain when the pocket is being used. There are several ways to do this, some of which are quite decorative.

▶ **REVERSE STITCH**

1 Reinforce the corner with a reverse stitch. Make sure the stitches lie on top of one another.

2 Pull the threads to the reverse to tie off.

▶ **DIAGONAL STITCH**

1 This is a technique used primarily on shirts. When machining the pocket in place, stitch along horizontally for four stitches.

2 Turn and stitch diagonally back to the side, to create a triangular shape in the corner.

▶ **ZIGZAG STITCH**

1 Using a small zigzag stitch, width 1.0 and length 1.0, stitch diagonally across the corner.

2 Make a feature of this stitch by using a thread in a contrasting colour.

▶ **PARALLEL ZIGZAG STITCH**

1 Place a patch on the wrong side of the garment, behind the pocket corner, to stitch into for strength.

2 Using a small zigzag stitch, width 1.0 and length 1.0, machine a short vertical line next to the straight stitching.

PATTERN MARKING **pp.82–83** ● TACKING STITCHES **p.89** ● HAND STITCHES **pp.90–91** ● STITCHES MADE WITH A MACHINE **pp.92–93**

PAPER BAG POCKET

This pocket is so-named because it resembles a paper bag. It is found on cargo trousers and also bags. The pocket is attached to the garment with a gusset, which is a straight strip of fabric. A paper bag pocket is best made in a light or medium-weight fabric.

Difficulty level ✳✳✳✳✳

1 First neaten the upper edge of the pocket. Fold it over twice, making a double hem. Stitch along the edge close to the fold.

2 Place the gusset to the outer edge of the pocket, right side to right side.

3 Fold under the ends of the gusset and match the ends to the edge of the pocket.

4 Stitch the gusset to the pocket along the sides and bottom.

5 Clip the seam allowance in the curves.

6 Turn under the raw edge of the gusset. Mitre the corners. Tack to secure.

7 Place the tacked edge to the garment. Match the edge to the tailor-tack markings on the garment. Pin.

8 Machine the edge of the gusset to the garment. Stitch close to the folded edge.

9 Remove the tacking.

10 At the top edge, pleat the gusset under the pocket and place the top corner of the pocket and gusset together.

11 Stitch diagonally across the upper corners through the pocket, gusset, and garment. Leave the lower curved edges loose.

STITCHING CORNERS AND CURVES **pp.102–103** ● REDUCING SEAM BULK **pp.108–109**

TECHNIQUES

WELT POCKET

A welt pocket features a small, straight flap that faces upwards on a garment, with the pocket opening behind the flap. This kind of pocket is found on waistcoats and is the usual breast pocket on men's jackets, as well as being used on coats.

Difficulty level ★★★★★

RIGHT SIDE OF FABRIC

1 Mark the placement lines on the main fabric using trace tacks.

2 Apply fusible interfacing to the welt. Fold it in half, right side to right side, matching the tailor's tacks.

Raw edge

Fold

4 Layer the seams and remove the corners.

3 Machine the two short ends, following the shape of the welt.

RIGHT SIDE OF FABRIC

5 Turn the welt to the right side and press.

6 Align the top of the welt with the top line of tacks. Machine along the lower line of tacks. Trim away the bulk.

7 Place the lining pocket over the welt, right side to right side. Match the pattern markings.

8 Tack the lining in place over the welt.

9 Machine the lining over the welt. The upper row of machining will be shorter than the lower row, producing angled sides.

10 Slash through the centre of the machine-stitched box. Slash into the corners.

11 Push the lining through to the wrong side.

12 Pull the remaining lining through from the wrong side.

13 On the reverse, bring the lining together and machine around the edge to make the pocket bag.

WRONG SIDE OF FABRIC

14 The finished welt pocket on the right side.

RIGHT SIDE OF FABRIC

HOW TO APPLY A FUSIBLE INTERFACING **p.54** ● PATTERN MARKING **pp.82–83** ● TACKING STITCHES **p.89**

WELT POCKET ON TROUSER BACK

Difficulty level **★★★★**✳

A welt pocket on the back of a pair of trousers features a slim, elegant welt. For this reason, its construction is slightly different and you will need to reinforce the finished welt with stitches on the right side.

RIGHT SIDE OF FABRIC

1 Reinforce the wrong side of the pocket area with fusible interfacing (not shown on these samples).

2 On the right side, mark parallel stitching lines for the welt according to your pattern with tacks.

3 Apply fusible interfacing to the welt. Use tailor's tacks to transfer the dot markings on the welt pattern.

4 Fold the welt in half lengthways, wrong side to wrong side. Press.

5 Place the welt on the lower stitching line with the raw edges at the top. Align the tailor's tacks with the lower stitching line. Pin in place.

RIGHT SIDE OF FABRIC

6 Machine the welt onto the tacked stitching line between the tailor's tacks.

7 Trim back the seam to 5mm (³⁄₁₆in).

RIGHT SIDE OF FABRIC

8 Place the pocket fabric on the upper stitching line and pin in place.

9 Place the pocket lining on the lower stitching line over the welt. Pin in place.

RIGHT SIDE OF FABRIC

10 Machine both the pocket fabric and lining in place along the marked stitching lines.

11 The two rows must be parallel and exactly the same length as the stitched welt. Do not stitch across the short ends.

12 Trim away the bulk from both seams.

WRONG SIDE OF FABRIC

13 On the wrong side, slash through the centre of the welt.

14 Slash into the corners as shown.

WRONG SIDE OF FABRIC

15 Pull both pocket pieces and the welt through to the wrong side.

16 Make sure the triangles at the short ends are also on the wrong side.

17 Press in place with the welt over the triangles.

RIGHT SIDE OF FABRIC

18 Fold the pocket fabric down onto the pocket lining. Stitch the two pocket sections together on three sides to make a pocket sack or bag. Make sure you catch in the triangle end of the slash and the end of the welts.

19 Trim the corners to reduce bulk.

RIGHT SIDE OF FABRIC

20 On the right side, set the machine to a zigzag stitch, width 2.5 and length 0.5, and stitch across the short ends of the welt to reinforce.

STITCHES MADE WITH A MACHINE **pp.92–93** ● REDUCING SEAM BULK **pp.108–09**

JETTED POCKET WITH A FLAP

Difficulty level ✳✳✳✳✳

This type of pocket is found on tailored jackets and coats and men's wear. It is straightforward to make. The main components are the welts (the strips that make the edges of the pocket), the flap, and the lining that makes the pocket bag.

1 First make the upper welt. Apply fusible interfacing to the wrong side.

2 Fold in half lengthways, wrong side to wrong side. Tack down the centre to secure.

3 Next, make the pocket flap. Apply fusible interfacing to the wrong side of the fabric.

4 Place the right side of the lining to the right side of the flap. Pin, then machine around three sides, leaving the top edge open.

5 Remove the fabric from the bottom corners.

6 Turn the flap through to the right side. Press. Make sure the lining does not show on the right side.

7 If you like, top-stitch the flap around the three sides.

8 On the welt, trim the raw edge of the seam allowance down to half its width.

9 Place the welt to the right side of the pocket. Align the raw edges. Make sure the welt overhangs the flap by equal amounts at each end.

10 Machine together through the centre of the welt.

11 Place the right side of the welt and flap to the right side of the garment. Match the ends of the flap to the upper row of tailor's tacks on the garment. Pin in place.

12 Machine to the garment along the stitching line that is holding the welt and flap together.

13 Make up the lower welt in the same fabric as the upper welt.

14 Place the lower welt to the garment below the upper welt and flap.

15 Machine stitch in place. Make sure the two rows of stitching are exactly the same length. Also make sure the stitching lines are parallel.

16 Take the lining and press in half, right side to right side, matching the tailor's tacks, to produce a centre crease.

17 Place the right side of the lining over the welt and flaps, matching the tailor's tacks. The crease line should be sitting between the two welts. Pin in place.

HOW TO APPLY A FUSIBLE INTERFACING **p.54** ● PATTERN MARKING **pp.82–83** ● TACKING STITCHES **p.89** ● STITCHES MADE WITH A MACHINE **pp.92–93** ● REDUCING SEAM BULK **pp.108–109**

18 Tack the lining in position. Keep the tacking stitches about 1.5cm (⅝in) from the tailor's tacks that mark the welts.

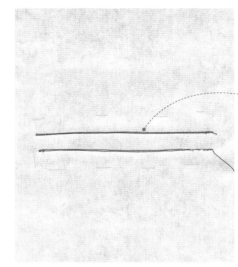

19 Working from the wrong side, machine the lining in place by stitching over the stitching lines that are holding the welts in place. The two rows of stitching should be exactly the same length. Secure at both ends.

20 Turn to the right side and remove the tacking.

21 Slash through just the lining along the pressed crease line. Cut through to the edge of the lining.

22 On the reverse, slash through the fabric of the garment. The slash line should cut through just the fabric and not the welts or flaps.

23 Slash into the corners right to the stitching lines.

24 Pull the lining through the slash to the wrong side. Push through the ends of the welts. The pocket flap will turn down.

25 To make the pocket, pull the ends of the welts out away from the slash lines. A small triangle of fabric should be on top of these welts.

26 Stitch across the welts and the triangle and around the pocket. Use pinking shears to neaten the seams on the lining.

27 Press everything in place, using a pressing cloth if necessary.

IN-SEAM POCKET

In trousers and skirts, the pocket is sometimes disguised in the seam line. There are two ways of making an in-seam pocket, either by adding a separate pocket shape or by the pocket shape being cut as part of the main fabric.

Difficulty level ✶✶✶✶✶

▶ SEPARATE IN-SEAM POCKET

1 Neaten the seam allowance on the garment.

FRONT PIECE OF GARMENT

2 Neaten the straight edge of the pocket.

3 Place the pocket to the garment, right side to right side. Match the tailor's tacks and the neatened edges. Pin in place.

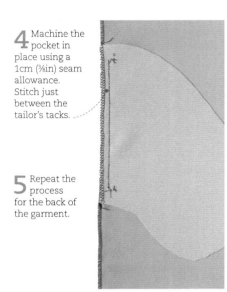

4 Machine the pocket in place using a 1cm (⅜in) seam allowance. Stitch just between the tailor's tacks.

5 Repeat the process for the back of the garment.

6 Open the pocket out and press the seam towards the pocket.

7 Place the back section of the garment to the front, right side to right side. Match the seams together above and below the pocket.

8 Stitch a 1.5cm (⅝in) seam to join the front and back of the garment together. Make sure the seam stitching extends past the pocket stitching before stopping.

9 Stitch around the pocket to join the two pieces together. Stop the stitching for the pocket at the pocket-to-garment stitching line.

10 Neaten the raw edges of the pocket.

11 On the garment back, clip the seam allowance to the pocket stitching line.

12 Press the seam open. Press the pocket towards the front of the garment.

13 On the right side, the pocket opening is discreet.

HOW TO APPLY A FUSIBLE INTERFACING p.54 ● **PATTERN MARKING pp.82–83** ● **TACKING STITCHES p.89**

▶ **ALL-IN-ONE IN-SEAM POCKET**

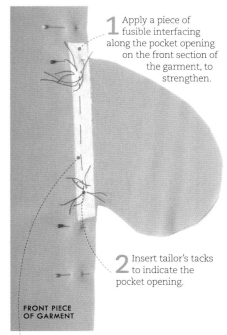

1 Apply a piece of fusible interfacing along the pocket opening on the front section of the garment, to strengthen.

2 Insert tailor's tacks to indicate the pocket opening.

FRONT PIECE OF GARMENT

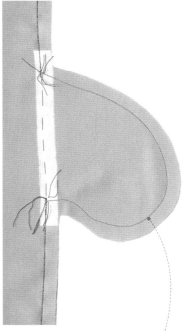

3 Place the back and front of the garment together, right side to right side. Tack the pocket opening closed over the interfacing, stitching between the tailor's tacks.

4 Stitch the back and front together with a 1.5cm (⅝in) seam allowance, above and below the pocket opening. Stop the stitching at the tailor's tack points.

5 Stitch around the pocket to join the two pieces. Start and finish the stitching at the tailor's tack points.

6 Clip the seam allowances above and below the pocket extension.

BACK PIECE OF GARMENT

7 Press the seams open. Neaten the edges of the seam allowances.

8 Neaten the raw edges of the seam allowances on the pocket together.

9 Remove the tacking on the interfacing. Press the pocket towards the front.

FRONT PIECE OF GARMENT

10 This is how the all-in-one pocket looks on the right side.

SEAM NEATENING **p.95** ● REDUCING SEAM BULK **pp.108–109**

FRONT HIP POCKET

Difficulty level ✱✱✱✱✳

On many trousers and casual skirts, the pocket is placed on the hipline. It can be low on the hipline or cut quite high as on jeans. The construction is the same for all types of hip pockets. When inserted at an angle, hip pockets can slim the figure.

1 Apply a piece of fusible tape on the garment along the line of the pocket.

WRONG SIDE OF GARMENT FRONT

2 Place the pocket lining to the front of the garment, right side to right side. Match any notches that are on the seam. Pin in place.

RIGHT SIDE OF GARMENT FRONT

3 Machine the lining in place taking a 1.5cm (⅝in) seam allowance.

4 Trim the lining side of the seam allowance down to half its width.

5 Open out the pocket and press the seam towards the lining.

6 Turn the lining to the inside. Press so that the lining is not visible on the outside.

7 Top-stitch 5mm (³⁄₁₆in) from the edge.

RIGHT SIDE OF GARMENT FRONT

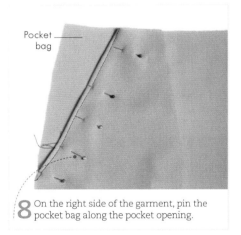

Pocket bag

8 On the right side of the garment, pin the pocket bag along the pocket opening.

9 Take the side front section that incorporates the pocket bag and place to the lining pocket section, right side to right side. Match any seams and tailor's tacks. Pin in place.

WRONG SIDE OF GARMENT

10 Machine the pocket bag together using a 1.5cm (⅝in) seam allowance. Press.

11 Neaten the raw edges of the seam allowance around the pocket.

12 Neaten the side seam allowance, stitching from the top down. Make sure that the fabric lies flat where it joins on to the side seam.

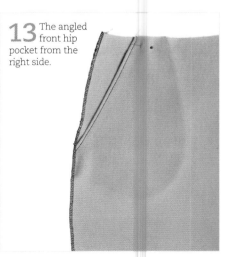

13 The angled front hip pocket from the right side.

CHINO POCKET

Difficulty level ✶✶✶✶✶

This is the style of pocket found on the front of chino trousers and jeans, but it can also be applied to skirts. The pocket is sometimes curved in shape rather than angular, as shown here. This pocket features a facing, which gives it a neat finish at the opening edge.

1 Apply fusible interfacing to the wrong side of the pocket facing.

Pocket facing

2 Neaten the raw edge along the bottom of the facing.

3 Tack the pocket facing right side up to the pocket lining.

4 Machine the pocket facing in place along the bottom edge only, next to the neatened edge.

Pocket lining

5 Place the pocket facing and lining right side to right side on the trouser or skirt front. Stitch together along the top edge.

6 Clip into the corner and along the top of the seam.

7 Trim the pocket side of the seam to half its width.

WRONG SIDE OF FACING AND POCKET LINING

RIGHT SIDE OF GARMENT FRONT

8 Turn the facing and pocket lining to the wrong side. Press in place.

WRONG SIDE OF GARMENT FRONT

9 On the right side of the garment, top-stitch using a 3.0 stitch length.

RIGHT SIDE OF GARMENT FRONT

10 On the wrong side of the skirt front, place the pocket fabric over the facing and lining.

11 Stitch around the pocket sack to join the lining to the pocket fabric.

Pocket fabric

WRONG SIDE OF GARMENT FRONT

12 Stitch the side seam together, through the skirt and pocket, using an overlock or zigzag stitch. The seam is left loose in order to allow extra room for the pocket.

KANGAROO POCKET

Difficulty level ★★☆☆☆

This is a variation on a patch pocket. It is a large pocket that is often found on aprons and the front of children's pinafore dresses. A half version of this pocket also features on casual jackets.

1 Neaten all the edges of the pocket.

2 Tie off the ends of the neatening at the corners.

3 Turn under the curved edges of the pocket to the wrong side. These will be the two pocket openings.

4 Press the curve and machine to secure.

WRONG SIDE OF POCKET

5 Turn under all the remaining edges of the pocket to the wrong side. If the fabric is bulky, mitre the corners. Press in place.

WRONG SIDE OF POCKET

6 Place the pocket to the garment, wrong side of the pocket to right side of the garment. Make sure the pocket is sitting flat and straight. Pin in place.

RIGHT SIDE OF FABRIC

RIGHT SIDE OF POCKET

7 Stitch the pocket along the upper edge.

8 Stitch the short straight sides and lower edge of the pocket. Press.

RIGHT SIDE OF FABRIC

RIGHT SIDE OF POCKET

9 Reinforce the corners of the pocket with a diagonal zigzag stitch.

10 If required, stitch one or two vertical lines down the centre of the pocket, to divide into two pockets. Press.

RIGHT SIDE OF FABRIC

RIGHT SIDE OF POCKET

MAKING A POCKET FLAP

On some styles of garment, there is no pocket, just a flap for decorative purposes. The flap is sewn where the pocket would be, but there is no opening under the flap. This is to reduce the bulk that would arise from having the rest of the pocket.

1 The flap consists of two pieces – a piece of lining and a piece of interfaced fabric. Place the two pieces together, right side to right side.

2 Match the tailor's tacks, then pin to secure.

Smooth curve stitched

3 Stitch the pocket flap together along three sides, using a 1cm (⅜in) seam allowance. Stitch through the tailor's tacks. Leave the upper edge open.

4 Layer the seam allowance, trimming away the lining side.

5 Remove the fabric from the point.

6 Use pinking shears to reduce the bulk through the curve. Press.

7 Turn the flap through to the right side. Push out the point.

8 Press the lining towards the back so that it does not show. Press a smooth curve.

9 Stitch across the upper open edge to hold together.

10 Place the flap to the garment, right side to right side. Match the edges of the flaps to the tailor's tacks on the garment.

11 Machine in place over the stitching line, holding the gap at the upper edge together.

12 Reduce the seam allowance by half. Press.

13 Press the flap into place. Do not pull too tight.

14 Top-stitch across the upper edge to secure.

STITCHING CORNERS AND CURVES **pp.102–103** • STITCH FINISHES **p.109** • REINFORCING POCKET CORNERS **p.242**

CHILD'S **REVERSIBLE JACKET**   *Difficulty level* ❋❋❋❋❋

This reversible jacket is the perfect opportunity for using fun craft cottons and co-ordinating prints. For practicality, choose a washable fabric. Light cottons would be great for spring and summer, while thicker fabrics such as needlecord or denim will provide added warmth in cooler months.

TECHNIQUES USED Attaching a patch pocket **p.242**, Flat sleeve construction **p.213**, Snaps **p.320**

YOU WILL NEED

- Pattern templates on pp.384–385. Choose your size using the Children's Sizing chart on p.368.
- For Fabric A and Fabric B: 150cm x 115cm (60 x 45in) or 100cm x 150cm (40 x 60in) light- to medium-weight dressmaking fabric. (Requirements for size 6–7 years; see pp.384–385 for other sizes).
- 50 x 90cm (20 x 36in) lightweight fusible interfacing
- 6 snap fasteners
- Matching thread

Front   Back

PIECES TO CUT

150cm (60in) folded

Back (unfold fabric and cut 1)   Front (cut 2)

Pocket (cut 2)   Pocket (cut 2)

Sleeve (cut 2)   Hood (cut 2)

Fold   Selvedge

Fabric A

115cm (45in) folded

Back (unfold fabric and cut 1)   Front (cut 2)

Sleeve (cut 2)

Hood (cut 2)   Pocket (cut 2)

Pocket (cut 2)

Fold   Selvedge

Fabric B

PREPARE THE PATTERN PIECES

1 Cut out the pattern pieces in the two fabrics.

2 Mark the position of the pockets on the four front pieces with tailor's tacks.

3 Apply a 5-cm (2-in) wide strip of interfacing to the centre front of each front jacket piece.

▶ **ASSEMBLE AND ATTACH THE POCKETS**

1 Place two different fabric pocket pieces together, right side to right side.

Gap for turning

WRONG SIDE OF POCKET PIECE

2 Machine all four sides using a seam allowance of 1.5cm (⅝in), leaving a 4cm (1½in) gap for turning on one edge.

3 Trim all four corners. Repeat to make four pockets.

3 Turn the pockets to the right side and press. Hand stitch the gap closed and fold down the top edge by 3cm (1¼in).

4 Using the tailor's tacks to position the pocket, top-stitch it to the jacket front, 6mm (¼in) from the edge.

5 Bar tack the flaps down. Repeat to attach one pocket to each front piece.

▶ **INSERT THE SLEEVES**

1 Machine stitch the front pieces to the back piece at the shoulder seams using a 1.5cm (⅝in) seam allowance. Press the seams open.

WRONG SIDE OF BACK PIECE

WRONG SIDE OF LEFT-HAND FRONT PIECE

WRONG SIDE OF RIGHT-HAND FRONT PIECE

TACKING STITCHES **p.89** ● HAND STITCHES **pp.90–91** ● REDUCING SEAM BULK **pp.108–109** ● TOP-STITCHING **p.109**

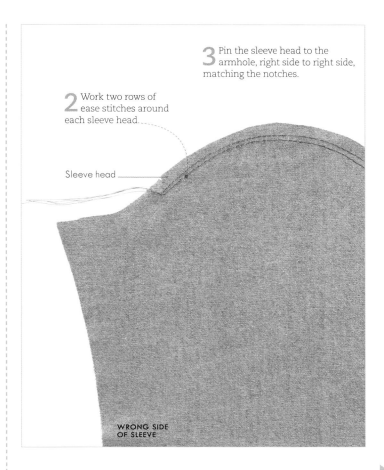

2 Work two rows of ease stitches around each sleeve head.

Sleeve head

3 Pin the sleeve head to the armhole, right side to right side, matching the notches.

WRONG SIDE OF SLEEVE

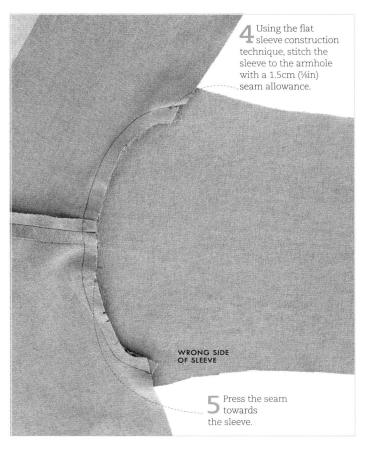

4 Using the flat sleeve construction technique, stitch the sleeve to the armhole with a 1.5cm (⅝in) seam allowance.

WRONG SIDE OF SLEEVE

5 Press the seam towards the sleeve.

6 Fold the garment and sleeve, right side to right side, bringing the side seams together. Align the underarm seam.

Underarm seam

7 Using a 1.5cm (⅝in) seam allowance, stitch the side seam and then continue along the sleeve.

8 Press the seam open and clip around the underarm.

Side seam

▶ **ATTACH THE HOOD**

1 With right sides together, machine the hood pieces together using a 1.5cm (⅝in) seam allowance.

2 Clip the seam and press it open.

WRONG SIDE OF HOOD

FLAT SLEEVE CONSTRUCTION **p.213** ● ATTACHING A PATCH POCKET **p.242**

3 Align the bottom edge of the hood with the top edge of the back and front pieces, right side to right side. Pin in place.

4 Stitch together using a 1.5cm (⅝in) seam allowance.

5 Clip the seam and press it open.

WRONG SIDE OF
RIGHT-HAND FRONT PIECE

WRONG SIDE OF
BACK PIECE

WRONG SIDE OF
LEFT-HAND FRONT PIECE

▶ ASSEMBLE THE JACKET

1 Make up the jacket in the second fabric, following the instructions above.

Hood

Centre front

Pockets

2 Place the two jackets together right side to right side, inserting one inside the other.

3 Machine around all the outer edges, from one side seam, up the centre front, around the hood, to the other side seam.

4 Leave a 15cm (6in) gap in the centre back hem for turning.

5 Clip the seams.

HAND STITCHES **pp.90–91** ● STITCHES MADE WITH A MACHINE **pp.92–93** ● REDUCING SEAM BULK **pp.108–109** ● TOP-STITCHING **p.109**

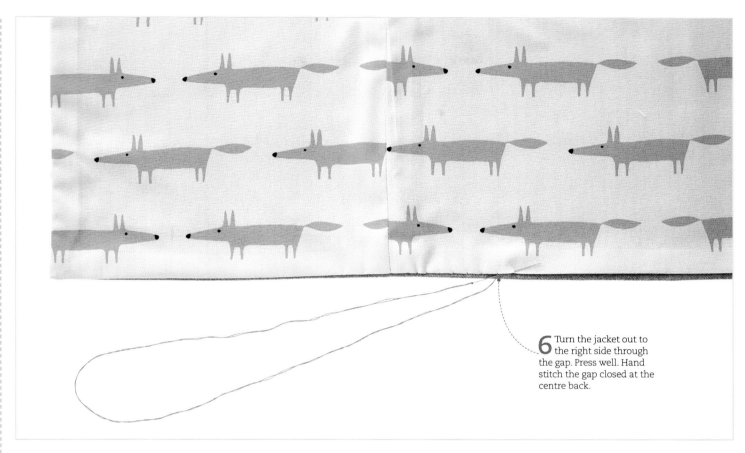

6 Turn the jacket out to the right side through the gap. Press well. Hand stitch the gap closed at the centre back.

7 Turn in the hem allowances on the sleeves and hand stitch the hem folds together.

▶ **ATTACH THE FASTENERS AND FINISH EDGES**

1 Attach the snaps in the positions marked on the pattern and following the manufacturer's instructions.

2 Top-stitch all around the jacket centre front, hood, and hems, 6mm (¼in) from the edge, using a contrasting thread, if desired.

SNAPS **p.320**

HEMS AND EDGES

The lower edge of a garment or of a curtain or other soft furnishing is normally finished with a hem. This is to give not only a neat finish but also to provide weight at the lower edge so that the garment or curtain hangs properly.

HEMS AND EDGES

The edge of a piece of fabric can be finished with a hem – which is normally used on garments – or with a decorative edge, which is used for crafts and soft furnishings as well as garments. Sometimes the style of what is being constructed dictates the finish that is used, and sometimes it is the fabric.

DIRECTORY OF HEMS

SINGLE-TURN HEM (p.266)

WRONG SIDE DURING STITCHING

RIGHT SIDE FINISHED HEM

BLIND HEM (p.266)

DOUBLE-TURN HEM (p.266)

ROLLED HEM (p.267)

MACHINED CURTAIN HEM (p.268)

FACED HEM (p.270)

BIAS-BOUND HEM (p.272)

INTERFACED HEM (p.273)

USEFUL EXTRAS **p.21** • TACKING STITCHES **p.89**

MARKING A HEMLINE

On a garment such as a skirt or a dress it is important that the hemline is level all around. Even if the fabric has been cut straight, some styles of skirt – such as A-line or circular – will "drop", which means that the hem edge is longer in some places. This is due to the fabric stretching where it is not on the straight of the grain. Poor posture will also cause a hem to hang unevenly.

▶ USING A RULER

1 You'll need a helper for this method. Put on the skirt or dress (without shoes). With the end of the ruler on the floor, measure straight up on to the skirt.

2 Use pins to mark where the crease line of the hem should be. Mark the hemline all the way around to the same point on the ruler.

▶ USING A DRESSMAKER'S DUMMY

1 Adjust the dummy to your height and measurements. Place the skirt or dress on the dummy.

2 Using the hem marker on the stand, mark the crease line of the hem. The hem marker will hold the fabric either side of the hemline.

Pin

3 Slide a pin through the slot in the marker, then gently release the marker.

TURNING UP A STRAIGHT HEM

Difficulty level ★★★★★

Once the crease line for the hem has been marked by the pins, you need to trim the hem allowance to a reasonable amount. Most straight hems are about 4cm (1½in) deep.

1 Gently press the crease line of the hem with the iron. Don't press too hard as you do not want a sharp crease.

2 Trim the seam allowance back to reduce the bulk. If wished, neaten the raw edge.

3 Turn up the hem at the crease. Match the seams together.

4 Tack the hem into position close to the crease line. The hem is now ready to be stitched in place by hand or machine.

TURNING UP A CURVED HEM

Difficulty level ★★★★★

When the hem on a shaped skirt is turned up, it will be fuller at the upper edge. This fullness will need to be eased out before the hem is stitched.

1 Mark the hemline, placing the pins vertically to avoid squashing the fullness out of the upper raw edge.

WRONG SIDE OF FABRIC

2 Tack the hem into position close to the crease line. Remove the pins.

3 Make a row of long machine stitches, length 5.0, close to the raw upper edge of the turned-up hem.

5 Use the steam iron to shrink out the remainder of the fullness. The hem is now ready to be stitched in place by hand or machine.

4 Pull on one of the threads of the long stitches to tighten the fabric and ease out the fullness.

HAND-STITCHED HEMS **pp.264–265** ● MACHINED HEMS **p.266**

TECHNIQUES

HAND-STITCHED HEMS

Difficulty level ✱✱✱✱✱

One of the most popular ways to secure a hem edge is by hand. Hand stitching is discreet and, if a fine hand sewing needle is used, the stitching should not show on the right side of the work.

TIPS FOR SEWING HEMS BY HAND

1 Always use a single thread in the needle – a polyester all-purpose thread is ideal for hemming.

2 Once the raw edge of the hem allowance has been neatened by one of the methods below, secure it using a slip hem stitch. For this, take half of the stitch into the neatened edge and the other half into the wrong side of the garment fabric.

3 Start and finish the hand stitching with a double stitch, not a knot, because knots will catch and pull on the hem.

4 It is a good idea to take a small backstitch every 10cm (4in) or so to make sure that if the hem does come loose in one place it will not all unravel.

▶ CLEAN FINISH

1 This is suitable for fine and lightweight fabrics. Lightly press the hem into position.

2 Turn the raw edge of the hem allowance to itself wrong side to wrong side and tack in place.

3 Open out the hem and machine the tacked edge.

4 Fold the hem back up and tack in place.

5 Roll the edge stitching back and stitch underneath it.

6 Using a small slip hem stitch, secure the edge of the hem to the wrong side of the fabric. Roll the edge back into place.

7 Remove the tacking and press lightly.

▶ OVERLOCKED FINISH

1 Using a 3-thread overlock stitch, stitch along the raw edge of the hem allowance.

2 Gently press the hem up into position and tack close to the crease.

3 Roll back the overlocked edge. Hand stitch to the wrong side of the fabric using a slip hem stitch.

4 Press carefully to prevent the overlocking from being imprinted through to the right side.

▶ BIAS-BOUND FINISH

1 This is a good finish for fabrics that fray or are bulky. Turn up the hem on to the wrong side of the garment and tack close to the crease line.

2 Pin the bias binding to the raw edge of the hem allowance.

3 Open out the crease in the bias and stitch along the crease line, keeping the raw edges level.

4 Turn down the bias over the raw edge and press.

5 Using a slip hem stitch, join the edge of the bias to the wrong side of the fabric. Remove the tacking and press lightly.

▶ ZIGZAG FINISH

1 Use this to neaten the edge of the hem on fabrics that do not fray too badly. Set the sewing machine to a zigzag stitch, width 4.0 and length 3.0. Machine along the raw edge. Trim the fabric edge back to the zigzag stitch.

2 Turn the hem on to the wrong side of the garment and tack in place close to the crease line.

3 Fold back the zigzag-stitched edge. Using a slip hem stitch, stitch the hem into place.

4 Roll the edge back into position. Remove the tacking and lightly press.

▶ PINKED FINISH

1 Pinking shears can give an excellent hem finish on difficult fabrics. Machine a row of straight stitching along the raw edge, 1cm (⅜in) from the edge. Pink the raw edge.

2 Turn up the hem to the wrong side of the garment and tack in place close to the crease line.

3 Fold back the edge along the machine stitching line and hand stitch the hem in place with a slip hem stitch.

4 Roll the hem edge back into place. Remove the tacking and lightly press.

▶ CURVED HEM FINISH

1 With a curved hem on a cotton or firm fabric, it is important that any fullness does not bulge on to the right side. Prior to turning up the hem into position, zigzag the raw edge, using stitch width 4.0 and stitch length 3.0.

2 Machine a row of straight stitching 3mm (⅛in) below the zigzag stitching, using stitch length 5.0.

3 Pin the hem into position, placing the pins vertically.

4 Tack the hem into position close to the crease line.

5 Pull on the straight stitching to tighten the fabric.

6 Roll the zigzagged edge back to the straight stitching line and hand stitch the hem in place using a slip hem stitch. Remove the tacking and press lightly.

STITCHES MADE WITH A MACHINE **pp.92–93** ● TURNING UP A CURVED HEM **p.263**

MACHINED HEMS

On many occasions, the hem or edge of a garment or other item is turned up and secured using the sewing machine. It can be stitched with a straight stitch, a zigzag stitch, or a blind hem stitch. Hems can also be made on the overlocker.

▶ **SINGLE-TURN HEM**

1 This is a popular technique. Turn up the hem to the wrong side of the work. Press in place.

2 Machine with a straight stitch close to the hem edge.

▶ **BLIND HEM**

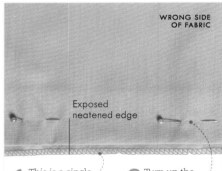

WRONG SIDE OF FABRIC

Exposed neatened edge

1 This is a single turn hem that is secured using the blind hem stitch on the machine. Neaten the raw edge of the fabric (here an overlock finish has been used).

2 Turn up the hem, then fold it to the right side of the fabric leaving the neatened edge exposed. Pin, but not too close to the fold.

WRONG SIDE OF FABRIC

Fold

3 Using the blind hem foot and the blind hem stitch, secure the hem to the fabric. The stitch line should be just below the neatened edge with only the points of the stitch going through the fold.

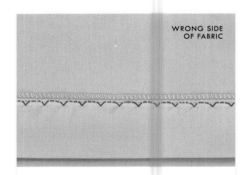

WRONG SIDE OF FABRIC

4 Fold the hem back into position and press lightly on the right side. The stitches will be barely visible on the right side.

▶ **DOUBLE-TURN HEM**

1 This hem will add weight at the edge. Fold up the raw edge of the fabric once and then fold again.

2 Pin in place, then press.

3 Machine using a straight stitch, close to the upper fold.

HEMS ON DIFFICULT FABRICS

Difficulty level ★★★★★

Some very fine fabrics or fabrics that fray badly require more thought when a hem is to be made. This technique works very well on delicate fabrics.

1 Turn up the hem with a single turn.

2 Tack to secure.

3 Set the machine to a zigzag stitch, width 3.5 and length 2.0, and zigzag close to the fold.

4 Trim away surplus hem allowance. Press.

ROLLED HEMS

Difficulty level ★★★★★

A rolled hem is used on lightweight fabrics. It is often found on soft furnishings as well as garments. To make it, the fabric is rolled to the wrong side by using the rolled hem foot on the sewing machine.

▶ STRAIGHT-STITCHED ROLLED HEM

Use the rolled hem foot on the sewing machine and a straight stitch.

▶ ZIGZAG-STITCHED ROLLED HEM

Use the rolled hem foot on the sewing machine and a zigzag stitch.

▶ OVERLOCKER ROLLED HEM

You will need to alter the settings on the overlocker to make this hem (consult the instruction book). Use a 3-thread stitch, with a bulky yarn on the upper looper.

▶ MANUAL ROLLED HEM

If you do not have a rolled hem foot for your sewing machine, or an overlocker, you can make a rolled hem manually. Turn the raw edge under once to make a very narrow hem and press. Stitch close to the fold. Turn under again and press, then machine on top of the previous stitching.

MACHINED CURTAIN HEMS

Difficulty level ✱✱✱✱✱

Curtains have hems at the bottom edge as well as at the sides. The hem at the bottom is treated differently from the side hems, using different techniques, although both types of hems are folded twice. The hems can be stitched using either machine or hand methods.

WRONG SIDE OF FABRIC

RIGHT SIDE OF FABRIC

1 A curtain bottom hem is turned up twice. Turn the fabric up to the wrong side by 10cm (4in) and press with the iron.

2 Turn up again by the same amount and press again.

3 Machine in place using a blind hem stitch on your sewing machine.

4 At each side, turn under the edge to the wrong side by 4cm (1½in) and press. Turn again by the same amount and press again.

Front of blind hem stitch

Back of blind hem stitch

5 Open out and turn the corner in at an angle to mitre it (see opposite page). Press.

WRONG SIDE OF FABRIC

6 Open out the corner and remove the fabric from under the mitre to reduce bulk.

WRONG SIDE OF FABRIC

7 Fold the doubled side hem back into position and pin in place.

8 Using a straight stitch, machine close to the folded edge.

HAND-STITCHED CURTAIN HEMS

Difficulty level ✱✱✱✱✱

Hand stitching is used on heavier curtain fabrics or where you do not want a machine stitch to show on the right side. Everything is pressed in place first.

WRONG SIDE OF FABRIC

1 Turn each side hem in to the wrong side by 4cm (1½in) and press, then turn in again by the same amount and press again.

2 Turn up the bottom hem to the wrong side by 10cm (4in) and press, then turn up again by the same amount and press.

3 Where the bottom hem and side hem meet, press under the hem at an angle to mitre it (see opposite page).

4 Open out all the crease lines and reduce some of the bulk.

5 Fold everything back into place and pin.

6 Use a herringbone stitch to stitch the bottom hem in place. Take shallow stitches that run along the folded edge.

7 Repeat the process down the side hems.

8 Stitch the mitred corner to match.

MITRED CORNERS

At the bottom corners of curtains, where the bottom and side hems meet, the fabric is folded at an angle. This is called a mitre. By pressing the mitre with the iron and then unfolding it, you can use the crease lines that have been formed as a guide for removing surplus fabric to reduce bulk. For lined curtains, where the lining is constructed separately, the side and bottom hems are machined in place. The same mitring technique is used for both curtains and linings.

1 After the bottom and side hems have been turned and pressed, fold back the corner at an angle. The angle runs between the outer corner of the curtain and the point where the hems meet, at the inner corner.

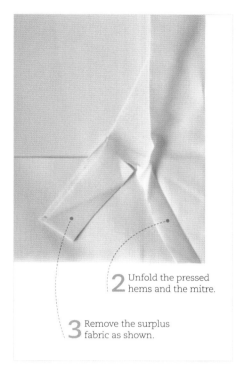

2 Unfold the pressed hems and the mitre.

3 Remove the surplus fabric as shown.

4 Refold the fabric into position and, if necessary, press again. Pin into place.

5 For curtain lining, machine the bottom and side hems using one continuous row of stitching, close to the folded edge and pivoting at the corner.

WEIGHTING CURTAINS

A weight is often inserted into the bottom hem of a curtain at the corners, to hold the curtain in place and make it hang properly. Specialist weights can be purchased, although a heavy coin can work just as well.

1 Measure the diameter of the weight. Cut a strip of curtain lining that is three times as long and twice as wide.

2 Press under the short edges of the lining to the wrong side and press. Fold the strip in half, matching the turned-under edges, to make a rectangle large enough to enclose the weight.

3 Using a zigzag stitch, machine the two long sides. Insert a coin or weight into the pouch.

4 Zigzag stitch across the open side.

5 Insert the weight pouch into the bottom corner of the curtain.

6 When stitching the hems for the side and bottom, place stitches through into the weight pouch to hold it in place.

TECHNIQUES

HEMS ON STRETCH KNITS

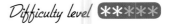
Difficulty level ★★✲✲✲

When making a garment with a stretch knit, the hem will need to stretch as well. There are two methods for stitching the hem on stretch knits, and the one you use depends on whether the fabric will ladder or not when it is cut.

▶ FABRIC THAT LADDERS

1 Neaten the raw edge using a 3-thread overlock stitch. If no overlocker is available, use a zigzag stitch on the sewing machine.

WRONG SIDE OF FABRIC

2 Turn up the hem to the wrong side.

3 Tack the hem close to the crease line.

4 Insert a twin needle into the sewing machine and thread the machine with two threads.

5 Working from the right side of the garment, machine the hem in place.

▶ FABRIC THAT DOES NOT LADDER

1 Insert the twin needle into the machine and thread the machine with two threads.

2 Turn up the hem to the wrong side and tack to hold in place.

3 Machine the hem in position.

Trimmed raw edge

RIGHT SIDE OF FABRIC

4 Trim the raw edge back to within 3mm (⅛in) of the stitching on the wrong side.

FACED HEM

Difficulty level ★★★★★

A faced hem is used on garments made from fabrics that may be too bulky to turn up without the hem showing, or on napped fabrics that may catch or ride up when they are worn. A faced hem is also used if there is not enough fabric to turn up to make a hem.

▶

1 Cut a bias strip of lining fabric 10cm (4in) wide to make a facing. Join the strips together until there is enough to go all around the hem.

2 Tack under 1cm (⅜in) along one long edge.

3 Pin the edge that has not been turned under to the lower edge of the garment, right side to right side.

4 Machine the bias facing in place. Use the edge of the machine foot as a guide to the seam width.

RIGHT SIDE OF FABRIC

5 Press the seam as stitched.

6 Open out the bias facing. Press the seam down on to the bias.

7 Roll the bias facing to the wrong side of the garment. Make sure the seam is not on the crease line but shows on the wrong side.

8 Using a herringbone stitch, stitch the folded edge of the bias strip in place.

WRONG SIDE OF FABRIC

DECORATIVE FACED HEM

Difficulty level ✶✶✶✶✶

If the edge of a garment, blind, cushion, or other item is to have a decorative effect, such as points or scallops (as shown in the photographs here), a faced hem is used.

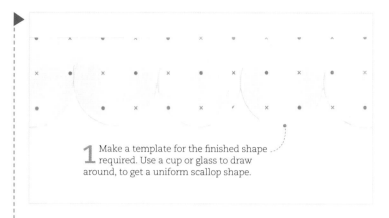

1 Make a template for the finished shape required. Use a cup or glass to draw around, to get a uniform scallop shape.

WRONG SIDE OF FABRIC

2 Cut a facing piece of fabric 10cm (4in) wide. Neaten one long edge with the overlocker or a zigzag stitch.

3 Pin the facing to the hem edge, right side to right side.

4 Place the template on the facing and use a marking pen or chalk pencil to draw the shaped hem. A seam allowance of 1.5cm (⅝in) is required between the lower edge of the template and the raw edge.

5 Stitch around the outline that you have drawn on to the fabric. Take one straight stitch between each scallop.

6 Working from the wrong side, trim close to the machining with pinking shears. Clip close into the machining at the top of the curves.

7 Turn through to the right side. Press the fabric as it is being turned, because you can work warm fabric into the required shape.

8 If required, secure the facing on each seam.

FUSED HEM

Difficulty level ✶✶✶✶✶

A fused hem is useful for a fabric that is difficult to hand stitch, as well as for an emergency hem repair. It uses a hemming tape that has a fusible adhesive on both sides.

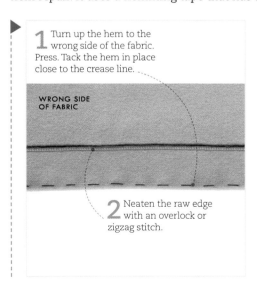

1 Turn up the hem to the wrong side of the fabric. Press. Tack the hem in place close to the crease line.

WRONG SIDE OF FABRIC

2 Neaten the raw edge with an overlock or zigzag stitch.

3 Insert the fusible hemming tape between the hem and the wrong side of the garment. Make sure the tape sits just below the overlock or zigzag stitch. Pin the tape in place.

4 Cover the hem allowance with a pressing cloth and, using a steam iron, press the edge of the hem to fuse the tape to the fabric. Once cool, the hem will be stuck in place. Remove the tacking stitches.

FUSIBLE TAPES **p.325**

BIAS-BOUND HEMS

Difficulty level ✱✱✱✱✱

A bias-bound hem will give a narrow decorative edge to a garment or an item of home furnishing. It is particularly useful for curved shapes, to finish them neatly and securely. On a bulky or chunky fabric a double bias is used so that it will be more substantial and hold its shape better. A double bias is also used on sheer fabrics as there will be no visible raw edges. The bias strip can be made from purchased bias binding or cut from a matching or contrasting fabric.

▶ SINGLE BIAS-BOUND HEM

1 Place the bias strip to the hem edge, right side to right side.

2 Machine the bias to the edge using the edge of the machine foot as a guide. Press as sewn.

3 Turn the bias to the wrong side of the fabric and roll the bias around the edge of the fabric.

WRONG SIDE OF FABRIC

4 Tack the bias down on to the wrong side of the fabric.

5 Working from the right side, stitch in the ditch formed by the seam.

6 On the wrong side, trim the bias back close to the stitching (bias-cut fabric hardly frays). Remove the tacking and press.

RIGHT SIDE OF FABRIC

▶ DOUBLE BIAS-BOUND HEM

1 Cut bias strips that are 8cm (3¼in) wide. Join them together until the required length is achieved.

2 Fold the bias in half, wrong side to wrong side. Tack along the bias to hold in place.

RIGHT SIDE OF FABRIC

3 Place the raw edge of the bias to the hem edge of the right side of the fabric.

4 Machine stitch in place, using the edge of the machine foot as a guide.

WRONG SIDE OF FABRIC

5 Wrap the folded edge of the bias to the wrong side of the garment. Place the folded edge to the machine stitching.

6 Use a slip hem stitch to secure the folded edge to the machining.

7 If preferred, machine stitch the bias in place using a stitch in the ditch technique.

RIGHT SIDE OF FABRIC

INTERFACED HEMS

On tailored garments, such as jackets and winter skirts, an interfaced hem can be used. It is only suitable for straight hems as it produces a heavy structured edge. A sew-in woven interfacing cut on the bias grain is used for this technique.

Difficulty level

1 Cut a bias strip of sew-in woven interfacing 5cm (2in) wide. If it requires joining, use a lapped seam.

2 Press up a 4cm (1½in) hem on the garment to the wrong side to make a hemline crease.

3 Place the interfacing to the crease line of the hem. Herringbone stitch the interfacing in place, stitching along the upper and lower edges.

4 Pin the hem up over the interfacing. A strip of interfacing should show at the upper edge of the hem.

5 Roll back the top edge of the hem. Herringbone stitch just to the interfacing.

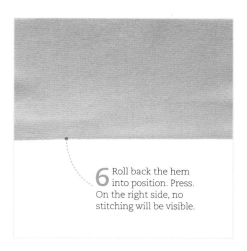

6 Roll back the hem into position. Press. On the right side, no stitching will be visible.

HORSEHAIR BRAID HEMS

On special-occasion wear, a horsehair braid is used in the hem edge as it will hold the edge out and give a look of fullness. Although once made from horsehair, the braid is now made from nylon. It is available in various widths. The braid is stretchy so try not to stretch it when applying.

Difficulty level ★★★★★

▶ **USING A NARROW HORSEHAIR BRAID**

Pinked edge of hem

1 Place one edge of the braid to the edge of the hem, wrong side to wrong side.

2 Using a narrow zigzag, stitch along the other edge of the braid to secure.

3 Fold the braid on to the wrong side of the fabric along the zigzag stitching. Press into position.

4 Machine stitch with a straight stitch, through the centre of the hem and braid. A row of machining will show on the right side.

▶ **USING A WIDE HORSEHAIR BRAID**

1 Overlay by 1cm (⅜in) the edge of the braid to the wrong side of the fabric. Use the edge of the braid that does not have the white stitching inserted. Pin in place.

2 Zigzag stitch in place, 5mm (³⁄₁₆in) from the edge of the braid.

3 On the right side, trim the fabric down to the zigzag stitching.

4 Press the hem and braid up on to the wrong side of the fabric.

5 Use a herringbone stitch to secure. If the hem is curved, pull up the white stitching at the edge of the braid to tighten the braid into shape.

STITCHES MADE WITH A MACHINE **pp.92–93** • HOW TO CUT BIAS STRIPS **p.154**

HEMS WITH BANDING

Banding is a term applied to a much wider bias strip. Some banding is visible by the same amount at the hem or edge on both sides of the work, while other bandings are surface-mounted to the edge of a fabric, such as for a decorative effect on a blind or a table runner. Dealing with the corners on banding needs accurate marking and stitching. Most of the following techniques are used primarily on craft and home furnishing items.

▶ BANDING AT INNER CORNERS

1 For this, the bias banding is machine stitched in place and hand finished. First reinforce the inner corner of the fabric by machine stitching 1cm (⅜in) from the edge.

2 Snip across the corner to the machine stitching.

RIGHT SIDE OF FABRIC

3 Cut a strip of bias banding 7cm (2¾in) wide. Press under 1cm (⅜in) on each side of the banding strip to the wrong side.

4 Stitch the strip to the fabric, right side to right side, using a 1cm (⅜in) seam allowance. Open out the clipped corner in the fabric as you stitch.

5 Snip through the banding seam at the corner.

WRONG SIDE OF FABRIC

6 Open out the banding. Press the seam towards the banding.

7 Fold the banding as illustrated and pin.

8 Tack a diagonal line as indicated by the dotted yellow line on the photograph.

WRONG SIDE OF FABRIC

9 Fold the banding to the wrong side. Place the folded edge of the banding to the machining.

10 Push the corners into place and remove the tacks.

11 Hand stitch using a flat fell stitch.

12 This is how banding looks on the right side. Press to finish.

▶ **BANDING AT OUTER CORNERS**

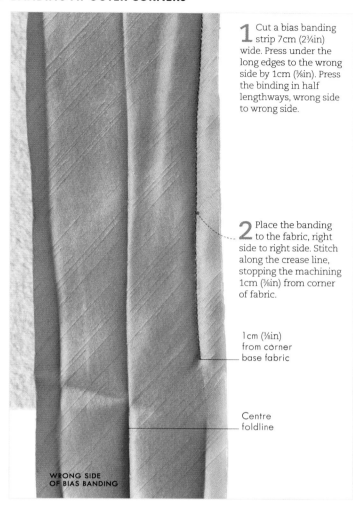

1 Cut a bias banding strip 7cm (2¾in) wide. Press under the long edges to the wrong side by 1cm (⅜in). Press the binding in half lengthways, wrong side to wrong side.

2 Place the banding to the fabric, right side to right side. Stitch along the crease line, stopping the machining 1cm (⅜in) from corner of fabric.

1cm (⅜in) from corner base fabric

Centre foldline

WRONG SIDE OF BIAS BANDING

3 Fold the banding on to itself diagonally, wrong side to wrong side.

4 Measure the distance from the centre foldline to the stitching line. Double this distance from the centre foldline (indicated by the dotted yellow line) and mark the point with a vertical pin.

5 Fold the banding at right angles on to itself, right side to right side, aligning edge to edge with the fabric. Make sure the vertical pin is at the fold.

6 Machine along the lower crease in the banding. Extend the machining through the folded part of the banding as well.

7 Stitch in the point for the banding corner as indicated by the dotted yellow lines. Trim to remove surplus fabric around the point.

8 Open out the banding and press the seams towards the banding.

9 Fold the banding to the wrong side of the fabric along the centre crease line.

10 Fold in the mitred corners on either side. Pin in place.

11 Finish on the wrong side with a flat fell stitch.

WRONG SIDE OF FABRIC

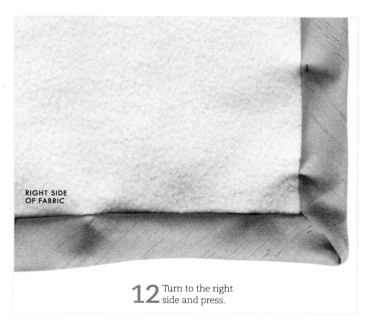

RIGHT SIDE OF FABRIC

12 Turn to the right side and press.

TECHNIQUES

▶ SURFACE-MOUNTED BANDING AT OUTER CORNERS

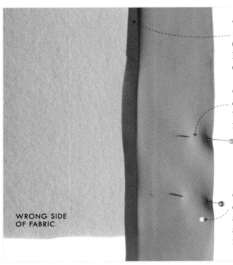

1 Cut a bias banding strip 6cm (2⅜in) wide. Press under one long edge by 1cm (⅜in).

2 Place the right side of the strip to the wrong side of the fabric. Pin in place.

3 Mark with a marker pen a point 1cm (⅜in) in and 1cm (⅜in) up from the corner.

WRONG SIDE OF FABRIC

4 Remove the banding from the fabric. Machine a row of stitches through the marked point.

5 Snip out a V notch from the edge to this point.

6 Place the banding back to the wrong side of the fabric. Pin in place.

7 Machine to secure, stretching out the banding as snipped to open it, and pivoting through the corner.

8 Fold the banding strip at an angle with the fold touching the stitching line. Keep the outer edge of the strip folded in place. Press to form crease lines.

9 Stitch along the crease lines. Ensure these edges are folded down.

10 Remove the surplus fabric and press the seam open. Make sure the folds meet exactly.

11 Turn the bias band to the right side of the fabric. Press.

12 Either machine or hand stitch in place.

▶ SURFACE-MOUNTED BANDING AT INNER CORNERS

1 Cut a bias banding strip 6cm (2⅜in) wide. Press under one long edge by 1cm (⅜in).

2 Place the unfolded edge of the banding to the raw edge of the fabric, right side of the strip to wrong side of the fabric. Pin in place.

WRONG SIDE OF FABRIC

3 Fold the banding strip on to itself, right side to right side, to align the strip with the other side of the angle. Press to form a crease. Keep the edges folded down.

4 Remove the banding from the fabric and stitch in the angle for the corner. Make sure the folded edges meet.

5 Remove surplus fabric and press the seam open.

6 Place the banding back in place on to the wrong side of the fabric. Pin in place, then machine to secure. Press.

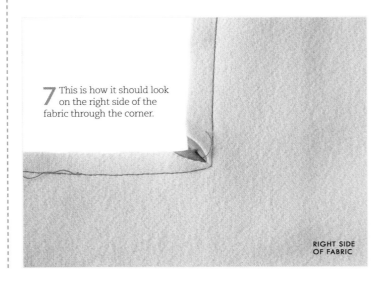

7 This is how it should look on the right side of the fabric through the corner.

RIGHT SIDE OF FABRIC

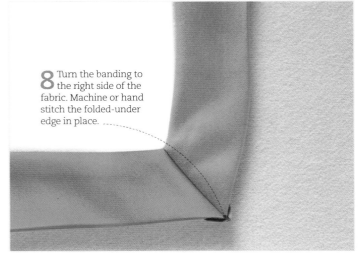

8 Turn the banding to the right side of the fabric. Machine or hand stitch the folded-under edge in place.

HOW TO CUT BIAS STRIPS p.154 ● **MITRED CORNERS p.269**

TECHNIQUES

APPLYING A FLAT TRIM

Difficulty level

On some items a flat trim braid or ribbon is added for a decorative effect. This may be right on the hem or edge, or placed just above it. To achieve a neat finish, any corners should be mitred.

1 Pin the trim to the fabric, wrong side of the trim to right side of the fabric.

2 At the corner point where the trim is to be mitred, fold the trim back on itself and secure with a pin.

3 Stitch across the trim at 45 degrees from the edge of the fold, through all layers.

4 Remove excess trim from the corner.

5 Open the trim out and press.

6 Machine stitch the inner and outer sides of the trim to the fabric, close to the edge. Be sure the stitching at the corners is sharp.

PIPED EDGES

Difficulty level

A piped edge can look very effective on a garment, especially if it is made in a contrasting colour or fabric. Piping is also an excellent way of finishing special-occasion wear as well as soft furnishings. The piping may be single, double, or gathered.

▶ **SINGLE PIPING**

1 Just one piece of piping is used. Cut a bias strip 4cm (1⅝in) wide.

2 Wrap the binding, wrong side to wrong side, around the piping cord. Pin in place.

3 Machine along the binding close to the cord, using the zip foot.

4 Pin the raw edge of the piping to the raw edge of the right side of the work.

5 Machine close to the stitching line on the piping, using the zip foot.

Piping

6 Place the other side of the fabric over the piping, right side to right side.

7 Machine in place close to the piping, using the zip foot.

8 On the right side of the work, the piping can be seen at the edge. Press to finish.

▶ DOUBLE PIPING

1 Different thicknesses of piping cord can be used for this. Make up single piping (see steps 1–3, opposite page).

2 Cut another bias strip, in a contrasting colour if you like.

WRONG SIDE OF SECOND BIAS STRIP

3 Join the bias strip to the single piping, right side to right side, stitching next to the piping.

Right side of single piping

4 Place a second piping cord to the wrong side of the contrast strip.

5 Wrap the contrast strip around the cord and stitch.

6 Attach to the edge of the work as for single piping (see steps 4–7 on the opposite page). On the right side, there is a double row of piping at the edge.

▶ GATHERED PIPING

1 This is a great technique to try on cushions. Cut a bias strip 5cm (2in) wide. Stitch the bias strip loosely around a piece of piping cord. Secure the cord to the bias at one end.

2 Push the bias along the cord to gather.

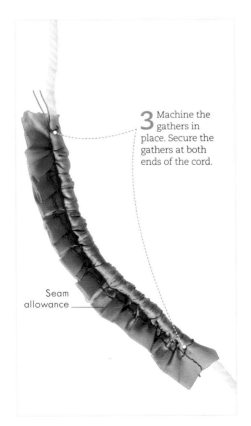

3 Machine the gathers in place. Secure the gathers at both ends of the cord.

Seam allowance

Gathered piping

4 Attach to the edge of the work as for single piping (see steps 4–7, opposite page).

HOW TO CUT BIAS STRIPS p.154 ● **MITRED CORNERS p.269**

TECHNIQUES

ATTACHING A LACE TRIM

Difficulty level ✶✶✶✶✶

A lace edge can give a look of luxury to any garment. There are many ways of applying lace, depending on how the lace has been made. A heavy lace trim has a definite edge to be sewn on to the fabric. Lace edging has a decorative edge and an unfinished edge, whereas a galloon lace is decorative on both edges.

▶ HEAVY LACE TRIM

1 Pin the lace to the right side of the fabric.

2 Using a small zigzag stitch, machine along the edge of the lace. All of the stitching should be on the lace.

3 Trim away surplus fabric behind.

▶ LACE EDGING

1 Place the lace to the fabric, right side to right side. Align the raw edges.

2 Machine using a straight stitch.

3 Turn the raw edges to the wrong side of the fabric. Press in place on to the wrong side.

4 Working from the right side of the fabric, zigzag stitch close to the fabric edge.

5 Trim away surplus fabric on the reverse side.

▶ GALLOON LACE

1 Place the complete piece of lace to the right side of the fabric. Align the edge of the lace with the raw edge of the fabric. Pin in place.

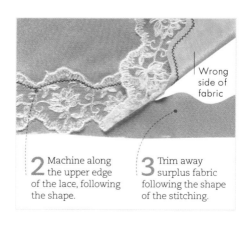

2 Machine along the upper edge of the lace, following the shape.

3 Trim away surplus fabric following the shape of the stitching.

4 The lace trim on the right side.

APPLYING OTHER TRIMMINGS

Difficulty level ✱✱✱✱✱

There are many kinds of trimmings – ribbons, braids, beads, feathers, sequins, fringes, and so on – that can be applied to a fabric edge. If a trim is made on a narrow ribbon or braid it can often be inserted into a seam during construction. Other trims are attached after the garment or item has been completed.

▶ INSERTING A TRIM IN A SEAM

1 Place the trim to the right side of one piece of fabric, with the beaded or other decorative edge pointing away from the raw edge. The edge of the trim should be on the 1.5cm (⅝in) stitching line. Tack in place.

2 Machine along the trim using the zip foot.

3 Place the other piece of fabric to the first one, right side to right side. Machine again to join them.

4 Turn to the right side. Press carefully. The trim should hang free.

▶ ATTACHING A TRIM TO AN EDGE

1 Pin the trim in position along the finished edge of the work. Be sure the trim is aligned to the edge. Tack in place.

2 Using the zip foot, machine in place close to the upper edge, leaving the lower edge of the trim free.

▶ HAND STITCHING A TRIM

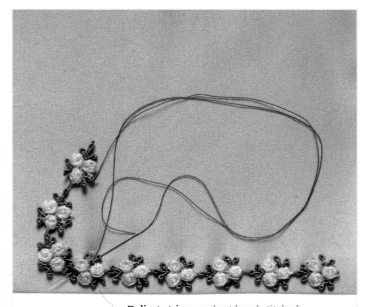

Delicate trims are best hand stitched in place because machining the trim may damage it. Place the trim in position and carefully stitch down with a flat fell stitch.

FASTENERS

There are many types of fastening available. Some of them are purely functional while others are more decorative as well as practical. A great many fastenings are hand stitched in place.

ZIPS

The zip is probably the most used of all fastenings. There are a great many types available, in a variety of lengths, colours, and materials, but they all fall into one of five categories: skirt or trouser zips, metal or jeans zips, concealed zips, open-ended zips, and decorative zips. Before attaching any zip, apply 2cm (¾in)-wide strips of fusible interfacing to the zip seam allowances on the wrong side of the fabric.

DIRECTORY OF ZIPS

LAPPED ZIP (p.286)

CENTRED ZIP (p.287)

FACED FLY-FRONT ZIP (pp.288–289)

CONCEALED OR INVISIBLE ZIP (p.290)

ZIP PLACKET (p.291)

OPEN-ENDED ZIP (p.292)

DECORATIVE ZIP (p.293)

MEASURING TOOLS AND MARKING AIDS **pp.18—19** • TACKING STITCHES **p.89** • STITCHES MADE WITH A MACHINE **pp.92—93** • HOW TO MAKE A PLAIN SEAM **p.94**

HOW TO SHORTEN A ZIP

Difficulty level ✳✳✳✳✳

Zips do not always come in the length that you need, but it is easy to shorten them. Skirt or trouser zips and concealed zips are all shortened by stitching across the teeth or coils, whereas an open-ended zip is shortened at the top and not at the bottom.

▶ **SHORTENING A SKIRT/TROUSER OR CONCEALED ZIP**

1 Using a zigzag stitch, width 5.0 and length 0.5, machine across the teeth of the zip.

2 Cut off the surplus zip below the stitching.

▶ **SHORTENING AN OPEN-ENDED ZIP**

1 Mark with a marker pen the place where the zip is to be shortened.

2 Open the zip past this point.

3 Using a zigzag stitch, width 3.0 and length 0.5, machine across each side of the opened zip. Cut off the surplus.

MARKING FOR ZIP PLACEMENT

Difficulty level ✳✳✳✳✳

For a zip to sit accurately in the seam, the seam allowances where the zip will be inserted need to be marked. The upper seam allowance at the top of the zip also needs marking to ensure the zip pull sits just fractionally below the stitching line.

▶

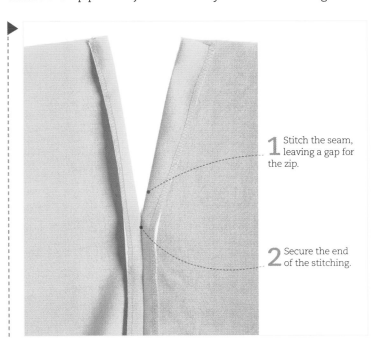

1 Stitch the seam, leaving a gap for the zip.

2 Secure the end of the stitching.

3 Place a row of tacks along the stitching line through the opening.

4 Place a row of tacks along the upper seam allowance.

Interfacing

REPAIRING A BROKEN ZIP **p.367**

TECHNIQUES

LAPPED ZIP

A zip in a skirt or a dress is usually put in by means of a lapped technique or a centred zip technique (see opposite page). For both of these techniques you will require the zip foot on the sewing machine. A lapped zip features one side of the seam – the left-hand side – covering the teeth of the zip to conceal them.

1 Stitch the seam, leaving enough of the seam open to accommodate the zip.

Interfacing ———

2 Secure the end of the stitching.

WRONG SIDE OF FABRIC

3 Insert the right-hand side of the zip first. Fold back the right-hand seam allowance by 1.3cm (½in). This folded edge is not in line with the seam.

4 Place the folded edge against the zip teeth. Tack.

RIGHT SIDE OF FABRIC

5 Using the zip foot, stitch along the tack line to secure the zip tape to the fabric. Stitch from the bottom of the zip to the top.

6 Fold back the left-hand seam allowance by 1.5cm (⅝in). Place the folded edge over the machine line of the other side. Pin and then tack.

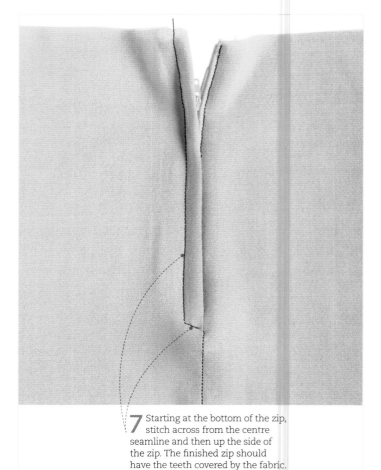

7 Starting at the bottom of the zip, stitch across from the centre seamline and then up the side of the zip. The finished zip should have the teeth covered by the fabric.

CENTRED ZIP

With a centred zip, the two folded edges of the seam allowances meet over the centre of the teeth, to conceal the zip completely.

1 Stitch the seam, leaving a gap for the zip.

2 Tack the rest of the seam allowance.

3 Press the seam open lightly.

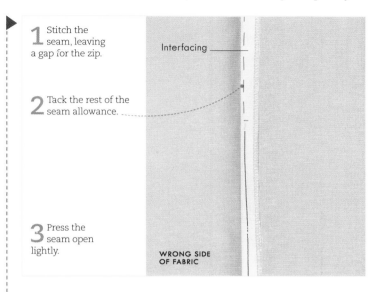

Interfacing

WRONG SIDE OF FABRIC

4 Centre the zip behind the tacked part of the seam. Pin and then tack in place along both sides.

5 On the wrong side, lift the seam allowance and the zip tape away from the main fabric. Pin.

6 Machine the zip tape to the seam allowance. Make sure both sides of the zip tape are secured to the seam allowances. Stitch through to the end of the zip tape.

7 Working from the right side of the work, stitch down one side, across the bottom, and up the other side of the zip.

8 Remove the tacks.

RIGHT SIDE OF FABRIC

9 The finished zip from the right side.

STITCHES MADE WITH A MACHINE **pp.92–93** ● HOW TO MAKE A PLAIN SEAM **p.94**

TECHNIQUES

FACED FLY-FRONT ZIP

Difficulty level ★★★☆☆

Whether it be for a classic pair of trousers or a pair of jeans, a fly front is the most common technique for inserting a trouser zip. The zip usually has a facing behind it to prevent the zip teeth from catching.

1 Stitch the seam, leaving a gap for the zip.

2 Using tailor's tacks, mark the centre front lines.

3 Trim the left-hand front (as worn) of the opening straight, to measure 1.5cm (⅝in) from the centre line.

4 Neaten the edges on both sides.

WRONG SIDE OF LEFT-HAND FRONT

5 Fold back 1.3cm (½in) on the left-hand front.

RIGHT SIDE OF LEFT-HAND FRONT

6 Place the fold adjacent to the zip teeth and pin in place. The zip may be too long and will extend beyond the top of the fabric.

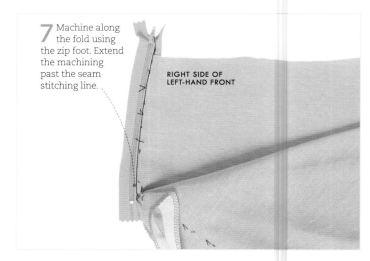

7 Machine along the fold using the zip foot. Extend the machining past the seam stitching line.

RIGHT SIDE OF LEFT-HAND FRONT

8 Fold the right-hand front along the centre front. Place the fold over the zip and pin the fold to the machine stitching on the left-hand side.

RIGHT SIDE OF RIGHT-HAND FRONT

RIGHT SIDE OF LEFT-HAND FRONT

9 On the wrong side, pin the zip tape to the fabric extension.

Fabric extension

10 Machine the zip tape to the fabric along the centre of the tape.

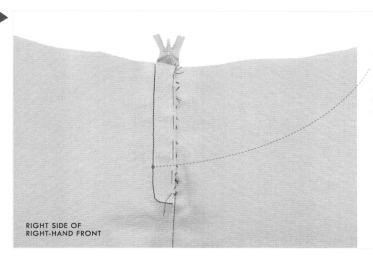

11 On the right side, top-stitch around the zip. Start stitching at the centre front. Stitch a smooth curve.

RIGHT SIDE OF
RIGHT-HAND FRONT

12 Neaten all the edges of the fly-front facing, leaving the top edge raw.

13 On the wrong side, pin the facing to the seam allowance on the left-hand side. Ensure that the facing covers the zip fully.

14 Machine to the seam allowance on the left-hand side.

WRONG SIDE OF
LEFT-HAND FRONT

15 Attach the waistband over the zip and the facings. Trim facing and zip.

16 Secure the lower edge of the facing on the right-hand side to the right-hand seam allowance.

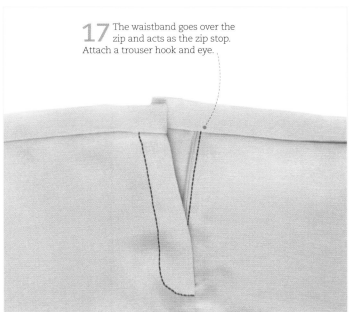

17 The waistband goes over the zip and acts as the zip stop. Attach a trouser hook and eye.

HOOKS AND EYES **p.319**

TECHNIQUES

CONCEALED OR INVISIBLE ZIP

Difficulty level ✱✱✱✱✱

This type of zip looks different from other zips because the teeth are on the reverse and nothing except the pull is seen on the front. The zip is inserted before the seam is stitched. A special concealed zip foot is required.

1 Mark the seam allowance with tacking stitches.

2 On the left-hand back place the centre of the zip over the tack line, right side of zip to right side of fabric. Pin in place.

3 Undo the zip. Using the concealed zip foot, stitch from the top of the zip down as far as possible. Stitch under the teeth. Stop when the foot hits the zip pull.

4 Do the zip up. Place the other piece of fabric to the zip. Match along the upper edge. Pin the other side of the zip tape in place.

5 Open the zip again. Using the concealed zip foot, stitch down the other side of the zip to attach to the right-hand side. Remove any tacking stitches.

Free end of zip tape

6 Close the zip. On the wrong side at the bottom of the zip, the two rows of stitching that hold in the zip should finish at the same place.

7 Stitch the seam below the zip. Use the normal machine foot for this. There will be a small gap of about 3mm (⅛in) between the stitching line for the zip and that for the seam.

8 Stitch the last 3cm (1¼in) of the zip tape to just the seam allowances. This will stop the zip pulling loose.

9 On the right side, the zip is completely concealed, with just the pull visible at the top. Apply waistband or facing.

ZIP PLACKET

The zip placket, or zip guard, can be placed behind any of the zips that are covered in this chapter. This type of placket sits behind the zip on the inside of the garment, and prevents the zip from catching on you or on your clothes.

Difficulty level ✸✸✸✸✸

1 Make a paper pattern for the placket in the shape shown. It should be 5cm (2in) wide and the same length as your zip tape.

2 Fold a piece of fabric wrong side to wrong side. Pin the pattern to the fabric and cut around it to give two pieces.

RIGHT SIDE OF FABRIC

Fold

3 Place the two placket pieces wrong side to wrong side.

4 Join both side edges and bottom edges together using a 3-thread overlock stitch or a zigzag stitch. Leave the top edge open.

Right side of fabric

5 Once the zip has been inserted into the garment, use the zip foot to attach the straight side of the placket to the seam allowance on the right-hand back (as worn).

6 Attach the curve of the placket to the zip tape at the bottom and secure using a double stitch.

Seam allowance of right-hand back piece

WRONG SIDE OF RIGHT-HAND BACK PIECE

WRONG SIDE OF LEFT-HAND BACK PIECE

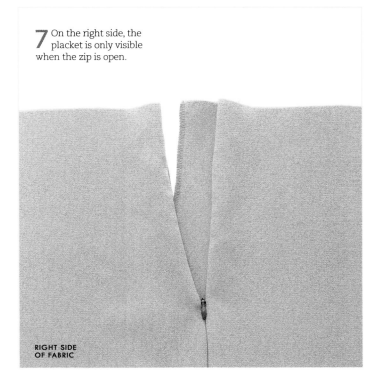

7 On the right side, the placket is only visible when the zip is open.

RIGHT SIDE OF FABRIC

STITCHES MADE WITH A MACHINE pp.92—93

TECHNIQUES

OPEN-ENDED ZIP

Difficulty level ✶✶✶✶✶

The open-ended zip is used on garments where the two halves need to be fully opened in order to put the garment on – for example, on a jacket or cardigan.

WRONG SIDE OF FABRIC

1 On both pieces of fabric, turn under the seam allowance at the centre front and tack.

2 Turn up the hem allowance and tack in place.

RIGHT SIDE OF FABRIC

3 Place the folded edge of the centre front about 3mm (⅛in) from the zip teeth to allow for the puller to move up and down. Pin in place.

4 Place the bottom of the zip at the hem edge.

RIGHT SIDE OF FABRIC

5 Using the zip foot, machine the zip in place. Start with the zip open. Stitch 5cm (2in), then place the machine needle in the work, raise the zip foot, and close the zip.

6 Stitch to the end of the zip tape and secure. Remove the tacks.

7 Pin the other side of the zip in place on the other piece of fabric. Make sure the fabric lines up top and bottom.

8 Undo the zip and, using the zip foot, machine in place as you did on the first side.

9 Once the zip is machined in place, check that the hems line up. If they do not, you will have to unpick and start again.

10 The zip should open completely.

MARKING AIDS p.19 • *SEWING-MACHINE ACCESSORIES* **p.33** • *ORGANZA* **p.49** • *TACKING STITCHES* **p.89**

EXPOSED ZIP

Some zips are meant to be seen – they may have crystals in the teeth, or they may have decorative coloured teeth. Metal zips can become design features when exposed using this technique.

1 Place a piece of silk organza on the right side of the work, positioning it where the zip will be.

2 Mark a rectangle on the organza the length and width of the zip.

3 Stitch around the rectangle.

RIGHT SIDE OF FABRIC

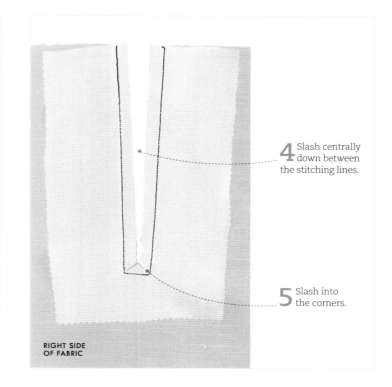

4 Slash centrally down between the stitching lines.

5 Slash into the corners.

RIGHT SIDE OF FABRIC

6 Pull the organza through to the wrong side and press.

7 Place the zip behind the opening. Pin in place along one side.

RIGHT SIDE OF FABRIC

WRONG SIDE OF FABRIC

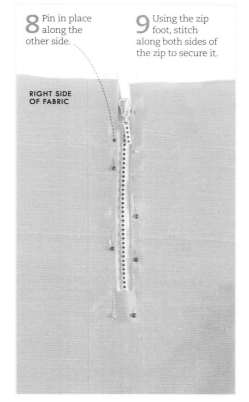

8 Pin in place along the other side.

9 Using the zip foot, stitch along both sides of the zip to secure it.

RIGHT SIDE OF FABRIC

10 On the right side, the zip is exposed.

TOILETRIES **BAG**

Difficulty level ✱✱✱✱✱

Inserting a zip is a rite of passage for many sewists, but it is nothing to fear. The zip on this lined toiletries bag is attached in the same way as an open-ended zip to help it open wide, but is neatened with a zip cover. With its flat bottom, the bag will sit beautifully on a dressing table or bathroom shelf.

TECHNIQUES USED How to apply a fusible interfacing **p.54**, Open-ended zip **p.256**

YOU WILL NEED

- Pattern template on p.386
- 50 x 110cm (20 x 43in) quilting-weight cotton for outer fabric
- 50 x 110cm (20 x 43in) quilting-weight cotton for the lining
- 50 x 90cm (20 x 36in) woven cotton fusible interfacing
- 25 x 90cm (10 x 36in) medium-loft fusible fleece batting
- 25cm (10in) closed-end nylon dress zip
- Matching thread
- Zip foot

PIECES TO CUT

Outer fabric

110cm (43in) folded

6.5cm (2½in)

5cm (2in)

Zip cover

50cm (20in)

Selvedge

Selvedge

15cm (6in)

Outer side 1 (cut on fold)

21.5cm (8½in)

19cm (7½in)

Fold

15cm (6in)

Outer side 2 (cut on fold)

21.5cm (8½in)

19cm (7½in)

Single layer · Double layer

Lining fabric

110cm (43in) folded

6.5cm (2½in)

5cm (2in)

Zip cover

Selvedge

Selvedge

15cm (6in)

Lining side 1 (cut on fold)

21.5cm (8½in)

19cm (7½in)

Fold

15cm (6in)

Lining side 2 (cut on fold)

21.5cm (8½in)

19cm (7½in)

Single layer · Double layer

▷ PREPARE THE ZIP

1 At the zip head end, fold back the excess fabric and hand-stitch in place.

2 Cut a 6.5 x 5cm (2½ x 2in) zip cover piece from each fabric, to give two pieces.

3 At the opposite end of the zip, take the two zip cover pieces and, with right sides facing the zip, sandwich the zip end between them.

4 Make sure the outer fabric is on the right side of the zip.

5 Align the zip cover pieces with the end of the zip, and pin. Stitch them down 6mm (¼in) from the zip edge.

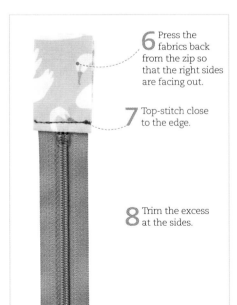

6 Press the fabrics back from the zip so that the right sides are facing out.

7 Top-stitch close to the edge.

8 Trim the excess at the sides.

▶ **ATTACH THE ZIP TO THE SIDES**

1 Cut four pieces of woven cotton interfacing using the template. Apply to the two outer pieces and two lining pieces according to the manufacturer's instructions. Leave to cool for 20 minutes.

2 Cut two pieces of fusible fleece batting using the template, then trim 18mm (¾in) on the top and 6mm (¼in) on all the other sides. Apply to the outer fabric only, positioning so that the top of the fleece is 18mm (¾in) below the top edge. Leave aside to cool for 20 minutes.

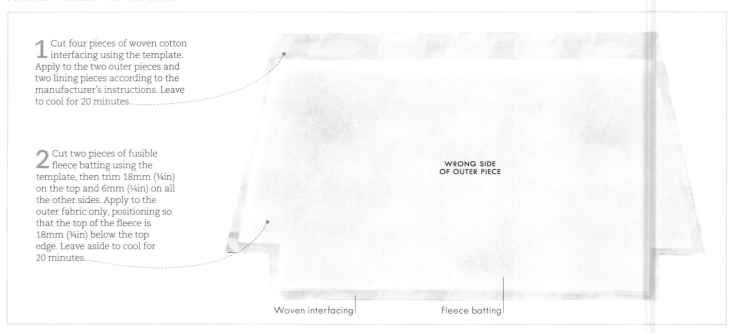

WRONG SIDE OF OUTER PIECE

Woven interfacing | Fleece batting

3 Take one outer piece and, with the right side facing up, pin the zip (facing down) to the top edge, positioning the zip head 1.2cm (½in) from the left-hand side edge.

1.2cm (½in)

Wrong side of zip

RIGHT SIDE OF OUTER PIECE 1

4 Lay one lining piece on top, right side down, sandwiching the zip. Make sure the side edges are flush. Tack or pin in place.

5 Mark a line 1.2cm (½in) from the right-hand side edge – you will start sewing from here.

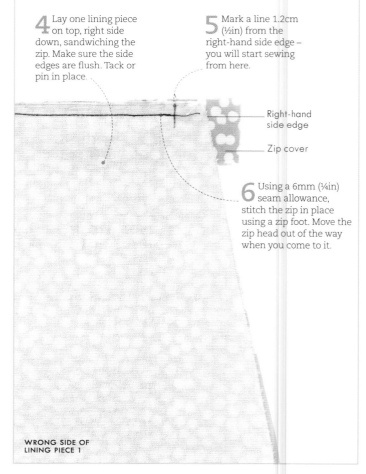

Right-hand side edge

Zip cover

6 Using a 6mm (¼in) seam allowance, stitch the zip in place using a zip foot. Move the zip head out of the way when you come to it.

WRONG SIDE OF LINING PIECE 1

7 Press back the outer and lining pieces, away from the zip.

Lining piece 1 and outer piece 1 are now wrong sides together

RIGHT SIDE OF
LINING PIECE 1

8 Repeat steps 4–7 to sandwich the other edge of the zip between the other outer and lining pieces.

9 This time, place the lining pieces right sides together on one side of the zip, and the outers right sides together on the other side of the zip. Ensure the side edges are lined up, pin, and stitch as before.

Outer pieces are right sides together on other side of zip

WRONG SIDE OF
LINING PIECE 2

Right side of lining piece 1

1.2cm (½in) from side edge

RIGHT SIDE OF
OUTER PIECE 2

RIGHT SIDE OF
OUTER PIECE 1

10 Fold both outers and linings away from the zip and press well so that you have very crisp edges.

11 Top-stitch either side of the zip, about 3mm (⅛in) from the fold, starting and stopping 1.2cm (½in) from both side edges. Press to set the stitching.

12 Using a hand needle, take the thread ends on the outer and linings from the right to wrong sides of the fabrics to give a tidy finish.

STITCHES MADE WITH A MACHINE **pp.92–93** ● TOP-STITCHING **p.109** ● OPEN-ENDED ZIP **p.292**

PROJECT

▶ **STITCH THE SIDES TOGETHER**

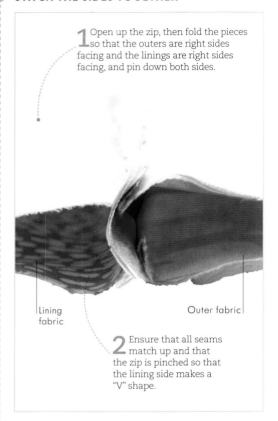

1 Open up the zip, then fold the pieces so that the outers are right sides facing and the linings are right sides facing, and pin down both sides.

Lining fabric

Outer fabric

2 Ensure that all seams match up and that the zip is pinched so that the lining side makes a "V" shape.

WRONG SIDE OF LINING PIECES

WRONG SIDE OF OUTER PIECES

3 Mark a 10cm (4in) turning gap at the bottom of the lining.

4 Starting at the lining side, stitch both sides using a 1cm (⅜in) seam on the lining and a 6mm (¼in) seam on the outer.

5 Go slowly over the zip edges where the fabric is a little bulkier.

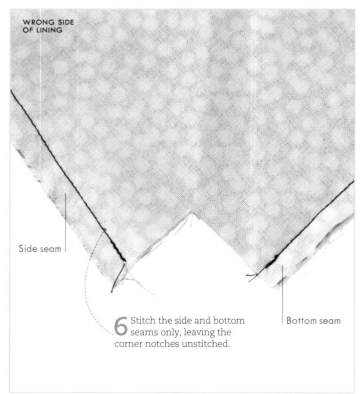

WRONG SIDE OF LINING

Side seam

Bottom seam

6 Stitch the side and bottom seams only, leaving the corner notches unstitched.

▶ **MAKE THE CORNER SEAMS**

WRONG SIDE OF LINING

Side seam

Bottom seam

1 On each of the four corner notches, pinch the fabric to bring the bottom and side seams together. Make sure the seams align.

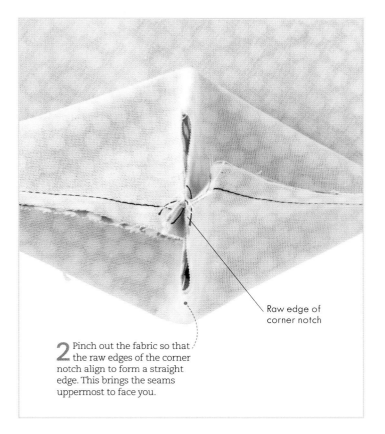

Raw edge of
corner notch

2 Pinch out the fabric so that the raw edges of the corner notch align to form a straight edge. This brings the seams uppermost to face you.

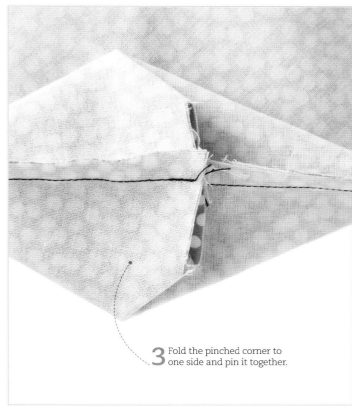

3 Fold the pinched corner to one side and pin it together.

4 Working from the raw edges of the corners, stitch a seam at 6mm (¼in) on the outer fabric corners and 1cm (⅜in) on the lining corners.

5 Backstitch across the central seam on each corner to reinforce it.

▶ **TURN AND FINISH**

1 Trim the ends of the zip covers and turn the bag right side out.

2 Close the turning gap by hand using a ladder stitch. Press well.

BUTTONS

Buttons are one of the oldest forms of fastening. They come in many shapes and sizes, and can be made from a variety of materials including shell, bone, plastic, nylon, and metal. Buttons are sewn to the fabric either through holes on their face, or through a hole in a stalk called a shank, which is on the back. Buttons are normally sewn on by hand, although a two-hole button can also be sewn on by machine.

DIRECTORY OF BUTTONS

TWO-HOLE BUTTON (p.301)

FOUR-HOLE BUTTON (p.301)

SHANKED BUTTON (p.302)

REINFORCED BUTTON (p.302)

OVERSIZED AND LAYERED BUTTON (p.302)

COVERED BUTTON (p.303)

SEWING ON A 2-HOLE BUTTON

This is the most popular type of button and requires a thread shank to be made when sewing in place. A cocktail stick will help you to sew on this type of button.

1 Position the button on the fabric. Start with a double stitch and double thread in the needle.

2 Place a cocktail stick on top of the button. Stitch up and down through the holes, going over the stick.

3 Remove the cocktail stick.

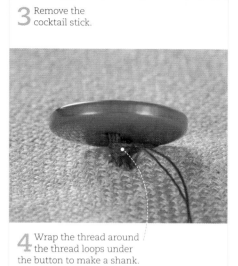

4 Wrap the thread around the thread loops under the button to make a shank.

5 Take the thread through to the back of the fabric.

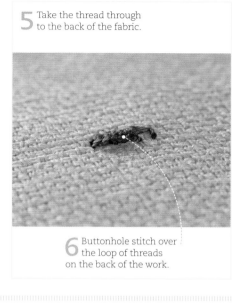

6 Buttonhole stitch over the loop of threads on the back of the work.

SEWING ON A 4-HOLE BUTTON

This is stitched in the same way as for a two-hole button except that the threads make an "X" over the button on the front.

1 Position the button on the fabric. Place a cocktail stick on the button.

2 Using double thread, stitch up and down through alternate sets of holes, over the cocktail stick. Make an "X" shape as you stitch.

3 Remove the cocktail stick.

4 Wrap the thread around the thread loops under the button to make the shank.

5 On the reverse of the fabric, buttonhole stitch over the thread loops in an "X" shape.

SEWING ON A SHANKED BUTTON **p.302** ● REPAIRING FABRIC UNDER A BUTTON **p.363**

TECHNIQUES

SEWING ON A SHANKED BUTTON

Difficulty level

When sewing this type of button in place, use a cocktail stick under the button to enable you to make a thread shank on the underside of the fabric.

1 Position the button on the fabric. Hold a cocktail stick on the other side of the fabric, behind the button.

2 Using double thread, stitch the button to the fabric, through the shank.

3 Be sure each stitch goes through the fabric and around the cocktail stick beneath.

4 Remove the cocktail stick. Work buttonhole stitch over the looped thread shank.

SEWING ON A REINFORCED BUTTON

Difficulty level ✱✱✱✱✱

A large, heavy button often features a second button sewn to it on the wrong side and stitched on with the same threads that secure the larger button. The smaller button helps support the weight of the larger button.

1 Position the large button on the right side of the fabric. Hold a smaller button beneath the fabric, in line with the large button.

2 Sew on the large button, stitching through both buttons to secure.

3 When the stitching is complete, wrap the thread around the thread loops beneath the larger button. Secure with a double stitch.

OVERSIZED AND LAYERED BUTTONS

Difficulty level ✱✱✱✱✱

There are some huge buttons available, many of which are really more decorative than functional. By layering buttons of varying sizes together, you can make an unusual feature on a garment or item of soft furnishing.

1 First position the oversized button on the fabric.

2 Top with a smaller button and stitch the two together to the fabric.

3 Place a small one-hole button on the layered buttons and attach to the thread using a buttonhole stitch.

BUTTONS **p.26** • HOW TO APPLY A FUSIBLE INTERFACING **p.54** • SECURING THE THREAD **p.88**

COVERED BUTTONS

Covered buttons are often found on expensive clothes and will add a professional finish to any jacket or other garment that you make. A purchased button-making gadget will enable you to create covered buttons very easily.

Button back Button top

1 On the pattern, select the size of button you want to make.

2 Cut out the button pattern from interfaced fabric.

3 Stitch a gather thread around the edge.

4 Place the button top on the interfaced side of the fabric.

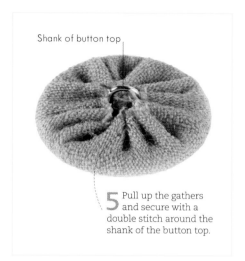

Shank of button top

5 Pull up the gathers and secure with a double stitch around the shank of the button top.

Button-maker

6 Put the button in the correct hole in the button-maker. Push well in.

7 Place the button back on top of the button.

8 Take the other side of the button-maker and press down on the button back until it clicks into position.

9 Remove the button from the button-maker and check to be sure the back is firmly in place.

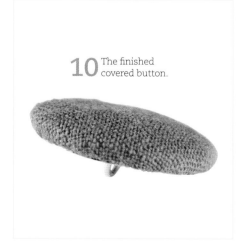

10 The finished covered button.

HAND STITCHES **pp.90—91** ● HOW TO MAKE AND FIT GATHERS **p.135**

BUTTONHOLES

A buttonhole is essential if a button is to be truly functional, although for many oversized buttons a snap fastener on the reverse is a better option, because the buttonhole would be just too big and could cause the garment to stretch.

DIRECTORY OF BUTTONHOLES AND BUTTON LOOPS

BASIC BUTTONHOLE
(p.113)

ROUND-END BUTTONHOLE
(p.306)

KEYHOLE BUTTONHOLE
(p.306)

MACHINE-CORDED BUTTONHOLE
(p.306)

PIPED BUTTONHOLE
(p.307)

PATCH METHOD BOUND BUTTONHOLE
(pp.308–309)

TRIANGULAR BOUND BUTTONHOLE
(p.310)

IN-SEAM BUTTONHOLE
(p.308)

ROULEAU LOOP
(p.316)

BUTTON PLACKET
(p.311)

CORDED LOOP
(p.316)

FROG FASTENING
(p.317)

MEASURING TOOLS **p.18** ● SEWING-MACHINE ACCESSORIES **pp.32–33** ● TACKING STITCHES **p.89** ● STITCHES MADE WITH A MACHINE **pp.92–93**

STAGES OF A BUTTONHOLE

A sewing machine stitches a buttonhole in four stages. The stitch can be slightly varied in width and length to suit the fabric or item, but the stitches need to be tight and close together.

1 Machine the first side of the buttonhole.

2 Stitch a bar tack at one end.

3 Machine the second side below the first.

4 Bar tack at the other end.

POSITIONING BUTTONHOLES

Difficulty level ✱✱✱✱✱

The size and position of the buttonhole is determined by the button size and needs to be worked out prior to any type of buttonhole being made.

1 Place the button on a sewing gauge and use the slider to measure the button's diameter.

2 On the right-hand side of the garment, work a row of tacking stitches along the centre front line.

3 Work a second row of tacks the diameter of the button away.

4 Position the buttons between the tack lines. Stitch lines at right angles where the buttonholes are to be placed.

VERTICAL OR HORIZONTAL?

As a general rule, buttonholes are only vertical on a garment when there is a placket or a strip into which the buttonhole fits. All other buttonholes should be horizontal. Any strain on the buttonhole will then pull to the end stop and prevent the button from coming undone.

▶ HORIZONTAL BUTTONHOLES

These are positioned with the end stop on the tacked centre line.

▶ VERTICAL BUTTONHOLES

These are positioned with the buttonhole centred on the tacked centre line.

REPAIRING A DAMAGED BUTTONHOLE **p.363**

TECHNIQUES

MACHINE-MADE BUTTONHOLES

Difficulty level ✱✱✱✱✱

Modern sewing machines can stitch various types of buttonhole, suitable for all kinds of garments.
On many machines the button fits into a special foot, and a sensor on the machine determines the correct
size of buttonhole. The width and length of the stitch can be altered to suit the fabric. Once the buttonhole
has been stitched, always slash through with a buttonhole chisel, to ensure that the cut is clean.

▶ **BASIC BUTTONHOLE**

The most popular shape for a
buttonhole is square on both ends.

▶ **ROUND-END BUTTONHOLE**

A buttonhole featuring one
rounded end and one square end
is used on lightweight jackets.

▶ **KEYHOLE BUTTONHOLE**

This is also called a tailor's buttonhole.
It has a square end and a keyhole end,
and is used on jackets and coats.

MACHINE-CORDED BUTTONHOLE

Difficulty level ✱✱✱✱✱

This buttonhole has a cord of heavier sewing thread running through it. You may have
to consult your sewing machine manual for the positioning of the cord.

▶

1 Place the cord into the buttonhole foot
as directed by your machine manual.

2 Work the buttonhole on the
machine – the machine will
stitch the buttonhole over the cord.

3 Gently pull on the ends of the
cord to eliminate the loop.

4 Thread the ends of the
cord into a large needle.

5 Take the cord to the back
of the fabric. Secure with
a hand stitch.

PIPED BUTTONHOLE

Difficulty level ✱✱✱✱✱

A buttonhole can also be made using piping cord. This is a type of buttonhole that is worked early in the construction of the garment. Very narrow piping cord needs to be used, otherwise the buttonhole will be too bulky.

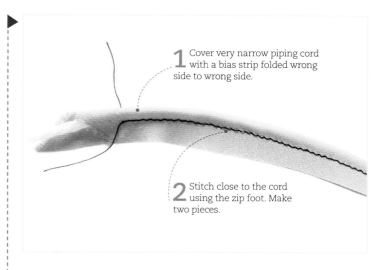

1 Cover very narrow piping cord with a bias strip folded wrong side to wrong side.

2 Stitch close to the cord using the zip foot. Make two pieces.

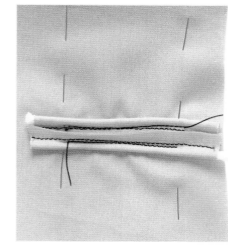

3 Align the machine stitches on the cord pieces with the buttonhole markings on the right side of the fabric, with the raw edges towards each other. Make sure the distance between the two rows of stitches is twice the diameter of the piping. If not, adjust until it is.

4 Use the zip foot to machine close to the cord. Stop stitching at the markings on the garment.

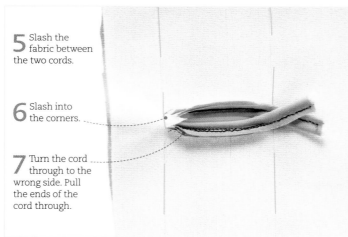

5 Slash the fabric between the two cords.

6 Slash into the corners.

7 Turn the cord through to the wrong side. Pull the ends of the cord through.

8 On the wrong side, stitch the end of the slash lines to the ends of the cord.

9 Trim away surplus cord to 1cm (⅜in).

Piping cord

10 The finished piped buttonhole.

RIGHT SIDE OF FABRIC

TECHNIQUES

IN-SEAM BUTTONHOLE

Difficulty level ★☆☆☆☆

This is a buttonhole formed in a seam allowance. It is found down decorative centre fronts that feature seam detailing. It is a very discreet buttonhole.

1 Reinforce the seam with a fusible tape on one side.

2 Tack the opening closed.

3 Press the seam open. The tacks will show.

4 Remove the tacking stitches to form the buttonhole.

PATCH METHOD BOUND BUTTONHOLE

Difficulty level ★★★★☆

Another method of creating a buttonhole is to use a patch of fabric stitched on to the main fabric. The technique is ideal for jackets and coats. A contrast fabric can be used for an attractive detail. This is known as a bound buttonhole.

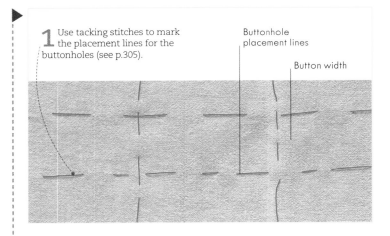

1 Use tacking stitches to mark the placement lines for the buttonholes (see p.305).

Buttonhole placement lines

Button width

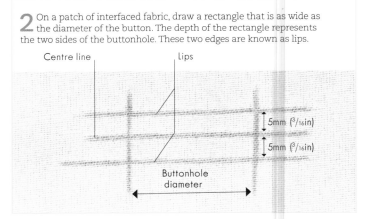

2 On a patch of interfaced fabric, draw a rectangle that is as wide as the diameter of the button. The depth of the rectangle represents the two sides of the buttonhole. These two edges are known as lips.

Centre line

Lips

5mm (^{3}/₁₆in)

5mm (^{3}/₁₆in)

Buttonhole diameter

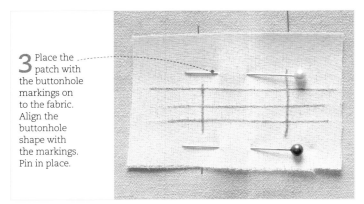

3 Place the patch with the buttonhole markings on to the fabric. Align the buttonhole shape with the markings. Pin in place.

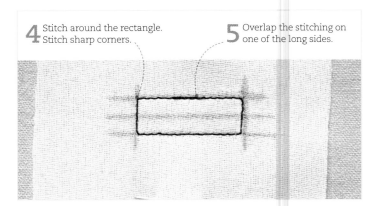

4 Stitch around the rectangle. Stitch sharp corners.

5 Overlap the stitching on one of the long sides.

6 Slash through the centre of the buttonhole.

7 Slash into the corners.

8 Pull the patch through to the wrong side. The patch should make a rectangular hole in the fabric.

9 Press down the lip on one side of the buttonhole, then press the patch back over the lip.

10 Repeat on the other side of the buttonhole. The patch will fold over the lips to meet in the centre.

11 Turn to the right side and press.

12 On the wrong side, stitch the end of the slash lines over the folded patch.

13 Whip stitch the folded edges of the buttonhole together.

14 Hand stitch in the ditch along the long edges of the buttonhole.

15 Press the finished buttonhole. Remove the whip stitches.

INTERFACINGS pp.324–325

TRIANGULAR BUTTONHOLE

A triangular buttonhole makes a nice feature on coats, jackets, waistcoats, or even bags, where you are using a large button. The method must be adapted from the bound buttonhole method to suit the triangle shape.

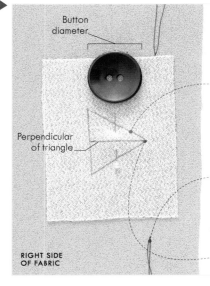

Button diameter

Perpendicular of triangle

RIGHT SIDE OF FABRIC

1 Apply interfacing to the wrong side of your garment or main fabric.

2 On a patch of interfaced fabric, draw your triangle shape. The perpendicular of the triangle must match the diameter of your button as the buttonhole will open through the centre.

3 Mark the centre front line on the right side of the garment with tacking stitches.

4 Place the patch right side down, aligning one point of the triangle with the centre front line. Pin in place.

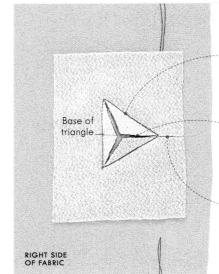

Base of triangle

RIGHT SIDE OF FABRIC

5 Stitch around the shape, starting on a side not a corner to make it easier to pivot.

6 Slash through both layers of fabric inside the shape as shown, going right into the corners.

7 At the sharp point of the triangle, snip the outer patch fabric to the stitch line. This will help it turn.

WRONG SIDE OF FABRIC

8 Push the buttonhole fabric through the hole to the wrong side.

WRONG SIDE OF FABRIC

9 Fold one half of the buttonhole fabric toward the centre. Pin in place

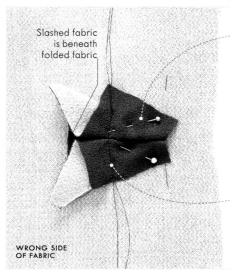

Slashed fabric is beneath folded fabric

WRONG SIDE OF FABRIC

10 Fold the other half of the buttonhole fabric to the centre line to meet the first fold. Pin in place.

11 On the right side, check that the buttonhole opening is straight and equal on both sides. Reposition if necessary.

12 Turn up the patch fabric at the base of the triangle and stitch across the slashed fabric underneath to join it to the patch. Don't stitch through to the right side of the main fabric.

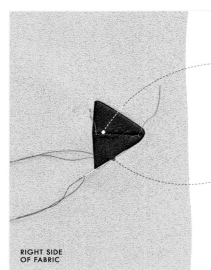

RIGHT SIDE OF FABRIC

13 On the right side, whip stitch the folded edges of the buttonhole together.

14 Hand stitch in the ditch along all sides of the shape using a prick stitch. This holds the buttonhole flat.

15 Press the finished buttonhole. Remove the whip stitches.

HOW TO APPLY A FUSIBLE INTERFACING p.54 ● **PATTERN MARKING pp.82–83** ● **TACKING STITCHES p.89**

BUTTON PLACKET

Difficulty level ✱✱✱✱✱

A hidden button placket is a great addition to a shirt, a shirt dress, or a coat. It creates a discreet fastening that hides the buttons completely from view behind a fold. Top-stitching the edge of the fold is optional but will produce a neat finish.

1 On the right front (or left front for menswear), mark the fold lines and crease lines as indicated on your pattern.

2 Use different coloured tacking stitches to distinguish the different lines.

Fold lines

Crease line

RIGHT SIDE OF FABRIC

3 Fold the placket along the crease line, bringing the fold line tacks together.

4 Make sure the raw edge is folded under to the wrong side.

5 Press the folds into place.

6 On the bottom fold of the placket, mark positions for vertical buttonholes along the centre line.

7 Stitch the buttonholes using an automatic buttonhole foot. The stitching will begin at the bottom left corner of each buttonhole.

8 On the top fold only, top stitch 2mm (1/16in) from the edge to create a crisp finish.

9 Machine through all layers to hold them together.

10 On the left front (or right front for menswear), attach the buttons so they align with the buttonholes.

11 On the finished front, the buttons will be hidden from view behind the placket.

HAND STITCHES **pp.90—91** ● TOP-STITCHED SEAM **p.98** ● MACHINE-MADE BUTTONHOLES **p.306**

ENVELOPE **CUSHION**

Difficulty level ✶✶✶✶✶

This attractive cushion with matching covered buttons is a quick, easy make, and is an ideal project for beginners. It is made using just three pieces – one front and two back pieces – to create the envelope, and requires just 50cm (20in) of fabric using an economical cutting layout.

TECHNIQUES USED Pattern layout **pp.78—81**, Seam neatening **p.95**, Double-turn hem **p.266**, Machine-made buttonholes **p.306**

YOU WILL NEED

- 50 x 115cm (20 x 45in) medium-weight cotton or linen
- 3 pieces 9 x 4cm (3½ x 1½in) lightweight non-woven fusible interfacing
- 3 covered buttons, 22mm (⅞in) in diameter (see p.303 for technique)
- 40 x 40cm (16in x 16in) cushion pad
- Matching thread
- Buttonhole foot

PIECES TO CUT

▶ PIN AND CUT THE FABRIC

1 Cut two paper pattern pieces: a front piece 42 x 42cm (16 x 16in) and a back piece 42 x 32cm (16 x 12¾in).

2 Fold the fabric in half, right sides together and matching the selvedge edges.

3 Place the back pattern piece as close to the selvedge edge as possible, avoiding the perforations. Make sure you match the grainline in the pattern to the grainline of the fabric. Pin and cut out. This gives two back pieces.

4 Open up the remainder of the fabric and place the front pattern piece along one of the cut edges. Pin and cut out.

▶ MAKE THE HEMS

WRONG SIDE OF BACK PIECE

1 On each of the back pieces, fold one long edge to the wrong side by 1cm (⅜in) and press. Fold by a further 2cm (¾in) to create a double-turn hem and press again. Pin in place.

2 Using an "edge" needle position setting on your machine, stitch from top to bottom on the hemmed edges, remembering to reverse stitch at the start and finish. Line up the fold of the hem against the left hand side of the presser foot as your guideline.

▶ MAKE THE BUTTONHOLES

RIGHT SIDE OF BACK PIECE

1 A 22mm (⅞in) button (used here) requires a 3cm (1¼in) buttonhole. Refer to your sewing machine manual for where to mark the start positions of the buttonholes.

2 For even spacing, place a pin at 9.5cm (9¾in), 19.5cm (17¾in), and 29.5cm (11¾in) from the bottom edge of one back piece to mark each of the three starting points.

3 If you want to position the buttons differently, or use buttons of a different size, sew a sample buttonhole on a scrap piece of fabric first. This will give you the size of the finished hole so you can position it accurately.

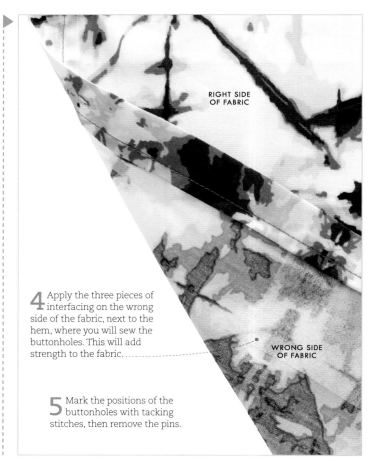

RIGHT SIDE OF FABRIC

WRONG SIDE OF FABRIC

4 Apply the three pieces of interfacing on the wrong side of the fabric, next to the hem, where you will sew the buttonholes. This will add strength to the fabric.

5 Mark the positions of the buttonholes with tacking stitches, then remove the pins.

RIGHT SIDE OF BACK PIECE

6 Adjust your machine to the correct settings and sew your buttonholes on the right side of the fabric. Ensure the needle starts accurately at the correct point.

7 Remove the tack stitches. Using a seam ripper or buttonhole chisel, carefully open up the centre of each buttonhole.

▶ **SEW THE CUSHION TOGETHER**

1 Place the front piece right side up on a table.

2 Place the back piece with the buttonholes right side down on top of the front, matching the outer raw edges.

WRONG SIDE OF BACK PIECE WITH BUTTONHOLES

WRONG SIDE OF BACK PIECE WITHOUT BUTTONHOLES

3 Place the second back piece on top, right side down, matching the outer raw edges. The hemmed edges should lie in the centre. Pin all around the four outside edges.

4 Starting just below a hemmed edge, sew all four sides of the cushion using a 1cm (⅜in) seam allowance, remembering to reverse stitch at the start and finish.

▶ **FINISHING TOUCHES**

1 Zigzag stitch around all four edges of the fabric to prevent any fraying.

2 Snip the corners diagonally to create a "crisp" corner when the fabric is turned right side out.

WRONG SIDE OF FABRIC

3 Turn the cushion the right side out and press the seams for a neat finish.

4 Sew the buttons on the underneath back panel, directly underneath each hole.

RIGHT SIDE OF FABRIC

STITCHES MADE WITH A MACHINE **pp.92–93** ● SEAM NEATENING **p.95** ● DOUBLE-TURN HEM **p.266** ● COVERED BUTTONS **p.303** ● POSITIONING BUTTONHOLES **p.305**

BUTTON **LOOPS**

A buttonhole is not the only way of using buttons. Buttons can also be fastened by means of a fabric loop, which is usually attached at the edge of a garment. Fabric loops are often found on the back of special-occasion wear, where multiple loops secure rows of small, often covered buttons. Loops called frog fasteners can also be made from decorative cord.

ROULEAU LOOP

Difficulty level ✹✹✹✹✷

This button loop is formed from a bias strip. Choose a smooth fabric for the strip as it will be easier to turn through. A rouleau loop is used with a round ball-type button.

1 Cut a bias strip 4cm (1½in) wide. Fold lengthways, right side to right side, and pin together.

2 Stitch along the strip, keeping the edge of the machine foot against the folded edge.

3 Stitch another row 2mm (⅛in) away from the first stitching. This is for strength.

4 Trim the bias close to the stitching.

5 Turn the bias strip to the right side, using a loop turner.

6 Pin the prepared loop strip to the ironing board and press with a steam iron.

CORDED LOOP

Difficulty level ✹✹✹✹✷

It is possible to make a very fine button loop that has a cord running through it. This type of loop is suitable for lightweight fabrics. Use a shanked button with a corded loop.

1 Cut a bias strip 4cm (1½in) wide. Cut a piece of cord twice the length of the strip.

2 Wrap the cord in the bias strip, folded right side to right side. Pin. Make sure the bias strip is near to one end of the cord.

3 Stitch along the bias strip, next to but not too close to the cord.

4 Machine another row 2mm (⅛in) away from the first stitching.

5 Trim away the bias strip close to the stitching.

6 Stitch through the cord and bias strip in the centre of the cord and near the end of the bias strip.

7 At the centre point, ease the fabric over the cord to turn it to the right side.

8 Trim off the exposed ends of cord from the fabric loop.

SPACING THE LOOPS

Once the loops have been made, the next step is to attach them to the garment. It is important that all the loops are the same size and positioned the same distance apart. To achieve this you will need to tack your fabric to mark the placement lines. The loops go on the right-hand front or the left-hand back of the garment or item you are making.

1 Mark the placement lines on the fabric using tacking stitches. Be sure the horizontal lines are equally spaced.

Diameter of button

Seamline

Raw edge

2 Place the loop to the fabric. The folded end of the loop should be on the inner tacking line and the cut ends to the raw edge. Centre the loop over the tack line.

3 Machine the loops just inside the seam allowance at the centre line.

4 Stitch another row to ensure the loops are secure.

5 Place the facing or lining over the loops to finish.

6 The completed loop will extend from the edge of the fabric.

FROG FASTENINGS

A loop made from a decorative cord is often found on garments with an oriental influence. These so-called frog fastenings can be purchased, although they are straightforward to make. A matching ball button can be made from cord as well, by twisting the cord over and under itself.

▶ MAKING A FROG FASTENER

1 Twist the cord into this shape and secure the raw ends together under the centre of the shape with fabric glue.

Loop to go over the button

2 Secure the cord by stitching along each edge with a small hand stitch. Use a matching thread.

▶ TYING A BALL BUTTON

1 Start by making a loop in the cord.

2 Twist the cord to make another loop over the first loop. The end of the cord goes under the first side.

3 Take the cord over, under, over, and under all the other loops.

4 Pull the two ends to tighten into a ball button.

5 Stitch the ends into a decorative pattern to match the frog fastener.

HOW TO CUT BIAS STRIPS **p.154** ▪ SEWING ON A SHANKED BUTTON **p.302**

OTHER **FASTENINGS**

There are many alternative ways to fasten garments, craft projects, and other items, some of which can be used instead of or in conjunction with other fasteners. These include hooks and eyes, snaps, tape fasteners, and laced eyelets.

DIRECTORY OF OTHER FASTENINGS

HOOK AND EYE (p.319)

TROUSER HOOK AND BAR (p.319)

SNAP FASTENER (p.320)

VELCRO™ (p.320)

SNAP TAPE (p.321)

HOOK AND EYE TAPE (p.321)

EYELETS (p.321)

HOOKS AND EYES

There are a multitude of different types of hook and eye fasteners. Purchased hooks and eyes are made from metal and are normally silver or black in colour. Different-shaped hooks and eyes are used on different garments – large, broad hooks and eyes can be decorative and stitched to show on the outside, while the tiny fasteners are meant to be discreet. A hook that goes into a hand-worked eye produces a neat, close fastening.

▶ ATTACHING HOOKS AND EYES

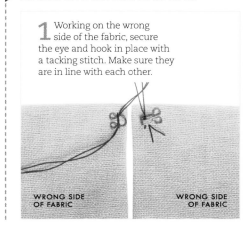

1 Working on the wrong side of the fabric, secure the eye and hook in place with a tacking stitch. Make sure they are in line with each other.

WRONG SIDE OF FABRIC   WRONG SIDE OF FABRIC

2 Stitch around each circular end with a buttonhole stitch on both hook and eye.

3 Place a few over-stitches under the hook to stop it moving.

▶ HAND-WORKED EYE

1 Using a double thread, work several small loops into the edge of the fabric.

RIGHT SIDE OF FABRIC

2 Buttonhole stitch over these loops.

RIGHT SIDE OF FABRIC

3 The completed loop will have a neat row of tight buttonhole stitches.

RIGHT SIDE OF FABRIC

▶ TROUSER HOOK AND BAR

1 The hook and bar fastener for trouser and skirt waistbands is large and flat. Tack the hook and bar in position. Do not tack through the holes that are used for securing.

2 Buttonhole stitch through each hole on the hook and bar.

HOOK AND EYE TAPE **p.321**

TECHNIQUES

SNAPS

Difficulty level ✱✱✱✱✱

A snap is a ball and socket fastener that is used to hold two overlapping edges closed. The ball side goes on top and the socket side underneath. Snaps can be round or square and can be made from metal or plastic.

▶ **METAL SNAPS**

▶ **PLASTIC SNAPS**

1 Tack the ball and socket halves of the snap in place.

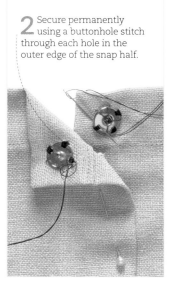

2 Secure permanently using a buttonhole stitch through each hole in the outer edge of the snap half.

3 Remove the tacks.

A plastic snap may be white or clear plastic and is usually square in shape. Stitch in place as for a metal snap (see left).

TAPE FASTENERS

Difficulty level ✱✱✱✱✱

In addition to individual small fasteners, there are fastenings in the form of tapes that can be sewn on or stuck on. Velcro™, a hook and loop tape, is available in many colours and types. Sewn-on Velcro™ is ideal for both clothing and soft furnishings, while the stick-on variety can be used to fix curtain pelmets and blinds to battens on windows. Plain cotton tape with snap fasteners is used primarily in soft furnishings. Hook and eye tape is found in underwear or down the front of a shirt or jacket, where it can be very decorative.

▶ **VELCRO™**

1 Pin the Velcro™ in place. The loop side should be underneath and the hook side on top.

2 Stitch around all the edges.

◀ USEFUL EXTRAS **p.21** ● BONING **p.27** ● TACKING STITCHES **p.89**

▶ **SNAP TAPE**

1 Pin the tape in position. Make sure that the snaps align.

2 Use the zip foot to stitch around all sides of the tape.

▶ **HOOK AND EYE TAPE**

1 The eye side of the tape features a slot into which the fabric is inserted. Pin in place.

2 Stitch along the edge using either a stretch stitch or a narrow 3-step zigzag stitch.

3 Wrap the hook side of the tape over the raw edge of the fabric.

4 Stitch to match up with the eye side.

EYELETS

Difficulty level ✳✳✳✳

An eyelet fastening can be very decorative and is often found on bridal wear and prom dresses. A piece of boning needs to be inserted into the fabric between the edge and the eyelets, to give strength. You will require eyelet pliers to punch the holes and then insert the eyelets.

▶ **1** Using the pliers, punch out the holes for the eyelets at 3–4cm (1¼–1½in) intervals.

2 Place an eyelet in each hole. Change the heads on the pliers and squeeze the eyelet in place.

3 Insert a row of eyelets on either side of the back opening.

Boning channel

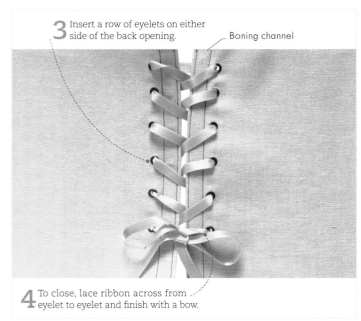

4 To close, lace ribbon across from eyelet to eyelet and finish with a bow.

HAND STITCHES **pp.90–91** ● STITCHES MADE WITH A MACHINE **pp.92–93**

LININGS AND INTERFACINGS

Interfacings provide shape and structure in a garment or in soft furnishing, while a lining will make any garment more comfortable to wear as well as hiding the inside seams and stitching from view.

TECHNIQUES

INTERLININGS AND INTERFACINGS

Interlinings are similar to interfacings, the difference being that an interfacing is an extra layer of fabric attached in a small area, while an interlining is attached to a whole garment or item. Interlinings and interfacings may be woven, knitted, or non-woven and can be applied with heat (fusible) or sewn in. Always try to buy products recommended for domestic use. Be sure to cut all these fabrics on the straight of the grain even if they are non-woven.

INTERLININGS

These are fabrics that cover the inside of an entire garment. They are cut to the same pattern pieces and joined to the main fabric by means of tacking stitches around the edges. The two layers are treated as one during construction.

▶ **MUSLIN**

This is a cotton muslin. Use it to interline wools and cottons, for jackets, skirts, and dresses.

▶ **SILK ORGANZA**

An interlining of silk organza will give shape and structure. Use in special-occasion wear and silk fabrics as well as wool in tailored skirts.

▶ **DRESS NET**

Net is used for bounce and rustle! Use in special-occasion wear for effect and to prevent creasing.

INTERFACINGS

Difficulty level ★★★★★

An interfacing may be fusible or non-fusible (sew-in) and is only attached to part of a garment or item. Sections of a garment normally interfaced include the collar and cuffs and the facings. In addition to fusible interfacings, there are also fusible tapes available, which are used to prevent a fabric from stretching and will support edges, and fusible webs that provide stiffening.

▶ **NON-FUSIBLE INTERFACINGS**

All of these interfacings need to be tacked to the main fabric around the edges prior to construction of the work or seam neatening.

Muslin

Silk organza

Non-woven interfacing

Alpaca tailoring canvas

Sometimes the interfacing does not cover the whole pattern piece, which occurs in tailored garments. Tack to the main fabric along the outer edges and herringbone stitch the inner edges.

INTERFACINGS pp.54–55 • **TACKING STITCHES p.89** • **HAND STITCHES pp.90–91** • **APPLYING INTERFACING TO A FACING p.153**

▶ **FUSIBLE INTERFACINGS**

A fusible interfacing is used in the same areas as a sew-in interfacing. To prevent the fusible interfacing from showing on the right side of the work, use pinking shears on the edge of the interfacing.

Lightweight woven fusible interfacing

Knitted fusible interfacing

Non-woven fusible interfacing

▶ **INTERFACINGS AND INTERLININGS COMBINED**

Muslin interlining

Alpaca interfacing

On structured garments there may be both interlining and interfacing. The interlining is applied first and the interfacing is attached on top. Tack around the outside edge and herringbone stitch the inner edges.

▶ **FRAME FUSING**

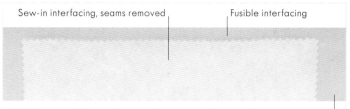

Sew-in interfacing, seams removed

Fusible interfacing

Seam allowance

This is a technique that combines a sew-in interfacing with a fusible. It is used in more structured garments to create tailored collars and cuffs. The fusible interfacing is placed on top to seal the sew-in interfacing in place in the seam allowances.

▶ **STRAIGHT FUSIBLE TAPE**

Straight grain tape is about 2cm (¾in) wide and has little give in it. Use it to stabilize edges. On some seams it may replace stay stitching. To fuse around curves, snip through the tape at 90 degrees.

▶ **BIAS FUSIBLE TAPE**

Bias tape has a machined straight stitch through it. As the tape is cut on the bias, it will bend around curves. When fusing the tape in position, the stitching line in the tape should be on the fabric stitching line.

▶ **SLOTTED FUSIBLE TAPE**

Slotted fusible is wider than other fusible tapes, and has a slotted edge. The tape is used to shape pocket tops and hems on jackets. Fuse in position so that the slots correspond to the foldline in the fabric.

INTERFACINGS, FACINGS, AND LININGS

Difficulty level ✹✹✹✹✹

On tailored and more structured garments, the facing will be interfaced and this is then attached to the lining.

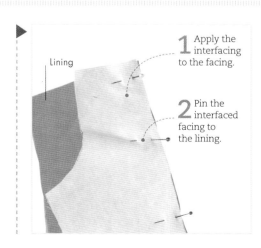

Lining

1 Apply the interfacing to the facing.

2 Pin the interfaced facing to the lining.

3 Stitch together.

4 Press the seam towards the lining.

STORAGE **BASKETS**

Difficulty level ✱✱✱✱✱

Encourage children to have fun tidying their toys into this set of fabric baskets. Heavyweight interfacing creates the boxy shape of each basket, and handles make them portable.

Of course, the baskets are ideal for storing all sorts of other objects, too, including your sewing items.

TECHNIQUES USED Stitching corners and curves **p.102**, Layering a seam **p.108**, Interlinings and interfacings **p.324–325**

YOU WILL NEED

- 70 x 137cm (28 x 54in) medium-weight cotton for large basket outer
- 70 x 110cm (28 x 43in) medium-weight cotton for large basket inner
- 60 x 137cm (24 x 54in) medium-weight cotton for small basket outer
- 60 x 110cm (24 x 43in) medium-weight cotton for small basket inner
- 120 x 90cm (48 x 36in) firm fusible interfacing
- 280 x 30cm (110 x 12in) ultra-heavy fusible interfacing
- Matching thread for each fabric

PIECES TO CUT

Outer fabric for large basket

70cm (28in)

26cm (10¼in)

Outer side panel 1	32cm (12¾in)
Outer side panel 2	32cm (12¾in)
Outer side panel 3	32cm (12¾in)

32cm (12¾in)

| Outer side panel 4 | Outer base | 32cm (12¾in) |

26cm (10¼in)

137cm (54in)

Selvedge

Inner fabric for large basket

70cm (28in)

Handle 1	9cm (3½in)
Inner side panel 1	
	26cm (10¼in)
	Handle 2	9cm (3½in)
Inner side panel 2	Inner side panel 3	32cm (12¾in)
Inner side panel 4	Inner base	32cm (12¾in)
26cm (10¼in)	32cm (12¾in)	

110cm (43in)

Selvedge

For outer small basket
Side panels: 28 x 22cm (11 x 9in)
Base: 28 x 28cm (11 x 11in)

For inner small basket
Side panels: 28 x 22cm (11 x 9in)
Base: 28 x 28cm (11 x 11in)
Handles: 9 x 26cm (3½ x 10¼in)

▶ **MAKE THE OUTER SIDES**

1 For each basket, cut a piece of firm fusible interfacing to the same size as the outer base and apply to the wrong side of the base.

2 Cut four pieces of ultra-heavy fusible interfacing to the same size as the four outer side panels.

3 Apply the ultra-heavy interfacing to the wrong side of each panel. As the interfacing is thick, you will need to press the fabric on the right side too.

4 Stitch the side panels together, right side to right side, in pairs along one short edge using a seam alowance of 1cm (⅜in). Finish the seam 1cm (⅜in) above the lower edge. Press the seams open.

WRONG SIDE OF OUTER SIDE PANEL

Stitching stops 1cm (⅜in) above lower edge

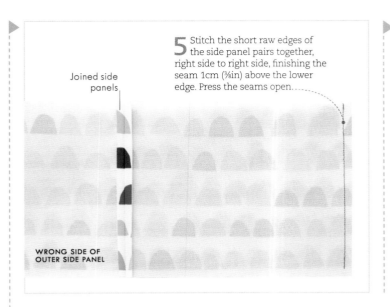

5 Stitch the short raw edges of the side panel pairs together, right side to right side, finishing the seam 1cm (⅜in) above the lower edge. Press the seams open.

Joined side panels

WRONG SIDE OF OUTER SIDE PANEL

▶ MAKE THE HANDLES

1 From ultra-heavy fusible interfacing, cut two 26 x 3cm (10¼ x 1¼in) rectangles for the handles for each basket. Press the interfacing handles to the wrong side of the fabric handles, 1.2cm (½in) inside one long edge. Press the raw edges over the interfacing.

2 Turn under the extending long raw edge so it is level with the handle edge. Pin in place.

3 Top-stitch both long edges close to the edge.

4 Pin the ends of one handle to the upper edge on the right side of one side panel. Make sure the inner edges of the handle are 8.5cm (3¼in) apart. Stitch using a 6mm (¼in) seam allowance.

5 Repeat to stitch the other handle to the opposite side panel on the other joined pair of side panels.

8.5cm (3¼in)

RIGHT SIDE OF OUTER SIDE PANEL

▶ ATTACH THE OUTER PANELS TO THE BASE

WRONG SIDE OF OUTER SIDE PANEL

Base

1 Pin, tack, and stitch the side panels to the base, right side to right side using a 1cm (⅜in) seam allowance. To pivot at the corners, lift the presser foot, turn the base so the next edge is facing you, and fold the side panel out of the way. Lower the presser foot and continue stitching.

2 Clip the corners, making sure you don't get too close to the stitching.

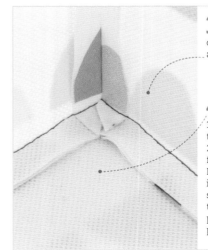

3 Turn the basket right side out. The interfacing will crease but it will smooth out flat again when ironed.

4 From ultra-heavy fusible interfacing, cut one 30 x 30cm (12 x 12in) square for the large basket base and one 26 x 26cm (10¼ x 10¼in) square for the small basket base. Position the interfacing base inside the basket on the base, slipping the interfacing under the seam allowance. Press in place, turn the basket over, and press the underside.

▶ MAKE THE INNER BASKET

WRONG SIDE OF
INNER SIDE PANEL

Turning gap in
base seam

1 Cut pieces of firm fusible interfacing to the same dimensions as the inner side panels and base, and apply to the wrong side of the pieces.

2 Repeat the steps for joining the side panels and base, without handles, to make the inner basket. Leave a 20–24cm (8–9½in) gap in the base seam, to turn through. Press the seams open.

▶ JOIN THE INNER AND OUTER BASKETS

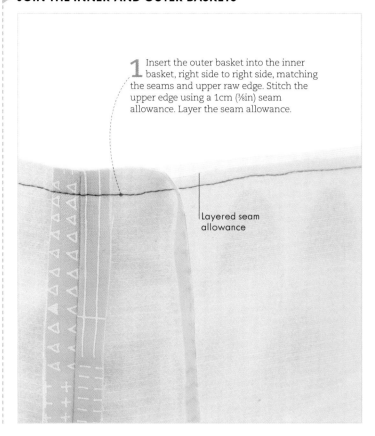

1 Insert the outer basket into the inner basket, right side to right side, matching the seams and upper raw edge. Stitch the upper edge using a 1cm (⅜in) seam allowance. Layer the seam allowance.

Layered seam allowance

2 Turn the basket right side out through the gap. Turn under the raw edges of the gap, and hand stitch the gap closed.

3 Turn the inner basket to the interior of the outer basket. Press the basket to remove the creases. Press the upper edge. Top-stitch 7.5mm (³⁄₁₆in) below the upper edge.

LININGS

A lining is placed inside a garment primarily to make the garment more comfortable to wear – it will prevent the garment from sticking to you. It will also make the garment last longer. Choose a good-quality lining made from rayon or acetate as these fabrics will breathe with your body. Polyester linings can be sticky to wear.

LINING A BODICE

Difficulty level ✱✱✱✱✱

On sleeveless dresses and fitted tops, a lined bodice is comfortable and it reduces bulk. The insertion of a lining is done prior to the centre back seam being joined and the side seams being joined.

1 Place the lining bodice to the fabric bodice, right side to right side. Match the shoulder seams and the neck and armhole edges.

2 Stitch together around the neck edge and the armhole edge using a 1.5cm (⅝in) seam allowance.

3 Clip the seam allowance around the neck and armhole.

4 To turn through to the right side, pull the back bodice through the shoulder.

5 Repeat for the other shoulder. Press.

6 Join the side seams by stitching through the fabric and lining in one continuous seam.

7 Press all the seams.

TACKING STITCHES p.89 ● **HAND STITCHES pp.90–91** ● **STITCHES MADE WITH A MACHINE pp.92–93**

LINING A SKIRT

Difficulty level ✱✱✱✱✱

Cut the lining out the same as the skirt, using the same pattern pieces, and join together, leaving a gap for the zip. Do not stitch in the darts.

1 Pin the lining to the skirt at the waist. Match all the seams.

2 Make tucks in the lining to correspond to the darts in the skirt.

Zip opening

3 Machine the lining to the fabric at the waist edge as the facing or waistband is being attached.

Centre back

HEMMING A LINING

Difficulty level ✱✱✱✱✱

The lining on a skirt or dress should be slightly shorter – about 4cm (1½in) – than the finished garment, so that the lining does not show when you are walking or sitting.

1 Machine the hem on the lining, making a double turn hem of 4cm (1½in).

2 Turn up the hem on the garment and stitch in place. The lining hem should sit about 4cm (1½in) from the hem fold.

LINING AROUND A SPLIT

Difficulty level ✱✱✱✱✱

If there is a split in a hemline, the lining will need to be stitched around it securely. First construct the skirt, with its split finished, corners mitred, and hemmed. Finish the lining hem in the same way.

1 Pin the lining to the fabric, wrong side to wrong side.

2 Secure the lining and fabric together at the top of the split, using a hand-worked bar tack.

3 Hand stitch the lining to the fabric around both sides of the split. The lining should be level at the hem edge.

REDUCING SEAM BULK **pp.108–109** ● ATTACHING A STRAIGHT WAISTBAND **p.192** ● MACHINED HEMS **p.266**

TECHNIQUES

LINING AROUND A VENT

Difficulty level ★★★★★

Some skirts and jackets feature a vent at the hemline, where the fabric overlaps to allow for movement. Lining around a vent can be tricky though, as the pattern pieces for the vent can be confusing.

1 On both back pieces, mark the top of the vent as indicated on your pattern using tailor's tacks.

2 Place the back pieces right side to right side, matching the tailor's tacks. Stitch the centre back seam of the garment, stopping at the tailor's tack.

3 On both back pieces, mark the fold line from the tailor's tack to the hem with a row of tacking stitches.

WRONG SIDE OF RIGHT-HAND BACK PIECE

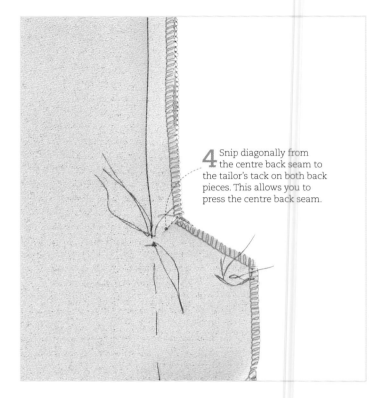

4 Snip diagonally from the centre back seam to the tailor's tack on both back pieces. This allows you to press the centre back seam.

5 Press open the centre back seam.

6 On the right-hand back (as worn), turn under 1.5cm (⅝in) on the vent extension in line with the tailor's tack. Hand stitch it in place using a herringbone stitch.

7 Turn up the hem and secure it using a blind hem stitch.

WRONG SIDE OF RIGHT-HAND BACK PIECE

WRONG SIDE OF LEFT-HAND BACK PIECE

WRONG SIDE OF RIGHT-HAND BACK PIECE

WRONG SIDE OF LEFT-HAND BACK PIECE

Vent extension

8 On the left-hand back, fold the vent extension along the tacked fold line.

9 Mitre the corner that meets the hem.

10 Fold the vent extension on the right-hand back down to overlap the left-hand back. Press the hem and vent.

PATTERN MARKING **p.82–83** ● TACKING STITCHES **p.89** ● HAND STITCHES **pp.90–91** ● STITCHES MADE WITH A MACHINE **pp.92–93**

11 Cut the lining pieces according to your pattern.

12 On both back pieces, mark the vent as indicated on your pattern using tailor's tacks.

13 Neaten the centre back edges using a 3-thread overlock stitch or zigzag stitch.

14 Reinforce the inner corners as shown, stitching through the tailor's tacks about 2cm (¾in) from, and parallel to, the edge.

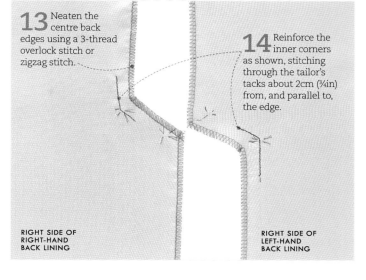

RIGHT SIDE OF RIGHT-HAND BACK LINING

RIGHT SIDE OF LEFT-HAND BACK LINING

WRONG SIDE OF LEFT-HAND BACK LINING

WRONG SIDE OF RIGHT-HAND BACK LINING

15 Place the back lining pieces right side to right side, matching the tailor's tacks. Stitch the centre back seam of the garment, stopping at the tailor's tack.

16 Press the centre back seam open then snip diagonally from the centre back edge into the reinforced corners.

17 At the bottom edge, make a double-turn hem and machine it in place.

RIGHT SIDE OF LEFT-HAND BACK LINING

RIGHT SIDE OF RIGHT-HAND BACK LINING

18 Place the lining to the skirt wrong side to wrong side, matching them at the centre back seam. Pin in place.

19 On the right-hand back lining (as worn), turn under the edge of the opening by 1.5cm (⅝in) and pin to the seam on the skirt vent extension.

RIGHT SIDE OF LEFT-HAND BACK LINING

RIGHT SIDE OF RIGHT-HAND BACK LINING

20 On the left-hand back lining (as worn), turn under the edge of the opening by 1.5cm (⅝in). This should fit alongside the right-hand side of the vent. Pin in place.

21 At the top of the vent, push the seam allowance of the right-hand back lining under the diagonal part of the left-hand-back lining.

22 Fold the diagonal part under and pin.

RIGHT SIDE OF RIGHT-HAND BACK LINING

RIGHT SIDE OF LEFT-HAND BACK LINING

23 Stitch the lining to the skirt around the vent using a flat fell stitch.

24 Machine diagonally from the centre back seam to the top of the vent, stitching through all layers. Pin in place.

25 Press to finish. The lining hem should remain unattached to the skirt hem.

REDUCING SEAM BULK **pp.108—09** • HAND-STITCHED HEMS **pp.264—265** • MACHINED HEMS **p.266** • MITRED CORNERS **p.269**

PROFESSIONAL TECHNIQUES

Once you have mastered the basics of sewing it is time to try some advanced techniques, such as those involved in modern tailoring or boning a bodice for special-occasion wear. These take a little more time and care to execute.

SPEED **TAILORING**

Speed tailoring is the term given to modern tailoring techniques that use fusible interfacings to give shape and structure to a jacket or coat. Choose woven fusible interfacings and cut on the same grain as the jacket fabric pieces. If possible, use two different interfacings – one a medium weight and one a light weight – in conjunction with fusible tapes to stabilize the edges of the jacket. If interfacings of different weights are not available, choose a lightweight product and use two layers if required in the front of the jacket.

COMPONENTS OF A JACKET

Difficulty level ✳✳✳✳✳

These photographs show where to place the fusible interfacing on a jacket or coat. Your pattern may be cut differently to this – the front and back may be one piece, not two as shown here, and you may have a two-piece sleeve – but the same principle will apply, of a heavier interfacing at the front and a lighter one at the back, with reinforcement through the shoulder.

▶ **FRONT**

Medium-weight fusible interfacing with 1.5cm (⅝in) seam allowances removed

Shoulder plate, cut on a bias grain to reinforce the shoulder

A 2cm (¾in) wide stitch-reinforced fusible tape to stop the leading edges of the jacket stretching

▶ **SIDE FRONT**

Medium-weight fusible interfacing with 1.5cm (⅝in) seam allowances removed

Bias tape fused through armhole

▶ **SIDE BACK**

Bias tape fused on through armhole

Section of medium-weight fusible 18cm (7¼in) deep to strengthen the armhole

Lightweight fusible all over the piece

Seam allowance removed on the medium-weight fusible

FUSIBLE INTERFACINGS p.54 ● **FABRIC GRAIN AND NAP p.76**

▶ BACK

Bias tape fused on at armhole

Bias tape fused on at neck edge

Medium-weight fusible over the shoulders to reinforce, cut 18cm (7¼in) deep at armhole edge and 25cm (10in) deep at centre back, seam allowances removed

Lightweight fusible all over

▶ SLEEVE

Lightweight fusible through upper part of sleeve

Edge of fusible cut with pinking shears

Slotted fusible hem tape to reinforce hem edge

▶ FRONT FACING

Lightweight fusible all over

▶ UPPER COLLAR

Lightweight fusible all over

▶ UNDER COLLAR

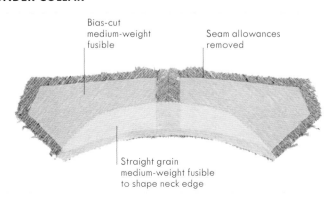

Bias-cut medium-weight fusible

Seam allowances removed

Straight grain medium-weight fusible to shape neck edge

▶ FINISHED JACKET

PATTERN LAYOUT **pp.78—79** ● INTERFACINGS **pp.324—325**

TECHNIQUES

JETTED POCKET

Difficulty level ✳✳✳✳✳

This is a professional pocket found on many suit jackets. Great care has to be taken when making this pocket because there is no flap for it to hide behind!

1 Cut out the welts (the strips that make the edges of the pocket). Apply lightweight fusible interfacing to them on the wrong side.

2 Transfer the marks from the pattern using tailor's tacks.

3 Press in half, wrong side to wrong side.

4 Mark the pocket position on the fabric, as indicated on your pattern, using tailor's tacks.

RIGHT SIDE OF FABRIC

5 Start with the upper welt. Place it to the right side of the jacket front. The raw edge of the welt is towards the hem, with the centre line of the welt over the top row of tacking stitches, matching the tailor's tacks. Pin in place.

6 Machine along the centre of the welt. Stitch between the tailor's tacks only.

7 Position the lower welt on the jacket, placing the raw edges together.

8 Stitch through the centre of the lower welt. Ensure both rows of stitching are exactly the same length.

9 Place the lining over the welts, raw edges to the centre. Pin to secure.

10 Stitch the lining in place over the stitching line of the welts – you can feel the indentation of welt stitching.

FUSIBLE INTERFACINGS p.54 • **PATTERN MARKING pp.82–83**

11 Slash through the jacket fabric between the welts (see Jetted pocket with flap, pp.246–247).

12 Push the lining and the ends of the welts through to the back.

WRONG SIDE OF FABRIC

13 Press the lining and welts on the wrong side as shown.

Square ends on welts

RIGHT SIDE OF FABRIC

14 On the right side, whip stitch the folds of the welts together.

15 On the reverse, fold the top layer of the pocket lining down to meet the bottom layer. Make the pocket bag by stitching from one end of the welts, around the bottom, to the other end of the welts.

16 Remove the whip stitches from across the pocket opening.

HAND STITCHES **pp.90–91** • STITCHES MADE WITH A MACHINE **pp.92–93** • JETTED POCKET WITH FLAP **pp.246–247**

TECHNIQUES

COLLAR APPLICATION

A notched collar is a sign of a tailored jacket. This type of collar consists of an upper and under collar, and a facing that folds back to form the rever on either side. Careful stitching and accurate marking are required.

1 Attach the upper collar to the front facing and back neck lining.

Upper collar

Back neck lining

3 Press the seam open over a tailor's ham.

2 Stop stitching at the tailor's tack at the front edge.

Front facing

4 Clip the seam as necessary.

5 Join the under collar to the jacket front and back.

Under collar

JACKET FRONT

6 Stop stitching at the tailor's tack at the front edge.

7 Press the seam open. Clip as necessary.

8 Place the jacket and the lining together. Match the collar sections.

UNDER COLLAR

JACKET FRONT

9 Stitch around the collar, stopping and starting the stitching at the tailor's tacks at the front edge.

10 Stitch the front facing to the jacket front. Start stitching at the tailor's tack at the front edge. The stitching line from the collar and the stitching line from the facing should line up but not cross each other.

11 Layer the seam.

JACKET FRONT

12 On the inside, herringbone stitch the neck seams together.

13 Turn the collar and revers to the right side.

14 Press using a steam iron and cloth. Roll the seam towards the back of the garment so that it does not show on the right side.

SET-IN SLEEVE

On a tailored jacket, the sleeve needs to be set in to have a rounded sleeve head, which is created with polyester wadding. The sleeve head will ensure that the sleeve hangs perfectly.

1 Cut a piece of polyester wadding to fit the sleeve head. The wadding should be approx 5cm (2in) deep at the centre. Pin in place.

2 Insert two rows of gather (ease) stitches to attach the wadding to the sleeve.

3 Make up the sleeve.

4 Insert the sleeve into the armhole, right side to right side. Pin in place.

5 Pull up the ease stitches to fit. The sleeve head will absorb the fullness.

6 Machine in place. Make a second row of machining close to the first stitching.

Back slope   Concave side   Front slope

7 The shoulder pad can now be inserted. The back slope of the shoulder pad is longer than the front slope. The concave side will face the jacket lining.

Concave side of shoulder pad

8 Attach the shoulder pad at the edge of the sleeve seam using a firm running stitch.

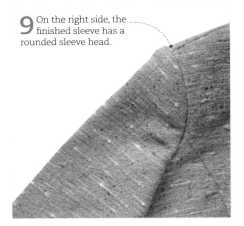

9 On the right side, the finished sleeve has a rounded sleeve head.

HEM AND LINING

When making a jacket, the jacket hem is turned up first and then the lining is hemmed. The jacket hem needs to be reinforced first with a fusible strip. Make sure that the hem edge is parallel to the ground.

1 Turn up the hem on the jacket by about 4cm (1½in). Pin to secure.

2 Roll back the edge of the hem and herringbone stitch in place.

3 Bring the lining down over the jacket hem. Turn up the hem of the lining so that it is level to the jacket hem, then push up to 2cm (¾in) from the hem edge. At the facing edge, the lining is level with the hem edge. Pin.

4 Use a slip hem stitch to secure the lining in place.

REDUCING SEAM BULK pp.108–109 ● **HOW TO MAKE AND FIT GATHERS p.135** ● **INSERTING A SET-IN SLEEVE p.211** ● **INTERFACINGS pp.324–325**

BONED **BODICES**

A strapless bodice will require boning to be inserted to prevent the bodice from falling down. The boning will also give extra structure to the bodice and prevent wrinkles. Boning can be a simple process, or more complex using interfacings for additional structure and shape.

COUTURE BONED BODICE

Difficulty level ★★★★✳

A couture boned bodice is the more complicated of the two methods of bodice construction, but it is well worth the extra work involved as the finished result is wrinkle-free and self-supporting. This technique can be used for bridal bodices and special-occasion wear.

▶ COMPONENTS OF THE BODICE

— Silk dupion

— Flat domette

— Cotton canvas

— Calico

1 On each piece of cotton canvas, stitch a piece of bias binding to make a boning channel. On the back, stitch bias binding in the centre.

2 On the side back and side front, stitch bias binding down the centre.

3 On the centre front, stitch bias binding below the bust to the waist.

4 Stitch across the top of each bias tape 2cm (¾in) from the top edge.

5 Insert nylon boning into the bias binding.

6 Layer the sections of the bodice together. Put the calico at the bottom, then the cotton canvas, boning uppermost, then the flat domette, and finally the silk dupion.

7 Tack around the edge to secure all the layers.

8 Place the bodice sections together, right side to right side. Stitch using a 1.5cm (⅝in) seam allowance.

9 Trim the cotton canvas from the seam allowance.

TECHNIQUES

10 Press all the seams open. Clip as required. Use a tailor's ham under the curves.

11 After pressing, the princess seams at the front will be smoothly tapered to the waist.

12 Join the lining together and press the seams open.

13 Pin the lining to the bodice around the top edge and down the centre back. Match all vertical seam allowances.

14 Clip and layer the seam, then turn to the right side. Press.

15 Press the seam allowances of the bodice and lining seam towards the lining. Understitch.

16 At the hem edge, turn up the silk bodice and herringbone stitch in place.

17 Turn up the lining hem and pin, then hand stitch to the silk.

18 The completed bodice will stand on its own!

A BASIC BONING TECHNIQUE

Difficulty level ★★★★★

For a simpler bodice on a dress or as a bodice on its own, this is a lightweight, quick technique.

1 Join the lining sections together.

2 Press the seam allowances together towards the centre.

3 Sew a piece of narrow polyester boning to each set of seam allowances. Use a zigzag stitch to secure.

4 Repeat on all seams to complete the lining.

5 Apply a fusible interfacing to all the bodice sections.

6 Join the bodice sections together. Press the seams open.

7 Join the bodice and lining together at the upper edge.

8 Press the seam towards the lining and understitch.

STITCHES MADE WITH A MACHINE **pp.92–93** • REDUCING SEAM BULK **pp.108–109** • STITCH FINISHES **p.109** • LINING A BODICE **p.330**

TECHNIQUES

APPLIQUÉ AND QUILTING

Simple finishing touches can be used to good effect on many items. The term appliqué applies to one fabric being stitched to another in a decorative manner. The fabric to be appliquéd must be interfaced to support the fabric that is to be attached. Appliqué can be drawn by hand, then cut and stitched down, or it can be created by a computer pattern on the embroidery machine. The embroidery machine can also be used to create quilting, or this can be done by hand or with a sewing machine.

HAND-DRAWN APPLIQUÉ

Difficulty level ★★★★★

This technique involves drawing the chosen design on to a piece of double-sided fusible web, after which the design is fused in place on fabric prior to being stitched.

1 Draw a decorative shape, such as a flower, on to a piece of double-sided fusible web.

2 Using the iron, fuse the web on to your chosen fabric.

3 Cut out the shape from the fabric.

4 Place the shape, fusible web-side down, where it is to be positioned on fabric and fuse in place.

5 Using a wide, close zigzag stitch, stitch around the shape.

6 For a flower, stitch on top of the fabric appliqué to make petal shapes.

MACHINE APPLIQUÉ

Difficulty level ★★★★★

There are designs available for appliqué if you have an embroidery machine. You will need to use a special fusible embroidery backer on both the fabric for the appliqué and the base fabric.

1 Place the base fabric and appliqué fabric in the embroidery hoop and stitch out the first part of the design.

2 Trim the appliqué fabric back to the stitching lines.

3 Complete the computerized embroidery.

QUILTING

This is a technique that involves stitching through two layers of fabric, one of which is a wadding. The stitching sinks into the wadding, creating a padded effect. Quilting can be done by hand, with a sewing machine, or using computerized embroidery.

Difficulty level ✱✱✱✱✱

▶ COMPONENTS OF QUILTING

Top fabric

Wadding

▶ HORIZONTAL QUILTING

Tack the wadding and top fabric together. Stitch double lines with spaces between. Use a stitch length of 4.0 on your machine.

▶ DIAMOND QUILTING

1 Diagonally tack the wadding and top fabric together.

2 Set the machine to a stitch length of 4.0, with the needle on the one side of the foot. Stitch rows of machining diagonally across. Use the width of the machine foot as a guide to keep the rows parallel.

3 Stitch parallel rows in the opposite diagonal directions, to create diamond shapes.

▶ FREEFORM QUILTING

Tack the wadding and top fabric together. Stitch at random.

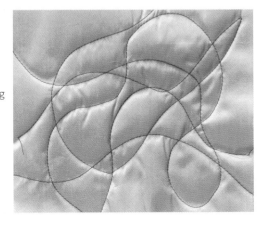

▶ COMPUTERIZED QUILTING

Tack the wadding and top fabric together, then stitch on a quilted pattern with the embroidery machine.

STITCHES MADE WITH A MACHINE **pp.92–93** ● INTERFACINGS **pp.324–325**

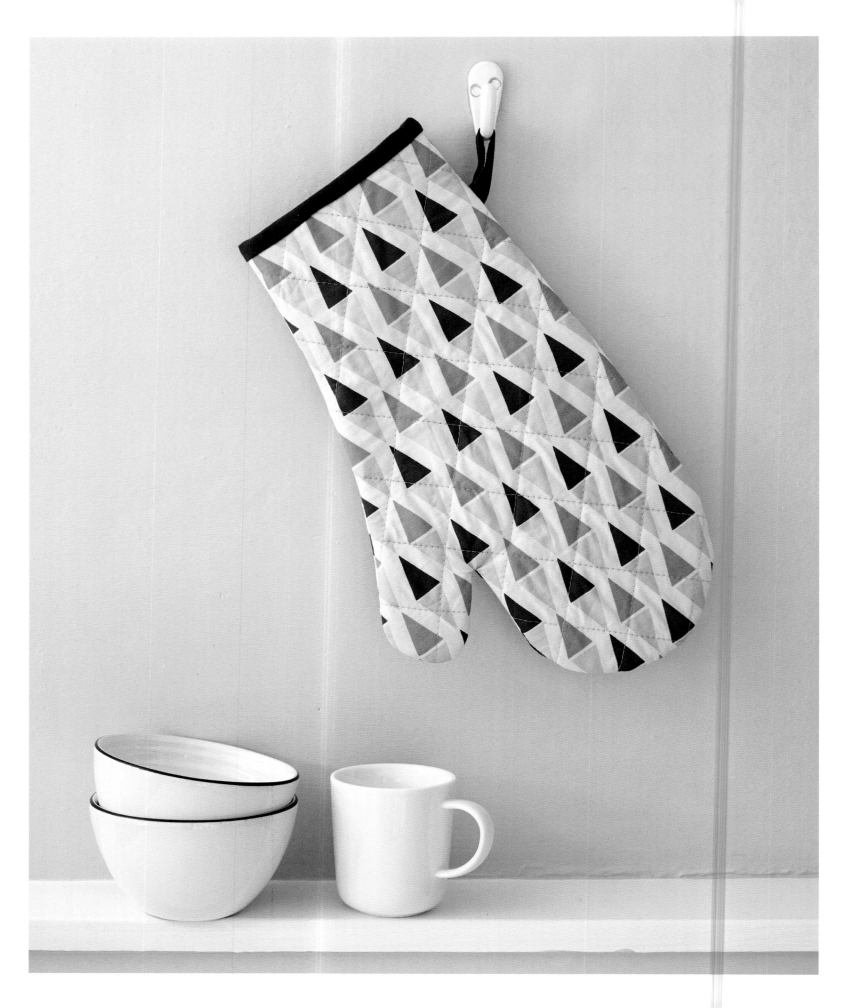

OVEN **MITT**

Difficulty level ✳✳✳✳✳

You can customize this attractive kitchen accessory with fabrics that coordinate with your kitchen, but this small-scale project is also great for using up spare fabric. Be sure to choose insulated wadding, which is heat-protective, so that your oven mitt is safe for handling hot items.

TECHNIQUES USED Zigzagged seam neatening **p.95**, How to cut bias strips **p.154**, Quilting **p.345**

YOU WILL NEED

- Pattern template on p.387
- 2 pieces of 40 x 27cm (15¾ x 10½in) medium-weight cotton for outer pieces
- 2 pieces of 40 x 27cm (15¾ x 10½in) medium-weight cotton for lining pieces
- 2 pieces of 40 x 27cm (15¾ x 10½in) insulated wadding
- 40 x 30cm (16 x 12in) medium-weight cotton for the bias binding
- Matching or contrast thread
- Tailor's chalk or air-soluble ink pen

PIECES TO CUT

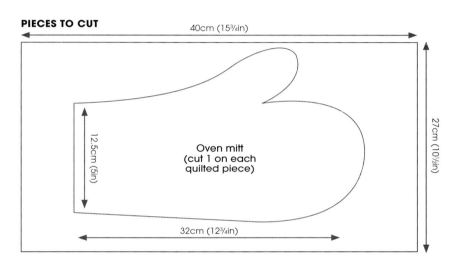

40cm (15¾in)

12.5cm (5in)

Oven mitt
(cut 1 on each
quilted piece)

27cm (10½in)

32cm (12¾in)

▶ **MAKE THE BIAS BINDING FOR THE TRIM AND LOOP**

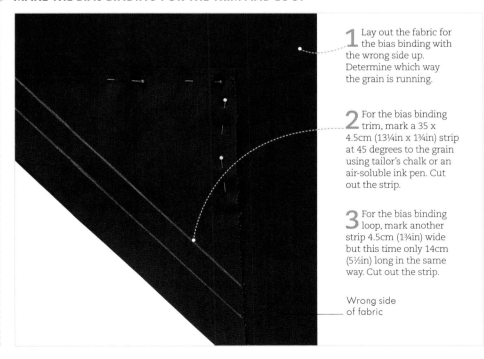

1 Lay out the fabric for the bias binding with the wrong side up. Determine which way the grain is running.

2 For the bias binding trim, mark a 35 x 4.5cm (13¼in x 1¾in) strip at 45 degrees to the grain using tailor's chalk or an air-soluble ink pen. Cut out the strip.

3 For the bias binding loop, mark another strip 4.5cm (1¾in) wide but this time only 14cm (5½in) long in the same way. Cut out the strip.

Wrong side of fabric

4 Thread the bias strip through a 2.5cm (1in) bias tape maker and press. Alternatively, fold 1cm (⅜in) under from each side by hand and press.

5 For the loop, fold the bias tape in half, pin, and machine stitch the open edge to close it.

PROJECT

▶ **MAKE THE QUILTED PIECES**

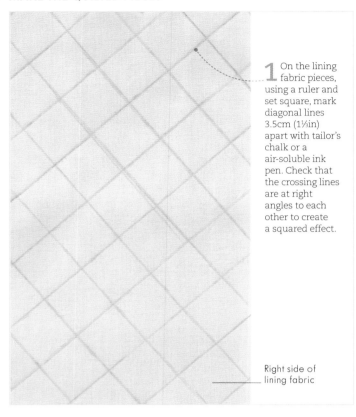

1 On the lining fabric pieces, using a ruler and set square, mark diagonal lines 3.5cm (1⅜in) apart with tailor's chalk or a air-soluble ink pen. Check that the crossing lines are at right angles to each other to create a squared effect.

Right side of lining fabric

2 Create two "sandwiches" of the pieces: place a patterned fabric piece wrong side up on a flat surface, lay a piece of the wadding on top, and finish with a piece of the lining fabric.

3 Pin the three layers together.

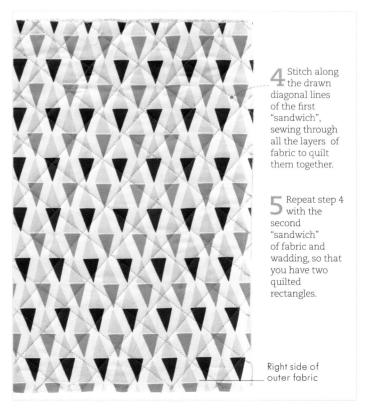

4 Stitch along the drawn diagonal lines of the first "sandwich", sewing through all the layers of fabric to quilt them together.

5 Repeat step 4 with the second "sandwich" of fabric and wadding, so that you have two quilted rectangles.

Right side of outer fabric

▶ **ASSEMBLE THE MITT**

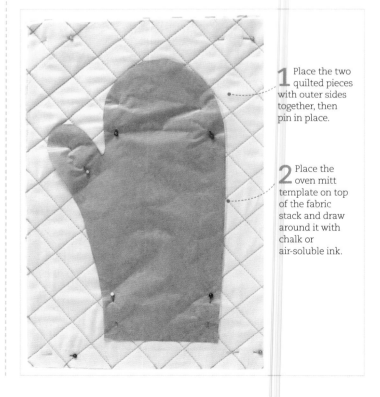

1 Place the two quilted pieces with outer sides together, then pin in place.

2 Place the oven mitt template on top of the fabric stack and draw around it with chalk or air-soluble ink.

4 Machine around the marked shape of the mitt, stitching through all layers. Stitch over the loop, but be sure to leave the bottom edge open.

6 Use a zigzag stitch to neaten the edge.

5 Trim around the outside of your stitching leaving a 5mm (³⁄₁₆in) seam allowance.

7 Snip into the fabric between the fingers and thumb, but take care not to cut any of the stitching.

Bottom of mitt

4cm (1½in)

3 Fold the bias tape for the loop in half lengthways. Place it between the quilted layers, with the looped end facing inwards. Pin it in place 4cm (1½in) from the bottom of the mitt, with raw edges extending past outline of the mitt by 1cm (³⁄₈in).

▶ BIND THE EDGE

1 Turn the mitt the right side out. Place the bias binding right side to right side on the bottom edge of the mitt, aligning the raw edges.

2 Pin in place, and stitch together in the crease of the binding.

3 Turn the mitt inside out and bring the binding to the inside. Hold the folded part of the tape down and sew in place by hand, using a slip stitch.

TECHNIQUES

ROSES AND BOWS

On special-occasion wear a rose can add a superb finishing touch. When the raw edges of a rose are exposed, as in version 2 below, it also looks great made in tweed and suiting fabrics, to add a decorative finish to a tailored jacket. A bow that is permanently fixed in place is a beautiful embellishment on bridal wear.

Difficulty level ★★☆☆☆

▶ ROSE VERSION 1

1 Cut a bias strip 10cm (4in) wide. Fold in half lengthways, wrong side to wrong side.

Angled end

2 Pin the raw edges together.

3 Insert two rows of gather stitches at the raw edge – one row at 1cm (⅜in) from the edge and the other row at 1.3cm (½in).

4 Pull up the gathers, grouping them together and leaving spaces between the groups. The groups and spaces will give the impression of petals.

5 Hold the lower edge of one end in your left hand and loosely wrap the strip around.

6 When you have a rose shape, tuck any raw edges that show into the base.

7 Secure at the base edge with hand stitches.

▶ ROSE VERSION 2

1 Cut a bias strip 10cm (4in) wide.

2 Insert two rows of gather stitches along the centre of the strip. Leave a gap of 3mm (⅛in) between the rows of stitching.

3 Pull up the gathers into groups and spaces (see step 4 above).

4 The groups and spaces will pull up to give a diagonal effect. Fold in half along the stitching lines.

5 Hold the end of the gathers in your left hand and wrap the strip around loosely.

6 Secure at the base with hand stitches. Although the edge is raw, fraying is minimal as the strip has been bias-cut.

▶ BOW

1 To make the loops, cut a piece of silk or other fabric that is four times the length of the loop required and twice the width plus seam allowances.

2 Interline with dress net to the wrong side. Tack the net around the raw edge.

3 Fold in half, right side to right side. Stitch along the raw edge leaving a 1.5cm (⅝in) seam allowance.

4 Turn through to the right side. Fold so that the seamline is in the centre.

5 Bring the short end to the centre. Pin in place.

6 Tack through the centre, using double thread.

7 Pull along the tacking stitches to gather the centre.

8 Next make the two ends. Cut two pieces of fabric the required finished length and twice the required width plus seam allowances.

9 Tack dress net to the wrong side of the fabric.

10 Fold each piece of fabric in half, right side to right side, and stitch along the long raw edge and at an angle at one end.

11 Remove bulk from the corners.

12 Turn through to the right side. Press. Make sure there are sharp points.

13 To assemble the bow, wrap a piece of fabric around the gathered centre of the loops and stitch in place by hand.

14 Scrunch the raw ends of the ends together and hand stitch behind the loop.

REDUCING SEAM BULK pp.108–109 ● **HOW TO MAKE AND FIT GATHERS p.135** ● **HOW TO CUT BIAS STRIPS p.154** ● **INTERLININGS p.324**

INTERLINING **CURTAINS**

A lined curtain that is also interlined will not only hang beautifully but will also be warm and keep out any draughts. This technique is for hand-sewn curtains and requires a large, flat table to work on. There are different weights of interlining available.

LINED AND INTERLINED CURTAINS

Difficulty level ✸✸✸✸✸

Preparation and accurate measuring of the window and the curtain fabric will ensure that this technique works every time. Choose a thicker quality curtain lining for interlined curtains because it will hang better.

1 Cut out the fabric, lining, and interlining.

Curtain fabric   Interlining   Lining

2 Tack lines to show where the foldlines of the hems will be. There is a double hem at the bottom and a single hem at the sides.

3 Cut interlining to fit between the lines of tacking stitches.

4 Pin in place.

5 Roll the interlining back. Starting at the centre, herringbone stitch the interlining to the curtain fabric. Repeat this approximately every 50cm (20in).

6 Fold the side of the curtain over the interlining and herringbone stitch down.

7 Mitre the corner.

8 Double turn the hem and attach to the interlining using a slip hem stitch.

9 Double turn the curtain lining and machine this hem.

10 Place the lining to the curtain and interlining. The hem of the curtain lining should sit 8cm (3¼in) above the curtain edge.

11 Turn under the sides of the lining and attach to the curtain side hems with a slip hem stitch.

12 On the right side the curtain corners will be sharp and there will be no visible stitching lines.

MITRED CORNERS p.269 • **INTERLININGS p.324**

PROJECT

ROMAN **BLIND**

Difficulty level ✳✳✳✳✳

A Roman blind is a simple, elegant way to dress a window and introduce accent colour or statement pattern to a room. It requires careful measurement of the window to begin with, but is quick and satisfying to assemble. A professional finish is easily achieved with the inclusion of interlining.

TECHNIQUES USED Hand-stitched hems **p.264–265**, Machined hems **p.266**, Interlining curtains **p.352–353**

YOU WILL NEED

- Fabric: to calculate the amount you need measure the window's width (at the widest part where the blind will hang) and also the drop (the finished length of the blind). Add 8cm (3¼in) to the width and 15cm (6in) to the drop for the hems (that's to cover 5cm/2in at the top edge and 10cm/4in at the bottom)
- Lining: add 2cm (¾in) to the width and 25cm (10in) to the drop (for hem and rod pockets)
- Interlining or cotton domette: cut to the desired blind width, with 5cm (2in) extra at the top
- Matching thread
- Sew-on Velcro™
- Roman blind fibreglass rods
- 3cm (1¼in) plastic or aluminium weight bar, cut to width of blind minus 4cm (1½in)
- Austrian blind rings 1cm (⅜in) diameter, and safety toggles/orbs
- Blind cord and breakaway cord connector
- Blind cord cleat
- Staple gun
- Screw eyes
- Wooden batten, to attach blind to window, cut to width of blind minus 1cm (⅜in)

Safety note: If babies or small children could come into contact with a blind, it is important to use safety toggles/orbs instead of blind rings on the bottom rod pocket to minimize risk of strangulation. You should also insert a breakaway cord connector, and install a cleat on the wall (see p.359).

PIECES TO CUT

Blind Fabric

5cm (2in)

Window/ finished blind size

4cm (1½in)   4cm (1½in)

10cm (4in)

Curtain lining

Window/ finished blind size

1cm (⅜in)   1cm (⅜in)

25cm (10in)

Interlining = same size as desired finished blind size, plus 5cm (2in) at the top.

▶ PREPARE THE HEMS

1 Press under 4cm (1½in) to the wrong side (a single-turn hem) along both side edges of the blind fabric.

2 On the bottom edge, press under 5cm (2in) twice to make a double-turn hem. Pin the side and bottom hems in place. Press.

WRONG SIDE OF FABRIC

▷ **ADD THE INTERLINING**

1 Unfold the side and bottom hems of the blind fabric.

2 Position the interlining fabric on the wrong side of the blind fabric; it should align with the creases of the side and bottom hems.

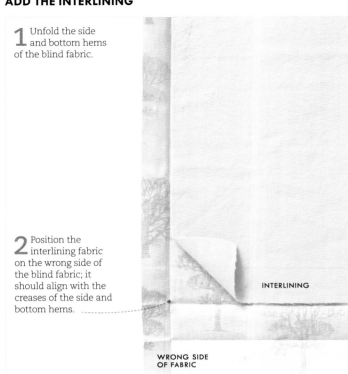

INTERLINING

WRONG SIDE OF FABRIC

3 Re-fold the side hems and then the bottom hem to enclose the interlining.

4 Tack the side seams with diagonal tacks and pin the bottom hem in place.

▷ **PREPARE THE LINING**

1 Press 2.5cm (1in) to the wrong side, down both side edges of the lining fabric. Pin.

2 Press a 4cm (1½in) hem along the bottom edge. Machine stitch close to the raw edge, at about 5mm (³⁄₁₆in).

▶ **MAKE THE ROD CASINGS AND ATTACH THE LINING**

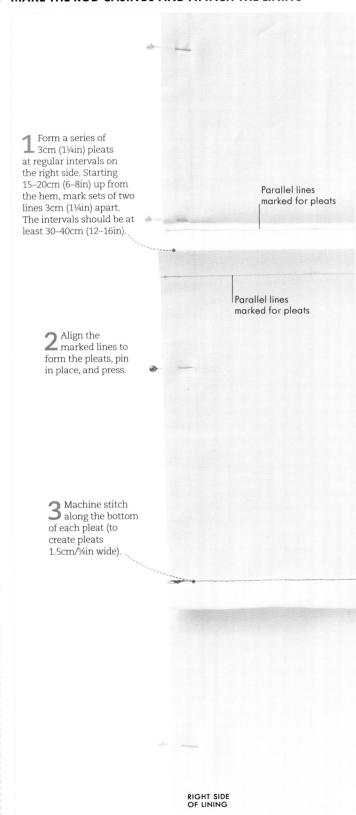

1 Form a series of 3cm (1¼in) pleats at regular intervals on the right side. Starting 15–20cm (6–8in) up from the hem, mark sets of two lines 3cm (1¼in) apart. The intervals should be at least 30–40cm (12–16in).

Parallel lines marked for pleats

Parallel lines marked for pleats

2 Align the marked lines to form the pleats, pin in place, and press.

3 Machine stitch along the bottom of each pleat (to create pleats 1.5cm/⅝in wide).

RIGHT SIDE OF LINING

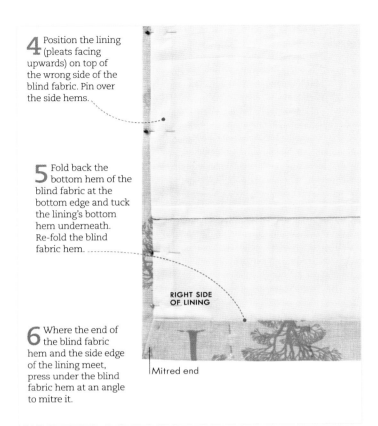

4 Position the lining (pleats facing upwards) on top of the wrong side of the blind fabric. Pin over the side hems.

5 Fold back the bottom hem of the blind fabric at the bottom edge and tuck the lining's bottom hem underneath. Re-fold the blind fabric hem.

RIGHT SIDE OF LINING

6 Where the end of the blind fabric hem and the side edge of the lining meet, press under the blind fabric hem at an angle to mitre it.

Mitred end

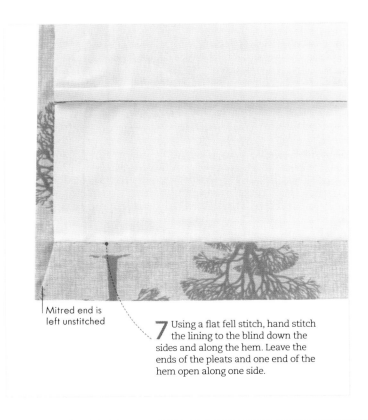

Mitred end is left unstitched

7 Using a flat fell stitch, hand stitch the lining to the blind down the sides and along the hem. Leave the ends of the pleats and one end of the hem open along one side.

MACHINED HEMS p.266 ● **MITRED CORNERS p.269** ● **INTERLININGS AND INTERFACINGS p.324–325** ● **INTERLINING CURTAINS pp.352–353**

▶ **ATTACH THE VELCRO™ AND BLIND RINGS**

1 Turn down the top edge so that the blind measures the required finished length. Pin in place.

2 Cut a piece of Velcro™ equal to the width of the blind. Stitch the soft loop side of the Velcro™ to the blind along the top hem edge.

3 Using a buttonhole stitch, sew a blind ring on either end of each rod casing, 5cm (2in) in from the blind edge. Sew additional rings at regular intervals in between, no more than 30cm (12in) apart.

4 Sew three small backstitches through both the lining fabric and the blind fabric, above the rod pocket at each ring location. Use a thread that matches your blind fabric colour.

5 Insert a rod into each casing and close the end of the casing using flat fell stitch.

Roman blind rod

6 Insert the weight bar into the lining fabric pocket in the bottom hem. Press the blind hem corner under to re-fold the mitred end and close it using flat fell stitch.

Weight bar

▶ **ASSEMBLE THE BLIND**

1 Cut a length of blind cord equal to twice the blind drop, for each vertical set of rings. Knot the cord around each ring nearest to the hem. Thread the cord up through each vertical line of rings.

2 Insert screw eyes to the underside of the batten to align with each vertical line of rings. Staple the other (hook) side of Velcro™ to the batten and fix the batten above the window.

3 Attach the blind to the batten and pass the cords through the screw eyes and along to one side (see illustration).

4 To comply with child safety regulations, insert a breakaway cord connector where the cords gather at the end of the batten, no more than 5cm (2in) below the batten when the blind is fully down. Install a cord cleat 1.5m (60in) from the floor and keep the cord wound around it.

HOW TO THREAD A ROMAN BLIND

MITRED CORNERS **p.269** ● TAPE FASTENERS **p.320**

MENDING

Mending can preserve the life of your favourite clothes or furnishings. Try to fix lost buttons or dropped hems as soon as possible. Here you will find more complex mending techniques for split seams, holes, tears, and broken zips.

MENDING

Repairing a tear in fabric, patching a worn area, or fixing a zip or a buttonhole can add extra life to a garment or an item of soft furnishing. Repairs like these may seem tedious, but they are very easy to do and well worthwhile. For some of the mending techniques shown here, a contrast colour thread has been used so that the stitching can be seen clearly. However, when making a repair, be sure to use a matching thread.

UNPICKING STITCHES

Difficulty level ✱✱✱✱✱

All repairs involve unpicking stitches. This must be done carefully to avoid damaging the fabric because the fabric will have to be restitched. There are three ways you can unpick stitches.

▶ **SMALL SCISSORS**

Pull the fabric apart and, using very small, sharply pointed scissors, snip through the stitches that have been exposed.

▶ **SEAM RIPPER**

Slide a seam ripper carefully under a stitch and cut it. Cut through every fourth or fifth stitch, and the seam will unravel easily.

▶ **PIN AND SCISSORS**

On difficult fabrics or on very small, tight stitches, slide a pin under the stitch first to lift it away from the fabric, then snip through with a pair of sharply pointed scissors.

DARNING A HOLE

Difficulty level ✱✱✱✱✱

If you accidentally catch a piece of jewellery in a sweater or other knitted garment, it may make a small hole. Or a moth could cause this. It is worth darning the hole, especially if the sweater was expensive or is a favourite. Holes can also occur in the heels of socks and these can be darned in the same way.

▶

1 Even if the hole is small, the sweater will be unwearable.

2 Work several rows of running stitches vertically around the hole.

3 Complete the repair by working horizontal rows of running stitches through the vertical stitches.

CUTTING TOOLS **pp.16–17** ● HOW TO APPLY A FUSIBLE INTERFACING **p.54** ● HAND STITCHES **pp.90–91**

REPAIRING FABRIC UNDER A BUTTON

Difficulty level

A button under strain can sometimes pull off a garment. If this happens, a hole will be made in the fabric, which needs fixing before a new button can be stitched on.

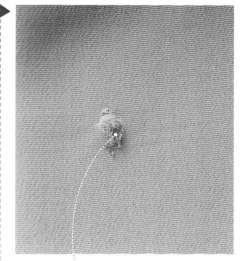

1 On the right side of the fabric, the hole where the button has pulled off is clearly visible.

2 Turn to the wrong side and apply a patch of fusible interfacing over the hole.

3 Work a machine straight stitch over the hole on the right side to strengthen the fabric.

4 Stitch the button back in place.

REPAIRING A DAMAGED BUTTONHOLE

Difficulty level

A buttonhole can sometimes rip at the end, or the stitching on the buttonhole can come unravelled. When repairing, use a thread that matches the fabric so the repair will be invisible.

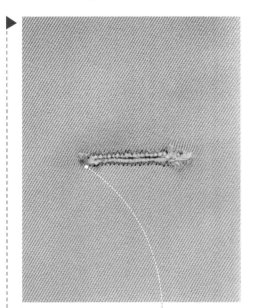

1 On the right side of the fabric, the edges of the buttonhole stitching have torn and come unravelled.

2 Stitch over the torn sections by hand using a buttonhole stitch.

3 Reinforce the ends using small over-sewing.

SEWING ON BUTTONS pp.301–303 ● BUTTONHOLES pp.304–311

MENDING A SPLIT IN A SEAM

Difficulty level

A split seam can be very quickly remedied with the help of some fusible mending tape and new stitching.

1 Where the split has occurred in the seam, unpick the stitching on either side. Press the fabric back into shape.

2 Apply a strip of fusible mending tape over the split and the seam on either side of the split.

3 Re-stitch the seam using a thread colour to match the fabric.

4 On the other side, the repair will not be visible.

MENDING A TEAR WITH A FUSIBLE PATCH

Difficulty level

Tears easily happen to clothing, especially children's wear, and they may occur on soft furnishings too. There are several methods for mending a tear. Most use a fusible patch of some kind, which may or may not be seen on the front, but you can also use a patch cut from matching fabric (see p.366).

▶ **FUSIBLE APPLIQUÉ PATCH**

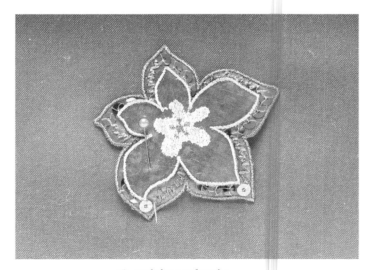

1 Place a fusible appliqué patch over the tear and pin in place.

2 Apply heat to fuse the decorative patch in place.

HOW TO APPLY A FUSIBLE INTERFACING **p.54** • HAND STITCHES **pp.90—91** • STITCHES MADE WITH A MACHINE **pp.92—93**

▶ VISIBLE FUSED PATCH

1 Measure the tear in the fabric.

2 Cut a piece of fusible mending fabric that is slightly longer and wider than the tear.

3 Fuse the fabric in place on the right side.

4 Using a zigzag stitch, machine all around the edge of the patch on the right side of the work.

5 On the reverse side of the fabric, the tear will be firmly stuck to the mending patch, which will prevent the tear getting any bigger.

▶ FUSED PATCH ON THE WRONG SIDE

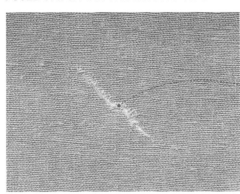

1 Measure the length of the tear. Cut a piece of fusible mending tape to fit.

2 On the wrong side of the fabric, fuse the mending tape over the tear.

3 Using a zigzag stitch, width 5.0 and length 0.5, stitch over the tear, working from the right side.

4 On the wrong side, the zigzag stitching will have gone through the fusible tape.

INTERFACINGS **pp.324—325** ● UNPICKING STITCHES **p.362**

MENDING A TEAR WITH A MATCHING PATCH

Difficulty level ✶✶✶✶✶

On a patterned fabric, such as a check or a stripe, it is possible to mend a tear almost invisibly by using a patch that matches the pattern.

1 Cut a square hole in the fabric, removing the damaged area.

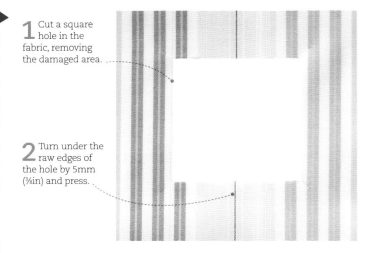

3 Cut a piece of fabric from matching fabric to fill the hole (this fabric could be taken from the hem). Match the stripes or checks. Tack in place.

2 Turn under the raw edges of the hole by 5mm (⅜in) and press.

4 Using a small flat fell stitch, stitch the patch into the hole, working from the right side of the fabric.

5 This is how it will look on the reverse.

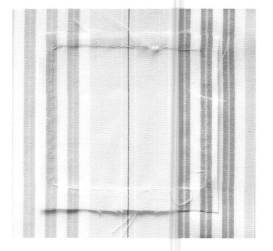

6 Remove the tacks and press.

REPAIRING OR REPLACING ELASTIC

Difficulty level ✹✹✹✹✹

Elastic can frequently come unstitched inside the waistband, or it may lose its stretch and require replacing. Here is the simple way to re-insert elastic or insert new elastic.

▶ **1** Carefully unpick a seam in the elastic casing.

Old elastic

2 Pull the old elastic through the gap in the seam and cut through it.

3 Attach new elastic to the old with a safety pin. Use the old elastic to pull the new elastic through inside the casing.

4 Secure the ends on the new elastic.

5 Hand stitch the unpicked seam back together.

REPAIRING A BROKEN ZIP

Difficulty level ✹✹✹✹✹

Zips can break if they come under too much strain. Sometimes the zip has to be removed completely and a new zip inserted. However, if only a few teeth have been broken far enough down so that the zip can still be opened sufficiently, you can make this repair.

▶ **1** Where there are broken teeth on the zip, the zip pull will be attached to one half only. Move the puller up so it is alongside the gap in the teeth on the other side.

Broken teeth

2 Carefully feed the teeth on the broken side into the top of the zip.

Broken part of zip

3 Just above the broken part, hand stitch over the zip teeth using double thread. This makes a stop for the puller and the zip will now have an extended life.

ZIPS **pp.284–293** • UNPICKING STITCHES **p.362**

USING THE **PATTERNS SECTION**

To create most of the projects in this book, you will first need to transfer the pattern to paper. You can do this in one of three ways: enlarge it on a photocopier, draw the pattern by hand onto pattern paper, or download it from our website. For garments, you will also need to find the correct size. It is always a good idea to make a garment in a toile first (see pp.74–75) to make sure that the size is right and the garment fits.

CHOOSING A SIZE

Take the relevant body measurements for the garment you are making and find the closest set of measurements in the tables below. If the measurements are between sizes, choose the larger of the two. Sizes may differ from what you would buy in a store.

▶ WOMEN'S SIZING

SIZE	6–8	8–10	10–12	12–14	14–16	16–18	18–20	20–22	22–24
BUST	82cm (32¼in)	84.5cm (33¼in)	87cm (34¼in)	92cm (36¼in)	97cm (38in)	102cm (40in)	107cm (42in)	112cm (44in)	117cm (46in)
WAIST	62cm (24½in)	64.5cm (25¼in)	67cm (26¼in)	72cm (28¼in)	77cm (30¼in)	82cm (32¼in)	87cm (34¼in)	92cm (36¼in)	97cm (38in)
HIP	87cm (34¼in)	89.5cm (35¼in)	92cm (36¼in)	97cm (38in)	102cm (40in)	107cm (42in)	112cm (44in)	117cm (46in)	122cm (48in)

▶ CHILDREN'S SIZING

SIZE	2–3 YRS	4–5 YRS	6–7 YRS
CHEST	54–56cm (21¼–22in)	57–60cm (22½–23⅝in)	61–64cm (24–25¼in)
WAIST	51–53cm (20–20⅞in)	54–58cm (21¼–22⅞in)	58–60cm (22⅞–23⅝in)
HEIGHT	96–98cm (37¾–38⅝in)	104–110cm (41–43¼in)	116–122cm (45⅝–48in)

▶ UNISEX SIZING

SIZE	CHEST
XS	84–86.5cm (33–34in)
S	91.5–96.5cm (36–38in)
M	101.5–106.5cm (40–42in)
L	112–117cm (44–46in)
XL	123–127cm (48–50in)
XXL	132–137cm (52–54in)

▶ PATTERN MARKINGS

The following markings are used on the patterns in this section.

———————— Cutting lines

– – – – – – –

················· Cutting lines

◀▬▬▬▬▶ Grainlines

◣▬▬▬◥ Place-to-fold line

⊢▬▬⊣ Buttonhole

⬡ Button position

= = = = ▬● Dart

⊕ Markings to be transferred from pattern pieces to the fabric for matching or to indicate detail

T Single notches

T T Double notches

▶ SEAM ALLOWANCE

Seam allowance is the amount of fabric that is taken up by the seam. It is usually given as the distance between the cutting line and the stitching line.

The garment patterns in this section include 1.5cm (⅝in) seam allowance. This means that to make a project that is the correct size and shape, you will need to cut along the line on the pattern, and stitch 1.5cm (⅝in) inside the cutting line. It can be helpful to mark a stitching line onto the pattern pieces before you begin.

Cutting line

Stitching line

COPY OR DOWNLOAD YOUR PATTERN

▶ METHOD 1: PHOTOCOPYING

1 To enlarge the pattern on a photocopier, begin by copying it at 100%. Find the line for your chosen size in the pattern, and draw along it in marker or pen. Enlarge the pattern by 200%.

2 Enlarge the pattern pieces again by 200% to reach full size. If you are using a photocopier that has a 400% setting, you can use this setting to enlarge the pieces in one step.

3 Once you have enlarged all parts of the original page, piece them together using the gridlines as a guide, and tape them down. Cut around the line for your chosen size.

▶ METHOD 2: DRAWING THE PATTERN BY HAND

1 Each grid square in the patterns represents a 5cm square at full size. To enlarge the patterns by hand, you will need pattern paper with either a 1cm or 5cm grid.

2 Begin by finding the line for your chosen size in the pattern. Enlarge the pattern onto your paper, mapping each square of the pattern onto a 5cm square on the pattern paper.

3 Depending on the size of your pattern paper, you may need to stick together several sheets to fit all the pieces for a single pattern. Once you have copied the pieces, cut them out.

▶ METHOD 3: DOWNLOADING FROM THE INTERNET

1 Check which pattern is needed to make the project. This is listed on the first page of the instructions. Then go to the website **www.dk.com/thesewingbook**

2 Find the correct PDF for your project. Download the PDF to your computer, and print it out. The pages will be labelled in the order that they fit together.

3 Trim the white margins from the printed pages, and tape the pages together, using the letters and gridlines as a guide. Find the line for your chosen size and cut around it.

A-LINE SHIFT DRESS PATTERN pp.166–171

ENLARGE BY 400% on a photocopier

FRONT
Cut 1

JOIN

NOTE: One square in the grid equals 5cm² at full size. A seam allowance of 1.5cm (⅝in) is included in the pattern pieces. After you have cut out the pattern pieces in your size, you may wish to add seamlines 1.5cm (⅝in) inside the cutting lines (see p.368).

JOIN

SLEEVE
Cut 2

A-LINE SHIFT DRESS PATTERN pp.166–171

ENLARGE BY 400% on a photocopier

BACK
Cut 2

POCKET
Cut 2

POCKET
Cut 2

SIZES

——————	6–8
················	8–10
—·—·—·—	10–12
·············	12–14
——————	14–16
················	16–18
··············	18–20
·············	20–22
——————	22–24

NOTE: One square in the grid equals 5cm² at full size. A seam allowance of 1.5cm (⅝in) is included in the pattern pieces. After you have cut out the pattern pieces in your size, you may wish to add seamlines 1.5cm (⅝in) inside the cutting lines (see p.368).

JOIN

FRONT
Cut 1 fabric
Cut 1 interfacing

BACK FACING
Cut 2 fabric
Cut 2 interfacing

WRAP SKIRT PATTERN pp.194–199

ENLARGE BY 400% on a photocopier

FABRIC REQUIREMENTS

SIZE	115cm (45in) wide	150cm (60in) wide
6–8	2.75m (110in)	1.75m (70in)
8–10	2.75m (110in)	1.75m (70in)
10–12	2.75m (110in)	1.75m (70in)
12–14	2.75m (110in)	1.75m (70in)
14–16	2.75m (110in)	1.75m (70in)
16–18	2.75m (110in)	1.75m (70in)
18–20	2.75m (110in)	2.50m (100in)
20–22	2.75m (110in)	2.50m (100in)
22–24	2.75m (110in)	2.50m (100in)

Place to fold

BACK
Cut 1 on fold

TAB
Cut 2

SIZES

——————	6–8
··············	8–10
— · — · —	10–12
············	12–14
— — — —	14–16
············	16–18
——————	18–20
············	20–22
— — — —	22–24

NOTE: One square in the grid equals 5cm² at full size. A seam allowance of 1.5cm (⅝in) is included in the pattern pieces. After you have cut out the pattern pieces in your size, you may wish to add seamlines 1.5cm (⅝in) inside the cutting lines (see p.368).

RIGHT-HAND FRONT
Cut 1

WRAP SKIRT PATTERN pp.194–199

ENLARGE BY 400% on a photocopier

RIGHT WAISTBAND
Cut 2

BACK WAISTBAND
Cut 2

LEFT-HAND FRONT
Cut 1

JOIN

RIGHT FRONT FACING
Cut 1

SIZES

——————	6–8
··············	8–10
— · — · —	10–12
·············	12–14
——————	14–16
··············	16–18
——————	18–20
··············	20–22
——————	22–24

NOTE: One square in the grid equals 5cm² at full size. A seam allowance of 1.5cm (⅝in) is included in the pattern pieces. After you have cut out the pattern pieces in your size, you may wish to add seamlines 1.5cm (⅝in) inside the cutting lines (see p.368).

JOIN

LEFT WAISTBAND
Cut 2

UNISEX DRESSING GOWN PATTERN pp.216–221

ENLARGE BY 400% on a photocopier

FABRIC REQUIREMENTS FOR SHORT GOWN

SIZE	115cm (45in) wide	150cm (60in) wide
ALL SIZES MAIN FABRIC	3.30m (130in)	3.30m (130in)
ALL SIZES CONTRAST FABRIC	2.30m (90in)	2.30m (90in)

FABRIC REQUIREMENTS FOR LONG GOWN

SIZE	115cm (45in) wide	150cm (60in) wide
ALL SIZES MAIN FABRIC	3.30m (130in)	3.30m (130in)
ALL SIZES CONTRAST FABRIC	4.00m (160in)	2.60m (102in)

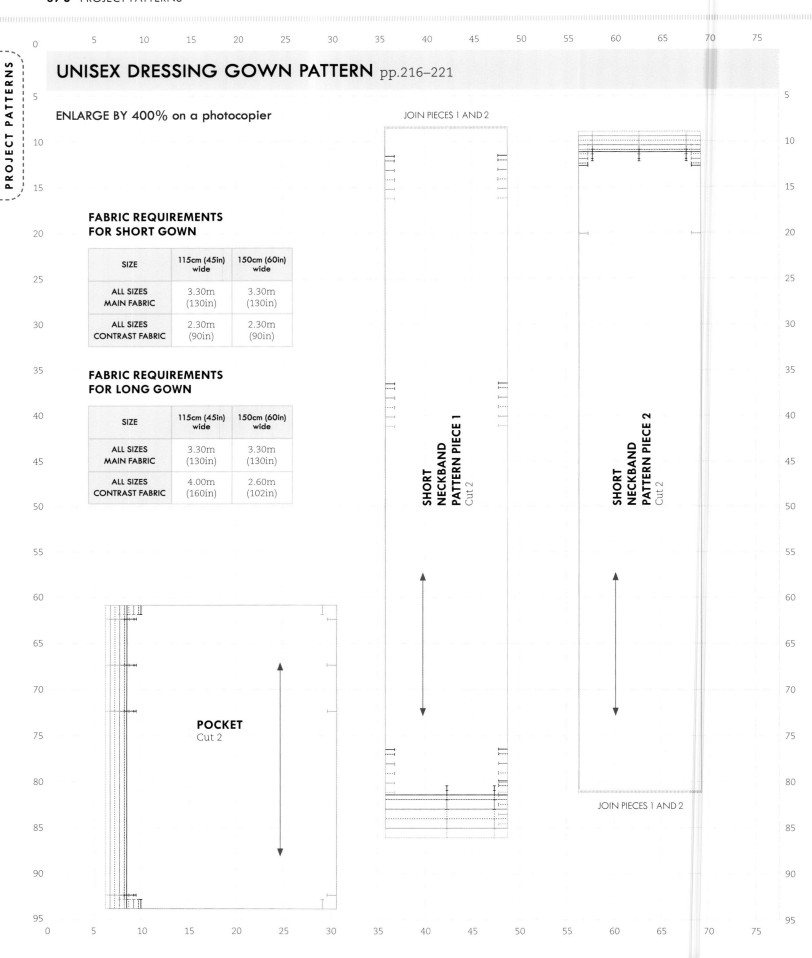

JOIN PIECES 1 AND 2

SHORT NECKBAND PATTERN PIECE 1
Cut 2

SHORT NECKBAND PATTERN PIECE 2
Cut 2

JOIN PIECES 1 AND 2

POCKET
Cut 2

JOIN PIECES 1 AND 2

LONG NECKBAND PATTERN PIECE 1
Cut 2

JOIN PIECES 1 AND 2

LONG NECKBAND PATTERN PIECE 2
Cut 2

BELT LOOP
Cut 1

BELT LOOP
Cut 1

HANGING LOOP Cut 1

SIZES
XS
S
M
L
XL
XXL

NOTE: One square in the grid equals 5cm² at full size. A seam allowance of 1.5cm (⅝in) is included in the pattern pieces. After you have cut out the pattern pieces in your size, you may wish to add seamlines 1.5cm (⅝in) inside the cutting lines (see p.368).

Place to fold

BACK HEM PANEL
Cut 1 on fold

UNISEX DRESSING GOWN PATTERN pp.216–221

ENLARGE BY 400% on a photocopier

SLEEVE
Cut 2

CUFF
Cut 2

JOIN PIECES 1, 2 AND 3

JOIN PIECES 1, 2 AND 3

SIZES

———	XS
··········	S
– – – –	M
··········	L
———	XL
··········	XXL

NOTE: One square in the grid equals 5cm² at full size. A seam allowance of 1.5cm (⅝in) is included in the pattern pieces. After you have cut out the pattern pieces in your size, you may wish to add seamlines 1.5cm (⅝in) inside the cutting lines (see p.368).

TIE BELT PATTERN PIECE 3
Cut 1

TIE BELT PATTERN PIECE 1
Cut 1

TIE BELT PATTERN PIECE 2
Cut 1

FRONT HEM PANEL
Cut 2

JOIN PIECES 1, 2 AND 3

JOIN PIECES 1, 2 AND 3

PROJECT PATTERNS

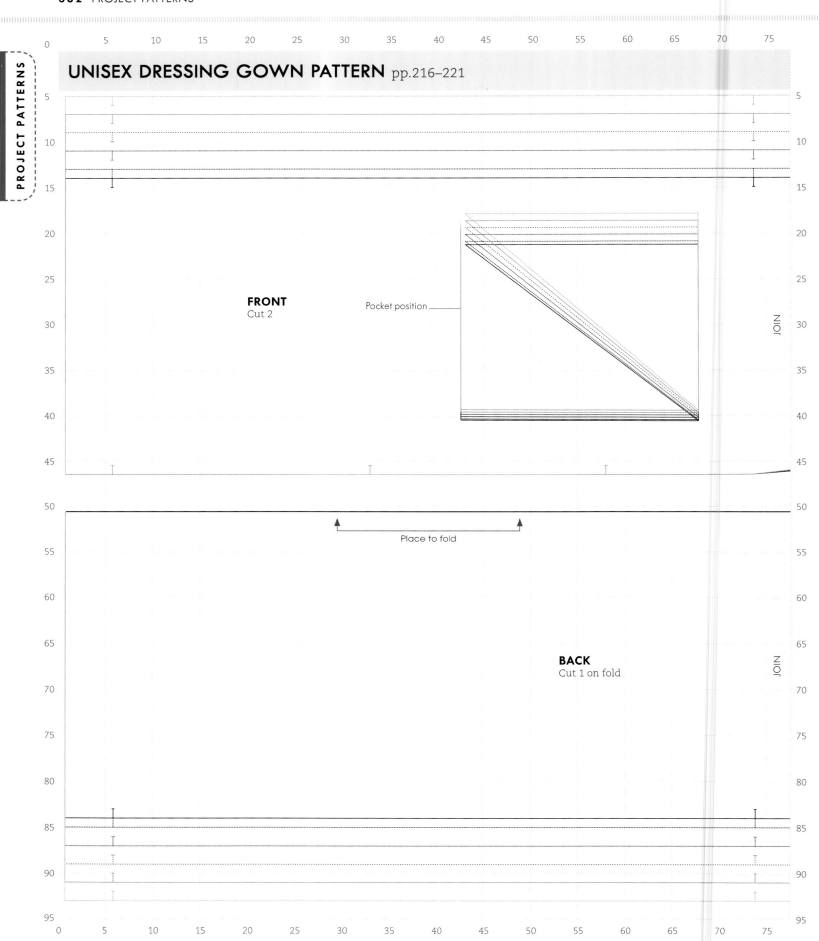

UNISEX DRESSING GOWN PATTERN pp.216–221

FRONT
Cut 2

Pocket position

JOIN

Place to fold

BACK
Cut 1 on fold

JOIN

SIZES

——————	XS
··············	S
———·———	M
·-·-·-·-·	L
—————	XL
············	XXL

NOTE: One square in the grid equals 5cm² at full size. A seam allowance of 1.5cm (⅝in) is included in the pattern pieces. After you have cut out the pattern pieces in your size, you may wish to add seamlines 1.5cm (⅝in) inside the cutting lines (see p.368).

JOIN

Place to fold

JOIN

JOIN

CHILD'S REVERSIBLE JACKET PATTERN pp.254–259

ENLARGE BY 400% on a photocopier

BACK
Cut 1 on
each fabric

FRONT
Cut 2 on
each fabric

Pocket
placement

SIZES

— 2–3 yrs

······· 4–5 yrs

– – – 6–7 yrs

NOTE: One square in the grid equals 5cm² at full size. A seam allowance of 1.5cm (⅝in) is included in the pattern pieces. After you have cut out the pattern pieces in your size, you may wish to add seamlines 1.5cm (⅝in) inside the cutting lines (see p.368).

FABRIC REQUIREMENTS FOR FABRICS A AND B

SIZE	115cm (45in) wide	150cm (60in) wide
2–3YRS	1.25m (50in)	90cm (36in)
4–5YRS	1.40m (56in)	1.00m (40in)
6–7YRS	1.50m (60in)	1.00m (40in)

HOOD
Cut 2 on each fabric

POCKET
Cut 4 on each fabric

SLEEVE
Cut 2 on each fabric

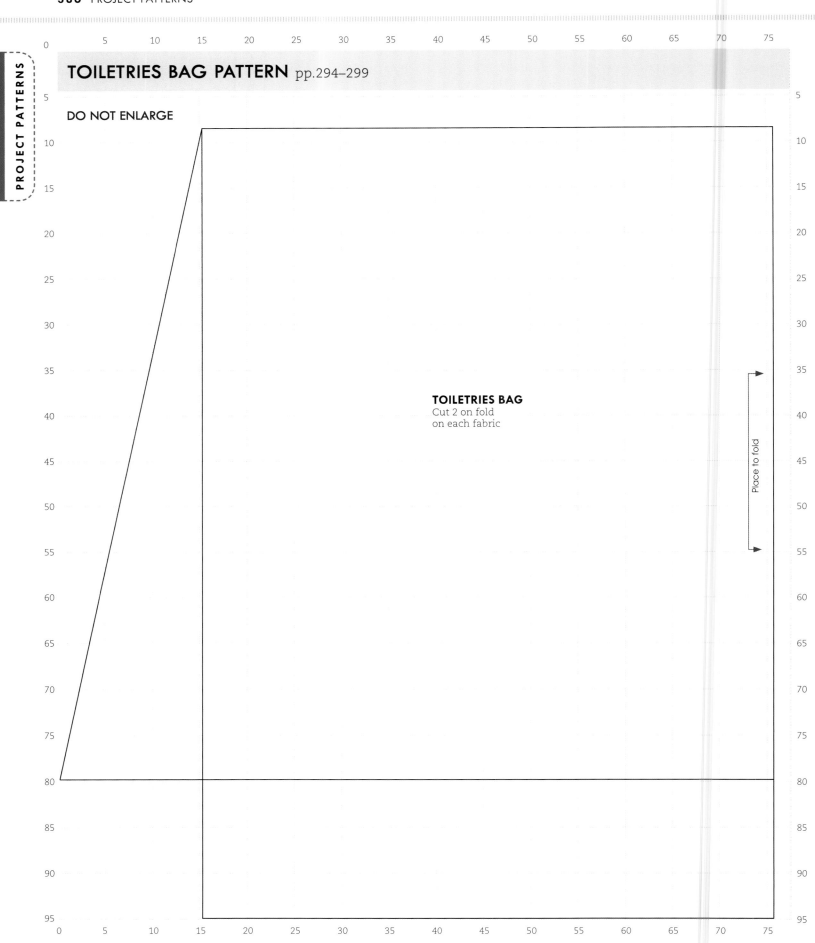

TOILETRIES BAG PATTERN pp.294–299

DO NOT ENLARGE

TOILETRIES BAG
Cut 2 on fold
on each fabric

Place to fold

OVEN MITT PATTERN pp.346–349

ENLARGE BY 200% on a photocopier

NOTE: One square in the grid equals 5cm² at full size. A seam allowance of 1.5cm (⅝in) is included in the pattern pieces. After you have cut out the pattern pieces in your size, you may wish to add seamlines 1.5cm (⅝in) inside the cutting lines (see p.368).

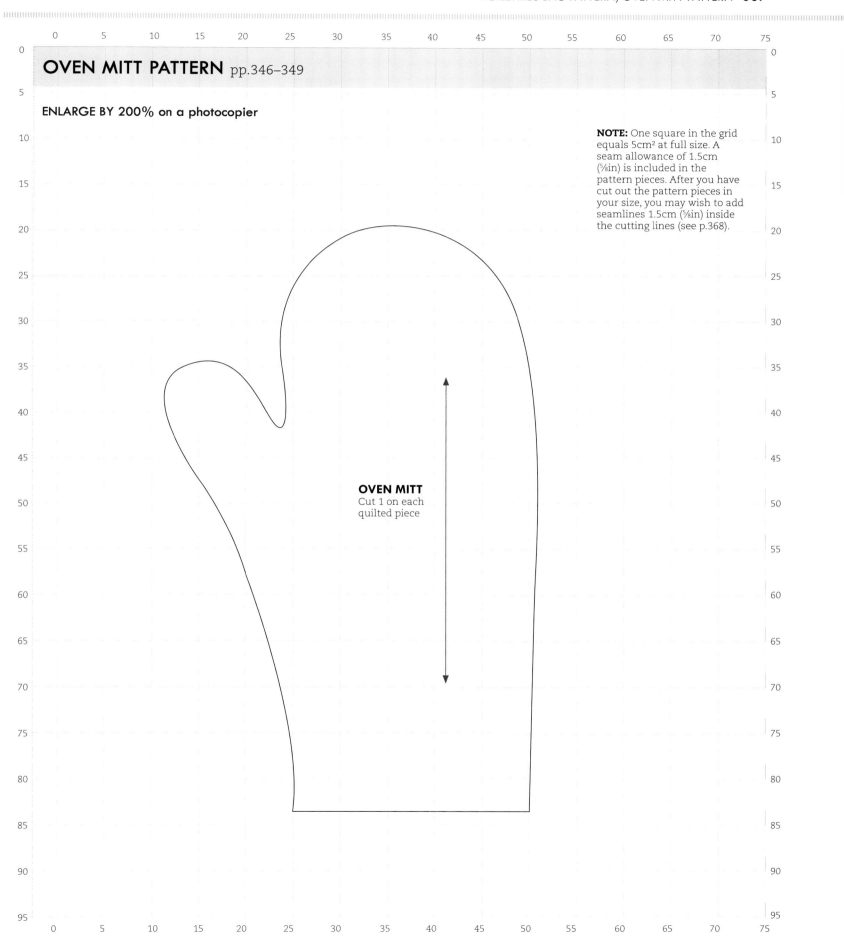

OVEN MITT
Cut 1 on each quilted piece

GLOSSARY

Acetate Man-made fabric widely used for lining.

Acrylic Man-made fabric resembling wool.

Alpaca Canvas made from wool and alpaca. This fabric can be used as a non-fusible interfacing.

Appliqué One piece of fabric being stitched to another in a decorative manner.

Armhole Opening in a garment for the sleeve and arm.

Arrowhead Small, triangular set of straight stitches worked either by hand or by machine across a seam to add strength at a point of possible strain (for example, at the top of a split).

Backstitch A strong hand stitch with a double stitch on the wrong side, used for outlining and seaming.

Balanced dart A dart with extra fabric added on the wrong side to distribute the fabric evenly on both sides of the dart stitching line.

Banding Method of finishing a raw edge by applying a wide strip of fabric over it. The strip can also be used to add length to a garment.

Bar tack A hand-worked bar of buttonhole stitches used to loosely attach two layers of fabric.

Belt carrier Loop made from a strip of fabric, which is used to support a belt at the waist edge of a garment.

Bias 45-degree line on fabric that falls between the lengthways and the crossways grain. Fabric cut on the bias drapes well. *See also* **Grain**.

Bias binding Narrow strips of fabric cut on the bias. Used to give a neat finish to hems and seam allowances.

Binding Method of finishing a raw edge by wrapping it in a strip of bias-cut fabric.

Blanket stitch Hand stitch worked along the raw or finished edge of fabric to neaten, and for decorative purposes.

Blind hem stitch Tiny hand stitch used to attach one piece of fabric to another, mainly to secure hems. Also a machine stitch consisting of two or three straight stitches and one wide zigzag stitch.

Blind tuck A tuck that is stitched so that it touches the adjacent tuck without machine stitches showing. *See also* **Tuck.**

Bobbin Round holder beneath the needle plate of a sewing machine on which the thread is wound.

Bodice Upper body section of a garment.

Bodkin Blunt-headed needle used for threading elastic or cord through a casing or heading.

Boning Narrow nylon, plastic, or metal strip, available in various widths, that is used for stiffening and shaping close-fitting garments, such as bodices.

Box pleat Pleat formed on the wrong side of the fabric, and fuller than a knife pleat. *See also* **Pleat.**

Broderie anglaise A fine plain-weave cotton embroidered to make small decorative holes.

Buttonhole Opening through which a button is inserted to form a fastening. Buttonholes are usually machine stitched but may also be worked by hand or piped for reinforcement or decorative effect.

Buttonhole chisel Very sharp, small chisel that cuts cleanly through a machine-stitched buttonhole.

Buttonhole stitch Hand stitch that wraps over the raw edges of a buttonhole to neaten and strengthen them. Machine-stitched buttonholes are worked with a close zigzag stitch.

Button shank Stem of a button that allows room for the buttonhole to fit under the button when joined.

Calico A plain weave, usually unbleached fabric.

Cashmere The most luxurious of all wools.

Casing Tunnel of fabric created by parallel rows of stitching, through which elastic or a drawstring cord is threaded. Often used at a waist edge. Sometimes extra fabric is required to make a casing; this can be applied to the inside or outside of the garment.

Catch stitch *See also* **Slip hem stitch.**

Challis Fine woollen fabric with uneven surface texture.

Chambray A light cotton with a coloured warp thread.

Chiffon Strong, fine, transparent silk.

Chintz Floral print or plain cotton fabric with a glazed finish.

Clapper Wooden aid that is used to pound creases into heavy fabric after steaming.

Contour dart Also known as double-pointed dart, this is used to give shape at the waist of a garment. It is like two darts joined together. *See also* **Dart.**

Corded gathers Gathers that are pulled up over a narrow cord or thick thread, used for thicker fabrics. *See also* **Gathers.**

Corded seam A seam with piping in it, often used to join together two different fabrics.

Corded shirring A method of shirring where a piece of piping cord is stitched into a fold in the fabric. *See also* **Shirring.**

Corded tuck Substantial fold of fabric that has a cord running through it. *See also* **Tuck.**

Corduroy A soft pile fabric with distinctive stripes.

Cotton Soft, durable, and inexpensive fabric widely used in dressmaking. Made from the fibrous hairs covering the seed pods of the cotton plant.

Crease Line formed in fabric by pressing a fold.

Crepe Soft fabric made from twisted yarn.

Crepe de chine Medium-weight fabric with uneven surface, often made from silk.

Crinkle cotton Cotton fabric with creases added by a heat process.

Cross stitch A temporary hand stitch used to hold pleats in place and to secure linings. It can also be used for decoration.

Cross tuck Tuck that crosses over another by being stitched in opposite directions. *See also* **Tuck.**

Curtain weight Weight inserted into the bottom hem of a curtain to hold the curtain in place and make it hang properly.

Cutting line Solid line on a pattern piece used as a guide for cutting out fabric.

Cutting mat Self-healing mat used in conjunction with a rotary cutter to protect the blade and the cutting surface.

Damask Woven cotton with a floral pattern.

Darning Mending holes or worn areas in a knitted garment by weaving threads in rows along the grain of the fabric.

Dart Tapered stitched fold of fabric used on a garment to give it shape so that it can fit around the contours of the body. There are different types of dart, but all are used mainly on women's clothing.

Darted tuck A tuck that can be used to give fullness of fabric at the bust or hip. *See also* **Tuck.**

Denim Hard-wearing twill weave fabric with coloured warp and white weft.

Double-pointed dart *See* **Contour dart**

Double ruffle Decorative trim made from two plain ruffles where one side is longer than the other. Also a ruffle made from doubled fabric.

Drape The way a fabric falls into graceful folds; drape varies with each fabric.

Dressmaker's carbon paper Used together with a tracing wheel to transfer pattern markings to fabric. Available in a variety of colours.

Drill Hard-wearing twill or plain-weave fabric with the same colour warp and weft.

Drop The length of fabric required to make a curtain, the "drop" being the measurement from top to bottom of the window.

Duchesse satin Heavy, expensive satin fabric.

Dupion Fabric with a distinctive weft yarn with many nubbly bits; made from 100 per cent silk.

Ease Distributing fullness in fabric when joining two seams together of slightly different lengths, for example a sleeve to an armhole.

Ease stitch Long machine stitch, used to ease in fullness where the distance between notches is greater on one seam edge than on the other.

Embroidery machine A machine that is capable of embellishing fabric with embroidery designs.

Enclosed edge Raw fabric edge that is concealed within a seam or binding.

Facing Layer of fabric placed on the inside of a garment and used to finish off raw edges of an armhole or neck of a garment. Usually a separate piece of fabric, the facing can sometimes be an extension of the garment itself.

Felt A natural wool fabric can felt when it is stimulated by friction and lubricated by moisture and the fibres bond together to form a cloth. Felting can also be done in a washing machine in a hot cycle.

Filament fibres Very fine synthetic thread, manufactured using plant materials and minerals.

Flannel Wool or cotton with a lightly brushed surface.

Flat fell seam *See* Run and fell seam.

Flat fell stitch A strong, secure stitch used to hold two layers together permanently. Often used to secure linings and bias bindings.

French dart Curved dart used on the front of a garment. *See also* Dart.

French seam A seam traditionally used on sheer and silk fabrics. It is stitched twice, first on the right side of the work and then on the wrong side, enclosing the first seam. *See also* Mock French seam.

Frog fastener Decorative fastener made from cord arranged into four overlapping loops stitched at the centre. Used with a Chinese ball button.

Fusible tape Straight grain tape used to stabilize edges and also replace stay stitching. The heat of the iron fuses it into position.

Gabardine Hard-wearing fabric with a distinctive weave.

Galloon lace Decorative lace trim shaped on both sides, used to edge a hem.

Gathers Bunches of fabric created by sewing two parallel rows of loose stitching, then pulling the threads up so that the fabric gathers and reduces in size to fit the required space.

Georgette Soft, filmy silk fabric.

Gingham Two-colour, checked cotton fabric.

Goblet pleat Decorative curtain heading in which the fabric is stitched into narrow tubes that are then stuffed with wadding. *See also* Pleat.

Godet A section that is inserted into a garment to give fullness at the hem edge. It is usually triangular in shape but it can also be a semi-circle. *See also* Pleat.

Grain Lengthways and crossways direction of threads in a fabric. Fabric grain affects how a fabric hangs and drapes.

Grosgrain Synthetic, ribbed fabric often used to make ribbons.

Gusset Small piece of fabric shaped to fit into a slash or seam for added ease of movement.

Haberdashery Term that covers all the bits and pieces needed to complete a pattern, such as fasteners, elastics, ribbons, and trimmings.

Habutai Smooth, fine silk originally from Japan.

Heading tape Wide fabric tape containing loops that is stitched to the top of a curtain. Hooks are inserted into the loops and then attached to a rail. The heading tape is drawn up to make pleats.

Hem The edge of a piece of fabric neatened and stitched to prevent unravelling. There are several methods of doing this, both by hand and by machine.

Hem allowance Amount of fabric allowed for turning under to make the hem.

Hemline Crease or foldline along which a hem is marked.

Hemming tape Fusible tape with adhesive on both sides. Iron in place to fuse and secure hems that are difficult to hand stitch.

Herringbone stitch Hand stitch used to secure hems and interlinings. This stitch is worked from left to right.

Herringbone weave A zigzag weave where the weft yarn goes under and over warp yarns in a staggered pattern.

Hong Kong finish A method of neatening raw edges particularly on wool and linen. Bias-cut strips are wrapped around the raw edge.

Hook and eye fastening Two-part metal fastening used to fasten overlapping edges of fabric where a neat join is required. Available in a wide variety of styles.

Horsehair braid A braid that is woven from strands of nylon thread and sewn into the hemlines of dressy garments to stiffen the lower edge.

Interfacing A fabric placed between garment and facing to give structure and support. Available in different thicknesses, interfacing can be fusible (bonds to the fabric by applying heat) or non-fusible (needs to be sewn to the fabric).

Interlining Layer of fabric attached to the main fabric prior to construction, to cover the inside of an entire garment to provide extra warmth or bulk. The two layers are then treated as one. Often used in jackets and coats.

Jacquard loom Device used in weaving to control individual yarns. This allows looms to produce intricately patterned fabric such as tapestry, brocade, and damask.

Jersey Cotton or wool yarn that has been knitted to give stretch.

Jetted pocket A type of pocket found on tailored jackets and coats. It consists of strips of fabric that form the edges of the pocket (welts) and the lining.

Keyhole buttonhole stitch A machine buttonhole stitch characterized by having one square end while the other end is shaped like a loop to accommodate the button's shank without distorting the fabric. Often used on jackets.

Kick pleat Inverted pleat extending upwards from the hemline of a narrow skirt to allow freedom when walking. *See also* Pleat.

Knife pleat Pleat formed on the right side of the fabric where all the pleats face the same direction. *See also* Pleat.

Lapped seam Used on fabrics that do not fray, such as suede and leather, the seam allowance of one edge is placed over the edge to be joined, then top-stitched close to the overlapping edge. Also called an overlaid seam.

Lightening stitch *See* Stretch stitch.

Linen Natural fibre derived from the stem of the flax plant, linen is available in a variety of qualities and weights.

Lining Underlying fabric layer used to give a neat finish to an item, as well as concealing the stitching and seams of a garment.

Locking stitch A machine stitch where the upper and lower threads in the machine "lock" together at the start or end of a row of stitching.

Madras Brightly coloured, unevenly checked cotton fabric from India.

Matka A silk suiting fabric with uneven yarn.

Mitre The diagonal line made where two edges of a piece of fabric meet at a corner, produced by folding. See also Mitred corner.

Mitred corner Diagonal seam formed when fabric is joined at a corner. After stitching, excess fabric is cut away.

Mock casing Where there is an effect of a casing, but in fact elastic is attached to the waist, or is used only at the back in a partial casing.

Mock French seam Similar to a French seam, but best used on cotton or firmer fine fabrics. It is constructed on the wrong side of the work. *See also* **French seam**.

Mohair Fluffy wool yarn cloth used for sweaters, jackets, and soft furnishings.

Multi-size pattern Paper pattern printed with cutting lines for a range of sizes on each pattern piece.

Muslin Fine, plain open-weave cotton.

Nap The raised pile on a fabric made during the weaving process, or a print pointing one way. When cutting out pattern pieces, ensure the nap runs in the same direction.

Needle threader Gadget that pulls thread through the eye of a needle. Useful for needles with small eyes.

Notch V-shaped marking on a pattern piece used for aligning one piece with another. Also V-shaped cut taken to reduce seam bulk.

Notion An item of haberdashery, other than fabric, needed to complete a project, such as a button, zip, or elastic. Notions are normally listed on the pattern envelope.

Nylon Hard-wearing, man-made fabric.

Organza Thin, sheer fabric made from silk or polyester.

Overedge stitch Machine stitch worked over the edge of a seam allowance and used for neatening the edges of fabric.

Overlaid seam *See* **Lapped seam**.

Overlocker Machine used for quick stitching, trimming, and edging of fabric in a single action; it gives a professional finish to a garment. There are a variety of accessories that can be attached to an overlocker, which enable it to perform a greater range of functions.

Overlock stitch A machine stitch that neatens edges and prevents fraying. It can be used on all types of fabric.

Over-stitch *See* **Buttonhole stitch**.

Pattern markings Symbols printed on a paper pattern to indicate the fabric grain, foldline, and construction details, such as darts, notches, and tucks. These should be transferred to the fabric using tailor's chalk or tailor's tacks.

Pencil pleat The most common curtain heading where the fabric forms a row of parallel vertical pleats. *See also* **Pleat**.

Petersham Stiff, ridged tape that is 2.5cm (1in) wide and curved. It can be used as an alternative finish to facing.

Pile Raised loops on the surface of a fabric, for example velvet.

Pill A small, fuzzy ball formed from tangled fibres which is formed on the surface of a fabric, making it look old and worn; it is often caused by friction. To remove fabric pills, stretch the fabric over a curved surface and carefully cut or shave off the pills.

Pinch pleat Decorative curtain heading in which groups of two or three pleats are stitched together. *See also* **Pleat**.

Pinking A method of neatening raw edges of fray-resistant fabric using pinking shears. This will leave a zigzag edge.

Pinking shears Cutting tool with serrated blades, used to trim raw edges of fray-resistant fabrics to neaten seam edges.

Pin tuck Narrow, regularly spaced fold or gather. *See also* **Tuck**.

Piped tuck *See* **Corded tuck**.

Piping Trim made from bias-cut strips of fabric, usually containing a cord. Used to edge garments or soft furnishings.

Pivoting Technique used to machine stitch a corner. The machine is stopped at the corner with the needle in the fabric, then the foot is raised, the fabric turned following the direction of the corner, and the foot lowered for stitching to continue.

Placket An opening in a garment that provides support for fasteners, such as buttons, snaps, or zips.

Plain weave The simplest of all the weaves; the weft yarn passes under one warp yarn, then over another one.

Pleat An even fold or series of folds in fabric, often partially stitched down. Commonly found in skirts to shape the waistline, but also in soft furnishings for decoration.

Pocket flap A piece of fabric that folds down to cover the opening of a pocket.

Polyester Man-made fibre that does not crease.

Presser foot The part of a sewing machine that is lowered on to the fabric to hold it in place over the needle plate while stitching. There are different feet available.

Pressing cloth Muslin or organza cloth placed over fabric to prevent marking or scorching when pressing.

Prick stitch Small spaced hand stitch with large spaces between each stitch. Often used to highlight the edge of a completed garment.

Raw edge Cut edge of fabric that requires finishing, for example using zigzag stitch, to prevent fraying.

Rayon Also known as viscose, rayon is often blended with other fibres.

Rever The turned-back front edge of a jacket or blouse to which the collar is attached.

Reverse stitch Machine stitch that simply stitches back over a row of stitches to secure the threads.

Right side The outer side of a fabric, or the visible part of a garment.

Rotary cutter Tool for cutting fabric neatly and easily, and useful for cutting multiple straight edges. It has different sizes of retractable blade.

Rouleau loop Button loop made from a strip of bias binding. It is used with a round ball-type button.

Round-end buttonhole stitch Machine stitch characterized by one end of the buttonhole being square and the other being round, to allow for the button shank.

Ruching Several lines of stitching worked to form a gathered area.

Ruffle Decorative gathered trim made from one or two layers of fabric.

Run and fell seam Also known as a flat fell seam, this seam is made on the right side of a garment and is very strong. It uses two lines of stitching and conceals all the raw edges, reducing fraying.

Running stitch A simple, evenly spaced straight stitch separated by equal-sized spaces, used for seaming and gathering.

Satin A fabric with a satin weave.

Satin weave A weave with a sheen, where the weft goes under four warp yarns, then over one.

Seam Stitched line where two edges of fabric are joined together.

Seam allowance The amount of fabric allowed for on a pattern where sections are to be joined together by a seam; usually this is 1.5cm (⅝in).

Seam edge The cut edge of a seam allowance.

Seamline Line on paper pattern designated for stitching a seam; usually this is 1.5cm (⅝in) from the seam edge.

Seam ripper A small, hooked tool used for undoing seams and unpicking stitches.

Seam roll Tubular pressing aid for pressing seams open on fabrics that mark.

Seersucker Woven cotton with a bubbly appearance due to stripes of puckers.

Self-bound seam Similar to the run and fell seam, except that it is stitched on the wrong side of the fabric.

Self-healing mat *See* Cutting mat.

Selvedge Finished edge on a woven fabric. This runs parallel to the warp (lengthways) threads.

Sewing gauge Measuring tool with adjustable slider for checking small measurements, such as hem depths and seam allowances.

Shantung Fabric with a distinctive weft yarn with many nubbly bits; made from 100 per cent silk.

Sharps General purpose needle used for hand sewing.

Shell tuck Decorative fold of fabric stitched in place with a scalloped edge. *See also* **Tuck**.

Shirring Multiple rows of gathers sewn by machine. Often worked with shirring elastic in the bobbin to allow for stretch.

Shirting Closely woven, fine cotton with coloured warp and weft yarns.

Silk Threads spun by the silkworm and used to create cool, luxurious fabrics.

Slip hem stitch Similar to herringbone stitch but is worked from right to left. It is used mainly for securing hems.

Slotted seam A decorative seam where the edges of the seam open to reveal an under layer, which can be in a contrasting fabric.

Smocking Traditional way of gathering fabric using multiple rows of parallel gathers, stitched by hand, to produce fine tubes in the fabric.

Smocking dots Heat-transfer dots that can be transferred to fabric to be used as a guide for hand gathers.

Snaps Also known as press studs, these fasteners are used as a lightweight hidden fastener.

Snips Spring-loaded cutting tool used for cutting off thread ends.

Spandex Lightweight, soft, stretchable fibre.

Staple fibres These include both natural and manufactured fibres such as cotton, wool, flax, and polyester. They are short in length, and relatively narrow in thickness.

Stay stitch Straight machine stitch worked just inside a seam allowance to strengthen it and prevent it from stretching or breaking.

Stay tape Tape sewn to a specific area of an item for reinforcement, for example to help strengthen a seam.

Stem stitch An embroidery stitch frequently used to outline other stitched decoration.

Stitch in the ditch A line of straight stitches sewn on the right side of the work, in the ditch created by a seam. Used to secure waistbands and facings.

Stitch ripper *See* **Seam ripper**.

Straight stitch Plain machine stitch, used for most applications. The length of the stitch can be altered to suit the fabric.

Stretch stitch Machine stitch used for stretch knits and to help control difficult fabrics. It is worked with two stitches forwards and one backwards so that each stitch is worked three times.

Tacking stitch A temporary running stitch used to hold pieces of fabric together or for transferring pattern markings to fabric.

Taffeta Smooth plain-weave fabric with a crisp appearance.

Tailor's buttonhole A buttonhole with one square end and one keyhole-shaped end, used on jackets and coats.

Tailor's chalk Square or triangular shaped piece of chalk used to mark fabric. Available in a variety of colours, tailor's chalk can be removed easily by brushing.

Tailor's ham A ham-shaped pressing cushion that is used to press shaped areas of garments.

Tailor's tacks Loose thread markings used to transfer symbols from a pattern to fabric.

Tape maker Tool for evenly folding the edges of a fabric strip, which can then be pressed to make binding.

Tape measure Flexible form of ruler made from plastic or fabric.

Tartan Fabric made using a twill weave from worsted yarns. Traditionally used for kilts.

Thimble Metal or plastic cap that fits over the top of a finger to protect it when hand sewing.

Toile A test or dry run of a paper pattern using calico. The toile helps you analyse the fit of the garment.

Top-stitch Machine straight stitching worked on the right side of an item, close to the finished edge, for decorative effect. Sometimes stitched in a contrasting colour.

Top-stitched seam A seam finished with a row of top-stitching for decorative effect. This seam is often used on crafts and soft furnishings as well as garments.

Towelling Cotton fabric with loops on the surface.

Trace tacking A method of marking fold and placement lines on fabric. Loose stitches are sewn along the lines on the pattern to the fabric beneath, then the thread loops are cut and the pattern removed.

Tracing wheel Tool used together with dressmaker's carbon paper to transfer pattern markings on to fabric.

Tuck Fold or pleat in fabric that is sewn in place, normally on the straight grain of the fabric. Often used to provide a decorative addition to a garment.

Tweed Traditional tweed is a rough fabric with a distinctive warp and weft. Modern tweed is a mix of chunky and bobbly wool yarns, often in bright colours.

Twill weave Diagonal patterned weave.

Underlay Strip of fabric placed under the main fabric to strengthen it, for example under a pleat or buttonhole.

Understitch Machine straight stitching through facing and seam allowances that is invisible from the right side; this helps the facing to lie flat.

Velcro™ Two-part fabric fastening consisting of two layers, a "hook" side and a "loop" side; when pressed together the two pieces stick together.

Velvet Luxurious pile-weave fabric.

Venetian Luxurious wool with a satin weave.

Waistband Band of fabric attached to the waist edge of a garment to provide a neat finish.

Warp Lengthways threads or yarns of a woven fabric.

Warp knit Made on a knitting machine, this knit is formed in a vertical and diagonal direction.

Weft Threads or yarns that cross the warp of a woven fabric.

Weft knit Made in the same way as hand knitting, this uses one yarn that runs horizontally.

Welt Strip of fabric used to make the edges of a pocket. *See also* **Jetted pocket**.

Whip stitch Diagonal hand stitch sewn along a raw edge to prevent fraying.

Wool A natural animal fibre, available in a range of weights, weaves, and textures. It is comfortable to wear, crease-resistant, and ideal for tailoring.

Wool worsted A light, strong cloth made from good quality fibres.

Wrong side Reverse side of a fabric, the inside of a garment or other item.

Yoke The top section of a dress or skirt from which the rest of the garment hangs.

Zigzag stitch Machine stitch used to neaten and secure seam edges and for decorative purposes. The width and length of the zigzag can be altered.

Zip Fastening widely used on garments consisting of two strips of fabric tape, carrying specially shaped metal or plastic teeth that lock together by means of a pull or slider. Zips are available in different colours and weights.

Zip foot Narrow machine foot with a single toe that can be positioned on either side of the needle.

ACKNOWLEDGMENTS

FIRST EDITION

AUTHOR'S ACKNOWLEDGMENTS No book could ever be written without a little help. I would like to thank the following people for their help with the techniques and projects: Jackie Boddy, Nicola Corten, Ruth Cox, Helen Culver, Yvette Emmett, Averil Wing, and especially my husband, Nigel, for his continued encouragement and support, as well as my mother, Doreen Robbins, who is responsible for my learning to sew. The following companies have also provided invaluable help, by supplying the sewing machines, haberdashery, and fabrics: Janome UK Ltd, EQS, Linton, Adjustoform, Guttermann threads, The Button Company, YKK zips, Graham Smith Fabrics, Fabulous Fabric, Simplicity patterns, and Freudenberg Nonwovens LP.

DORLING KINDERSLEY WOULD LIKE TO THANK: Heather Haynes and Katie Hardwicke for editorial assistance; Elaine Hewson and Victoria Charles for design assistance; Susan Van Ha for photographic assistance; Hilary Bird for indexing; Elma Aquino; Alice Chadwick-Jones; and Beki Lamb. Special thanks from all at DK to Norma MacMillan for her exceptional professionalism and patience.

PICTURE CREDITS: Additional photography Laura Knox p76 tl, tr, 78 t, 80 t/2 and 4, 81b; Alamy images: D. Hurst, front jacket c. Illustrator Debajyoti Datta. Patterns John Hutchinson, pp 58-9, 62 b row, 63 t and c row, 65, 66, 67 t row, br, 68, 69 t row, bl, 70 tr, bc, br, 71, 72 tl, b row, 73, 81. Additional artworks Karen Cochrane p59 r.

Project Editor Norma MacMillan
Project Designers Viv Brar, Nicola Collings, Mandy Earey, Heather McCarry
Photography Peter Anderson (Tools and Techniques), Kate Whitaker (Projects)

FOR DORLING KINDERSLEY

Project Editor Ariane Durkin **Project Art Editor** Caroline de Souza
Managing Editor Dawn Henderson **Managing Art Editor** Christine Keilty
Senior Jacket Creative Nicola Powling
Senior Production Editor Jenny Woodcock
Senior Production Controller Mandy Inness
Creative Technical Support Sonia Charbonnier

SECOND EDITION

AUTHOR'S ACKNOWLEDGMENTS For this revision of my book I would like to thank the following people for their help with the projects: Bethany Blight, Elisalex de Castro Peake, Georgina Jeffries, Emma May, Cheryl Owen, and Debbie Seton. I would also like to thank Tia Sarkar at DK for her continued patience and keeping me in check! Thanks also to Debbie Shepherd at Janome UK, and my students for their support. Finally, I would like to thank my husband, Nigel, not only for his encouragement but also for the endless cups of coffee.

DORLING KINDERSLEY WOULD LIKE TO THANK: Ruth Jenkinson and her assistants Sarah Merrett and Julie Stewart for the new photography; Keith Hagan and Patrick Mulrey for the illustrations; Steve Crozier for colour retouching; MIG Pattern Cutting for creating the garment patterns; Deborah Shepherd at Janome UK for lending us machines to photograph; Arani Sinha, Ishita Sareen, Madhurika Bhardwaj, Nisha Shaw, Priyadarshini Gogoi, Katie Hardwicke, and Bob Bridle for editorial assistance; Jomin Johny, Kanupriya Lal, Roshni Kapur, Shipra Jain, Amy Child, Louise Brigenshaw, Charlotte Johnson, and Alison Gardner for design assistance; Nityanand Kumar for DTP assistance; Angela Baynham for proofreading; and Vanessa Bird for creating the index.

DK UK

Project Editor
Shashwati Tia Sarkar
Senior Art Editor
Karen Constanti
Editorial Assistant
Alice Horne
Senior Jacket Creative
Nicola Powling
Producer
Rebecca Parton
Senior Production Editor
Tony Phipps
Managing Editor
Dawn Henderson
Managing Art Editor
Marianne Markham
Art Director
Maxine Pedliham
Publishing Director
Mary-Clare Jerram
**Special Sales
Creative Project Manager**
Alison Donovan

DK INDIA

Senior Art Editor
Chhaya Sajwan
Project Art Editor
Vikas Sachdeva
Art Editors
Anjali Sachar, Meenal Goel,
Sourabh Challariya
Assistant Art Editors
Anukriti Arora, Ankita Sharma,
Hansa Babra
Project Editors
Janashree Singha, Virien Chopra
Assistant Editors
Devangana Ojha, Nonita Saha
Managing Editor
Soma B. Chowdhury
Managing Art Editor
Arunesh Talapatra
Production Manager
Pankaj Sharma
Pre-production Manager
Sunil Sharma
Senior DTP Designers
Pushpak Tyagi, Tarun Sharma
DTP Designers
Anurag Trivedi, Manish Chandra
Upreti, Rajdeep Singh, Rajesh
Singh Adhikari, Satish Gaur,
Syed Md Farhan

This edition published in 2018

First published in Great Britain in 2009 by Dorling Kindersley Limited
DK, One Embassy Gardens, 8 Viaduct Gardens, London, SW11 7BW

For the curious
www.dk.com

ABOUT THE AUTHOR

ALISON SMITH MBE A trained fashion and textiles teacher, Alison taught for many years at one of the largest schools in Birmingham, where she was Head of Department. In 1992 she set up the School of Sewing – the first of its kind in the UK – teaching all aspects of sewing, including dressmaking, tailoring, and corsetry. Alison has also taught at the Liberty Sewing School in London and at Janome's sewing school in Stockport. In 2004, she opened a fabric shop in Ashby de la Zouch to complement the School of Sewing. In 2013, Alison was awarded an MBE for her services to sewing and corsetry. She also teaches online for Craftsy.com and writes regularly for sewing magazines, including *Love Sewing*. Alison lives in Leicestershire with her husband and has two adult children.

www.schoolofsewing.co.uk
www.sewwardrobe.co.uk
www.etsy.com/uk/shop/SewWardrobe

- *Alison's projects in the book are the A-line Shift Dress on pages 166–171 and the Child's Reversible Jacket on pages 254–259.*

CONTRIBUTORS

BETHANY BLIGHT Beth studied costume, set design, and animation at Central St Martins at the University of the Arts London. Since then, she has been an online contributor to several sewing and craft magazines, run sewing workshops in her local community, and worked as a dressmaker. She now divides her time between looking after her two boys and designing and making craft projects for blogs, magazines, and books. Beth has also contributed projects to DK's *Quilting*.

- *Beth contributed the Oven Mitt project on pages 346–349*

ELISALEX DE CASTRO PEAKE Co-founder of indie sewing pattern label By Hand London, Elisalex originally trained as a shoemaker, working in the fashion industry before turning her passion for sewing and self-sufficient style into a successful new career. She heads up the creative side of BHL, designing and sampling new patterns, creating online tutorials and blog content, and teaching sewing and handcrafts all over London. She is a regular contributor to a range of sewing publications.

- *Elisalex contributed the Wrap Skirt project on pages 194–99 and the Unisex Dressing Gown on pages 216–221.*

GEORGINA JEFFRIES Georgina graduated from Bath Spa University in 2008 with a degree in Fashion and Textiles. Since then she has worked as a designer and sewing tutor for various schools, social enterprises, and businesses, including Neema Crafts in Tanzania, Sew Over It in London, and Watts Gallery in Surrey. Georgina is currently Artist in Residence at Ochre Print Studio in Guildford, where she launched Fair Imprint – a business specializing in hand-made and printed organic homeware that donates a percentage of its profits to charities supporting refugees.

www.fairimprint.com
www.facebook.com/Georgiejaydesign
www.etsy.com/uk/shop/georgiejaydesign

- *Georgina contributed the Envelope Cushions project on pages 312–315.*

EMMA MAY Emma is a traditionally trained soft furnisher, making bespoke curtains, blinds, and cushions from her studio in Oxfordshire. She is passionate about passing on her skills and empowering other homemakers through inspiring and accessible sewing workshops. Emma is fascinated by colour and pattern, and the role they play in people's homes. She is a firm believer that, with dedication and a few simple, soft-furnishing techniques, you can create a beautiful, individual home at little cost.

www.emmamaystitching.co.uk

- *Emma contributed the Roman Blind project on pages 354–359.*

CHERYL OWEN An innovative and experienced crafter, Cheryl originally trained and worked in the fashion industry before applying her design and making skills to sewing – as well as other crafts such as paper crafts and jewellery making. She is the author of many craft books and is a regular contributor to magazines and partworks. Cheryl has also contributed craft projects to DK's *Craft* and *Quilting* books.

www.chirpymakes.com

- *Cheryl contributed the Storage Baskets project on pages 326–327.*

DEBBIE SETON Debbie has been a professional designer and maker since 2012, creating a variety of accessories for her small business, The Crimson Rabbit. Working from her home studio in Essex, she sews a variety of pieces – from bags to cat toys – and also knits and crochets luxurious wraps, cowls, and baby accessories. She's passionate about combining print and colour, sourcing beautiful fabrics and yarns, and incorporating traditional hand-stitching techniques into her designs.

www.etsy.com/shop/CrimsonRabbitBurrow

- *Debbie contributed the Two-tone Tote Bag project on pages 104–107 and the Toiletries Bag project on pages 294–299.*